A SAL

LETTERS TO A SALMON FISHER'S SONS

BY A. H. CHAYTOR

WITH DIAGRAMS AND ILLUSTRATIONS

ANDRE DEUTSCH

First published 1910
Fourth edition 1936

Reprinted 1983 by
André Deutsch Limited
105 Great Russell Street London WC1

Memoir Copyright © by Estate of Drewett Chaytor 1936

All rights reserved

ISBN 0 233 97604 3

Printed in Great Britain by
Ebenezer Baylis Limited, Worcester

INTRODUCTION

Considering the romance of the quarry there have been few books on salmon fishing which deserve the name of classic. Scrope, of course, is an honourable exception but there are not many others. As a subject it does not seem to attract authors in the same way as trout fishing, in particular trout fishing on the chalk streams. Even the finest authors, who were all round fishermen, and I am thinking particularly of Hills and Plunket-Greene, wrote little on salmon fishing.

In many ways Chaytor's book is the one exception. As with so many of the classic fishing books, its main aim and purpose is to give practical advice to the novice. It is written in the form of letters addressed to the author's two sons Drewett and Kit, but it is so full of enthusiasm and so descriptive that it has achieved a standing far beyond its original intention.

Letters to a Salmon Fisher's Sons was first published in 1910 and even today, more than seventy years later, it is worth reading for its advice. Study it closely and you will learn from a master who had thought deeply on the whole subject and had the rare gift of being able to put his thoughts into words. By the time the third edition was published in 1925 salmon fishing had been revolutionised by Arthur Wood whose advocacy of the greased line method of fishing, particularly in the summer has been universally followed ever since. Chaytor, indeed, makes reference to him in the notes appended to that edition. But it is obvious that while he did not use a greased line himself, he did use light lines and small flies in the summer and when water conditions were low. The story of the capture of the twenty-six-and-a-half pound fish which took sixty-five minutes to land makes this clear.

Chaytor was a great catcher of fish. We read in Drewett Chaytor's foreword to the fourth edition that his father's success, particularly in low water and poor conditions was often remarkable. And when we read the author's figures for the salmon he caught, which may not sound enormous, we have to remember that these were made on the Tyne which, fine river though it was, would never have been in the same league for catches as for instance the Spey or the Tweed.

Perhaps the best known passages in the book are contained in the chapter 'When and Where to Fish' starting with that memorable sentence, 'Cold winds and wretched weather, which send the trout fisher home empty handed, seem often to make little or no difference to the salmon . . .' and this should be read by everyone who fishes for salmon.

But the aspect of the book which I really like is the author's enthusiasm. I love his thoughts on spring salmon fishing, 'you are fishing for spring salmon in a time of hope and joy, and of budding leaves and singing birds, and at the beginning of a new salmon season when the mere casting of the fly again is a perfect holiday.' And, at the end of the same chapter, when you have landed your spring fish, 'As far as catching fish goes, you may now go home. Unless your lines are, indeed, cast in pleasant places you have had your only fish on the day, and you will catch no more. The memories of many days of spring fishing tell us so, and in our hearts we know it as we admire this shapely, shining fish. But, go home! do you say? Hang it, man, the day has only just begun. Go home! Don't you know that every cast that I make after this I shall feel certain that I am going to take another fish. I shall be fishing better than I have ever fished today. I've got one; nothing can make it a blank day now, and, with a little luck, I shall certainly get another.

'Well, this is called patience by those who don't know. But it is nothing at all like patience. It is hope, undying, unquenchable, the heart and the soul of salmon fishing.'

Surely no one has ever put it better.

ANTONY ATHA

TO

DREWETT ORMONDE DREWETT

A JUST MAN AND A GREAT SALMON FISHER

NOW IN THE LAND OF SILENCE

IN MEMORY OF UNNUMBERED KINDNESSES

. . . feriuntque summos fulgura montes

MEMOIR

THE third (revised) edition of this book has now reached its end, and since it was published the author, my father, has died. This memoir in the form of a preface to the new edition is written at the suggestion of the Publishers in the hope that those who enjoy the book may like to know something of the life of the man who wrote it.

In the year 1860 my grandfather and two of his brothers emigrated from Croft in Yorkshire to New Zealand, where they settled in the province of Marlborough in the South Island. There they started a cattle and sheep station, and there my father was born in 1869. He was the second of a numerous family of brothers and sisters, and his early years spent upon his father's farm in New Zealand made a great impression on his character for the whole of his life.

Their living was of the simplest kind, and sport very early took the place of games. The latter were of their own devising and sometimes led to curious consequences. One of their amusements was to blow up toy ships by means of churchwarden pipes filled with gunpowder, the bowl being stopped with clay and the powder-filled stem acting as a fuse. On one occasion a pipe, already charged with powder, broke off short near the bowl, and my father happened to have this in his pocket when he was made to stand in disgrace in school. The fire was close by and it occurred to him to drop the pipe bowl into it when the master was not looking. In a few moments there was a loud explosion and the burning contents of the fireplace were scattered over the floor. It is just possible that what happened might have passed for an accident except for one curious circumstance—that in the confusion and surprise which followed Alfred Chaytor was seen to be standing quite still in his place and was the only person there who had obviously noticed nothing unusual. He was soundly beaten and, I believe, expelled.

When he was fifteen years old my grandfather sent him to England at the suggestion of his uncle Henry Chaytor, and he went to Durham School, living in the holidays with his uncle and aunt at Witton, County Durham. They soon fell foul of their guest. His uncle said that he was impertinent, which I can well believe, and that he aimed a shotgun at his aunt, which to any one who ever knew him is quite incredible. Be that as it may, they refused to keep him any longer, and proposed that he should be sent back to New Zealand. At that time, most fortunately for him, his second cousins, Mr. and Mrs. Drewett, heard what his Uncle Henry proposed should be done. They thought it unfair that he should be sent away before his education was finished, and made a home for him at their house at Riding Mill in Northumberland. Grandpa and Granny they were to us. They had no children of their own, and treated my father as their son. It was at Riding Mill that he met my mother, who is Granny's niece, and as children we used always to be taken there during the Bar vacations. I have often, as a small boy, argued the possibility of having three pairs of grandparents, and called my own case to witness in the face of incredulous, but quite unconvincing, assertions of the other boys to the contrary.

For 'Grandpa' my father had the strongest affection and a sense of respect amounting to reverence. It was these feelings, as well as his gratitude, which caused him to dedicate this book to Grandpa in memory of unnumbered kindnesses. Not the least of those kindnesses was that he took the Dilston fishing on the Tyne principally for my father's amusement in his holidays, continuing the tenancy until he died, and it was there that most of my father's experience as a salmon fisher was gained. The fishing lay on the right bank from about a mile below Hexham to the bridge at Corbridge. The river was good in those days, though I believe it has fallen off considerably since then owing to the increasing pollution of its lower reaches.

Already a keen fisher, my father became really expert on this water, and his success, measured by the takes of others on the same river, was often remarkable. It was particularly noticeable in difficult conditions, such as a dead low water, that he seemed always to be able to catch fish when few others could do so.

From Durham School he went to Clare College, Cambridge, where, besides playing Rugby football for his College, he headed the first class in the Law Tripos and was given the Chancellor's gold medal. Later he became a fellow of the College and was called to the Bar by the Inner Temple.

At the Bar he acquired a good practice, mainly in Commercial cases. He was once briefed in order to rebuke a Judge in open Court. The late Mr. Justice Scrutton was at that time in charge of the Commercial list and had gravely offended a number of most respectable City solicitors by implying that they neglected their cases. One of these firms briefed my father in order to call attention to their grievances, the occasion being afforded by a summons, in itself of no great importance. It is said that he put the matter of complaint very clearly to the Judge, who thereafter considerably mended his manners.

In 1914 my father was a Captain in the Post Office Rifles. When the War broke out, he, like so many others who were over the age limit, volunteered to serve abroad, and was in France in 1915 and part of 1916. The exposure of the trenches resulted in his becoming a prey to asthma and bronchitis. He was transferred for a short time to the Divisional Headquarters Staff, but his health was broken, and in 1916 he was invalided out of the Army.

He greatly hoped that he would become strong enough to return to the Bar. In 1914 he had taken Silk, but owing to the War had never yet practised as a leader. The wish to do so, however, was not to be fulfilled, since he was never afterwards free for more than a few weeks at a time from attacks of the illness which finally caused his death.

Besides disabling him from practice at the Bar, his lack of health almost entirely prevented him from following the sport which he loved so well.

Except for a little shooting and very little fishing, he lived for his last years a life of enforced inactivity, which he found very galling. He took up as a hobby the growing and cultivation of fruit trees in his garden, but for a very large part of each summer he was confined to his room, and each winter he and my mother went to Teneriffe in the hope of getting some relief from his illness.

After Mr. Drewett's death in 1909 the house at Riding Mill had been given up, and with it the salmon fishing on the river Tyne. From then until 1922 we lived in Sussex, and my father's salmon fishing was confined to occasional days as a guest on other people's water. In 1922 his cousin, Sir Edmund Chaytor, felt obliged to sell the family place at Croft, and my father bought it rather than that it should go to strangers. The next year he went to live there, and made it his home until he died on the 20th July 1931.

All his life he had been a most generous man, always ready to help other people by unstinted gifts both of his time and money, although he was a great advocate to his children of personal economy, and he practised what he preached, living always with the greatest care and spending very little upon himself. It was typical of him that whilst still at Cambridge he saved enough out of a very moderate allowance to send one of his brothers to the same College for a year.

Although so good a teacher of fishing by the written word, yet as a teacher by the river-side my father was of too impatient a nature to make his pupil feel at ease. He had red hair and the hasty temper which so often goes with it. In the days of his health he was a very strong man, to wield a big rod was no strain on his trained muscles, and, the blunders of a learner appearing more stupid by comparison, he felt they must proceed from lack of attention to his instructions. Perhaps some of them did.

As a skinny boy of fifteen I have a vivid memory of his standing behind me and telling me, in somewhat flowery language, to 'hold up' a 17' 6" salmon rod on which I had hooked my first fish on the fly. After some hours of casting my back felt as if it would break, and no doubt the rod top did sag pretty badly. Though his criticism of the performance was severe, he never put upon me the indignity of offering to help with the rod, and somehow the fish was landed.

Whilst he professed to take an interest only in salmon fishing, my father knew a great deal about other branches of angling, and his hints to us about coarse fishing, when we were boys, often surprised us by showing that he knew much more about it than we imagined. He was a good trout fisher, if goodness in this respect is to be measured, as I think it should, by the angler's ability to fill his basket. His rod was one of the heavy 10' 6" weapons of the end of last century. Judged by modern standards it was an awful thing, but with it he could cast a fly with great delicacy, and he killed many salmon, including one of over 20 lbs., on that rod.

And now I must leave this memoir knowing that what I have written is very incomplete and mainly concerned with bare facts. It is surely true that the personality of an Author appears more plainly from his writings than from what is said of him by other people, and in this respect I can leave my father's book to speak for itself.

DREWETT CHAYTOR.

March 1936.

PREFACE

TO MY BOYS

My dear Sons, Drewett and Kit,

If in these matter-of-fact days there be any stars that still preside over our destinies, then you and I, my boys, must, I think, have been born under the sign *Pisces*, 'the fish with glittering scales'—unless, indeed, *Aquarius*, the water-carrier, is but the bearer of a celestial bait-can and intent upon his neighbouring fishes. And of you two, who each began your fishing before your seventh year was out, I have good hope of making salmon fishers, especially since that day when you, Drewett, were so fortunate as to hook and, with much luck and with some little help, to land your first grilse—a fish of 4½ lbs.—when worming for dace that very first season. One of you, indeed, began the taking of fish at the age of three by stealing, much to the joy of the proprietor, and to the detriment of your clothing, a small sea-trout from a fishmonger's slab, over which you, standing on tiptoe, were at that time barely able to peep.

I have written these letters for you in the hope

that they may tell you all that I can teach you about fishing. If they can teach you how to do it, I know well that you will like it. And for you two I need say nothing about myself, but as I begin to hope that these letters which I have written may help or amuse others, I must say something of my own fishing.

In the library of one enthusiastic angler—as Walton says—'now with God, a noted fisher both for Trout and Salmon,' there were no less than two thousand seven hundred books upon fishing. So, you see, when any one is found with pen in hand writing a book upon angling he may well be called upon, as the lawyers are when they join their circuits, to 'state his pretensions.' And if it were only to avoid the appearance of teaching those who exceed himself in experience and in skill he would probably wish to do so.

My own first experience of angling came very near to being also my last. As a very little boy I was fishing in the sea from a wooden landing-stage, and in trying to make a few feet of thread with a bent pin at the end of it reach out to some tiny prize, I tumbled in and was at once swept out by the tide. Luckily for me I had a brother, to call for help, and a mother—your grandmother—both able and willing, fully dressed as she was, to swim for me and to support me, although I was unconscious, until we were both rescued. Since then, though I have tried a great variety of sport, both in this country and in other parts of the world, fishing has always had a very large share of my affection, and of my holidays. Indeed, I was almost, as they say in the North, 'tied' to like it, for I learnt it partly from a grandfather who caught his first salmon at fifteen and his last at eighty-four, and still more from a cousin—more than a father to me—who had fished skilfully from his earliest boyhood, and who read all these pages in print, although— almost yesterday it was—he has since been called away to take his seat by that grim ferryman who awaits us all.

Of coarse fish I have no experience, and though I have fished for trout in many waters in this country, from the Exe and the Itchen up to the streams and lochs of Sutherland, and also in Norway and in New Zealand, yet it is mainly as a salmon fisher that I have loved to fish, and a great part of my salmon fishing has been upon a single river. I have never fished any of the extraordinarily good rivers either here or in Norway. How amazingly good some salmon waters can be, and how abundantly one may catch salmon in them, may, perhaps, be realised from the following little correspondence in the *Field* newspaper during the month of February 1909. On February the 20th a man writes to say that a lady, during the season lately over, has caught no less than seventy-five salmon to her own rod, and he asks is this not a 'record'—that curse of true sport. To him on February the 27th replies a proud husband; the partner of his joys has beaten this 'record,' and in six weeks of fishing has slaughtered no less than 104 salmon of the average weight of 19 lbs. But both these heroines have to yield the palm to a lady whose take for one season, tersely recorded by her husband, is the following:—Spring 55, summer 25, autumn 53, total 133 salmon, besides 750 sea-trout.

If to those whose lines are cast in such pleasant places my takes seem rather small, yet they represented very reasonable success upon the waters on which they were in fact obtained. Nor have they been left to the treachery of memory, for they were entered from day to day in Fishing Books kept with an almost religious care, and recording, with many details, every fish taken upon the water. So that if I am to be accused of lying, as commonly happens to the fisherman, it must be not merely the proverbial exaggeration of recollection, but deliberate, perverse, and pestilent.

PREFACE

Amongst people who have fished a great deal the following items together give a rough idea of the kind of experience that any salmon fisher has had. During upwards of twenty years of salmon fishing—in holidays only—my three best seasons have yielded me seventy-eight, seventy-three, and sixty-eight salmon, my best spring day five salmon, and my best autumn day nine salmon and two bull-trout, whilst my heaviest fish has been 40½ lbs.

As I undertake to teach you, my boys, I must, of course, set out very plainly my own opinion about theories held by many fine fishers, and criticise many things that they, perhaps, do. They may now be able to assure themselves that their experience is greater than mine ; and in any case, being anglers, I have little fear of annoying them, for they will be still quite sure that they are altogether right. But if I can hand on to you some of the skilful teaching and some of the ' wrinkles ' that have been always freely given to me by almost every good fisher that I have ever met—some of whom, I hope, may recognise their teaching here—I shall be more than repaid for the trouble of this little book. If from it you learn only a few of these things that I want you to know, how to tie your salmon gut with the knot that I have explained for you at page 187, how to save your flies on windy days by dressing them on a loop of soft fiddle-string (p. 167), how to recover your form at once when your casting is not satisfying you (p. 15), and how to hold your rod in a less strained and less tiring attitude than is commonly done by the salmon fisher (p. 24),—if you learn only those four things from these letters, I fancy that you will find yourselves content.

Many a time in reading books upon salmon fishing I have wished that their skilful writers would tell one a little more about the fish that they have caught—about the fights that they made for their liberty, their success or failure, and the angler's view of their desperate battles. When an author will write so for me I stand beside him in the river, my fingers feel the line, the reel screams in my ears, some fish of mine, lost or long dead, flings itself out with his or dashes down over the foaming rapids and our fish are lost together. When the fish is landed my interest ends, but if the fish is lost I know that angler's mind. My rod flies up with his, then comes a moment's doubt, a hope that the fish may only have turned, and in spite of all may still be on, then the sickening certainty that he has gone. It has always seemed to me strange that such trivial details can be interesting even to another fisherman—but they are so, and I suppose that it is only another proof of the extraordinary fascination that salmon fishing has for us.

Of course, many times—though your books will hardly tell you this—the playing of a salmon is as dull and uneventful as a thing can be. If that dulness were not varied, and pretty often, by the most brilliant contrasts, we should soon despise salmon fishing and abandon it altogether. But amongst every few fish comes one whose pluck and speed and dash keep your hands trembling the whole time that you are playing him, and wipe out all memory of his less active fellows.

Well, I have tried to give you a good many of such fishing days, and the actual details of the fights I had. In doing this it is useless to search back into one's memory, even aided by the best fishing records. You must, as I think, and have done, take a day that is still to-day or only yesterday and give the actual events from a fresh and precise recollection of them. If you find it dull to read these detailed accounts of playing fish, you must skip them, but I hope that when you can fish you will see something out of your own memory in them because you yourselves are salmon fishers and have dreamed dreams.

Not egotism, but the direct simplicity of using

the first and second person in speaking of scenes at which one has been present, and in giving any instruction, caused me to retain the form of letters directly to you.

I have put in two photographs of salmon and some others of typical salmon pools. The latter were all taken by my friend Bruce Williamson, to whom I am greatly indebted for them. I have to thank certain of my friends for reading several of these letters and helping me to knock out some fustian from what I had written. I dare say that there is much fustian left. I fear it is so. It is rather easy to be absurd when the very thought of a rod and a salmon pool can make one feel like a schoolboy going home for the holidays.

Your affectionate father,

A. H. C.

CONTENTS

	PAGE
INTRODUCTORY ESSAY,	1

CHAP.

I.	THE ROD, LINE, AND GUT,	6
II.	ON CASTING THE FLY. WHERE TO CAST. MOVING BETWEEN CASTS,	12
III.	HOW TO FISH,	27
IV.	ON FLIES,	34
V.	STRIKING THE FISH,	40
VI.	ON PLAYING A SALMON,	46
VII.	THE SENSE OF PAIN IN FISH,	55
VIII.	SPRING FISHING,	63
	ODE TO A SALMON RIVER,	76
IX.	A WEEK-END IN OCTOBER,	77
X.	MINNOW FISHING,	88
XI.	WORMING,	105
XII.	ONE OF OUR BEST DAYS,	114
XIII.	ON OTTERS AND OTHER POACHERS,	126
XIV.	SOME MORE POACHERS,	137
XV.	THE LAST DAY OF A SEASON,	145
XVI.	MY BEST FISH,	150
XVII.	WHEN AND WHERE TO EXPECT SALMON,	158

CONTENTS

CHAP.		PAGE
XVIII.	HINTS ON FLY TYING,	166
XIX.	KNOTS,	177
XX.	OF WADING, WADERS, AND CLOTHING,	192
XXI.	TACKLE AND ACCESSORIES,	201
XXII.	ON SPAWNING SALMON,	208
XXIII.	ON SPAWNING SALMON—*continued*,	220
XXIV.	TALES OF A GREAT-GRANDFATHER,	229
XXV.	NATURAL HISTORY AND OTHER POINTS,	253
XXVI.	THE OLD SALMON ACTS,	263
XXVII.	ON TAKING A FISHING,	273
XXVIII.	A POSTSCRIPT,	278
XXIX.	SOME BOOKS ON FISHING,	282
	APPENDIX ON PRAWNING AND NOTES,	286
	INDEX,	313

LIST OF ILLUSTRATIONS

THE THROAT OF A POOL,	*facing page*	36
A SALMON POOL,	,,	37
A HIGHLAND RIVER,	,,	68
A 25 LBS. FISH ON A SPINNING ROD,	,,	69
SEPTEMBER 7TH, 1908,	,,	164
A FORTY-POUNDER,	,,	165
AN ENGLISH RIVER,	,,	196
A ROCKY STREAM IN SCOTLAND,	,,	197

LETTERS
TO
A SALMON FISHER'S SONS

AN INTRODUCTORY ESSAY
ON FISHING

As Bacon said, 'God Almighty first planted a garden, and sure it is the purest of all humane pleasures.' The fisher constantly is as it were in a wild garden, and this very pleasure to be found in the beauty around him he has made a part of his sport itself. It has a spirit: it is not merely the sport of taking fish.

This was not always so, because it was not always realised, and even to this day in many countries angling is thought of merely as a humble drudgery. But in England, since the time of Walton, the first thought of your true fisher is of the fresh air, the rushing water in his ears, the cool evenings, the glowing sunsets, the flowers and trees, the birds, and all the river-loving things in furs or feathers. Small voices speak to him: the cheerful 'chit-chit' of the water ouzel, the droning of bees in the heather, the distant cry of curlew —that sweet quavering call which finds some unfailing echo in the soul of every man that knows the moorland—and always the swishing ripple of swift water,—these things fill him with a pleasure that he looks for as part of the very sport itself.

On sunny mornings in some quiet valley he sees the white-breasted 'dipper' curtsey to him from some stone ere she plunges in again to search for food upon the shallows, or the kingfisher skimming the water with his gleam of blue, or hovering, a flutter of blue and orange, over some luckless minnow. The swallow, sandmartin, water-wagtail, sandpiper are to be seen at every pool, and not seldom a great grey heron slowly and clumsily rises and flaps off at his approach. The stoat and the weasel he sees almost daily by the river-side. If very lucky, or very early, he may see the mole shuffle down to drink at the water's edge, or the otters' cubs playing like kittens by the willows, or perhaps at evening he may hear a hissing whistle, and if he keep still he will see the otters themselves slowly fishing upwards for their dinner.

The rose-pink flowers of the sea-thrift cover the banks wherever they are sanded by the winter's floods. Here and there his eye rests on a mass of wild pansies—the beautiful flower that we call 'heart's-ease'—on a nodding cluster of blue harebells, or on the pure five-pointed stars of the Grass of Parnassus. Amongst the dark firs the beeches are standing in their fresh spring dress, or perhaps the budding larches are putting out the softest green of all the year. Even in wild autumn weather he sees the flying leaves drift by like leaves of gold and burnished copper; and he hears the water ouzel then, and then only, singing a real and almost a blackbird's song.

These sights are his in a north-country landscape, but other sights as fair may be seen on any stream winding through southern meadows, or sparkling in the woodlands of a Devonshire valley. Does it matter that trout or salmon on such a day take ill or not at all? He will surely reckon this amongst his fishing days.

And then there is the joy of fishing itself; of throwing a line whether fish take or no. It seems impossible to convey the reality of this as a separate pleasure, to any but honest anglers. '*You fish?*' they say. '*What patience you must have.*' Not at all: hardly anything is less true. Some of the most impatient souls alive are untiring salmon fishers; men to whom blank days or lost fish are but as whetstones to keener fishing on the morrow.

The fact is that it is a keen pleasure not only to be fishing well oneself, but even to see another fishing well. If he is trouting, to see him laying his line softly on the water and dropping a tiny olive upon the very spot he chooses, to swim jauntily 'cocked' over the fish's nose; or it may be fishing quickly up-stream with a cast of wet flies, yet searching every swirl and nook, and taking incessant risks amongst rocks or branches.

If he is salmon fishing, to see him, with that slow recovery and easy action that lays the fly at the full stretch, even against a strong and gusty wind, casting a long, clean line and fishing every pool like a master of his craft.

Every cast well done is a separate and distinct effort with a distinct pleasure in its success. Every salmon fisher knows a few difficult or risky casts that delight him every time that he makes them neatly. Salmon love to lie against stakes or weiring or the points of jetties, and such places often require the most dexterous casting. And even the best salmon fisher varies in the nicety of his throw. On one day a happy judgment seems to pitch the fly almost within an inch or two of every danger; on another his gayest fly remains to ornament some snag or stake. The boldest cast goes right; the slightest hesitation hits the very danger that it feared.

But I wander from the point, which is that the act of fishing is itself a pleasure, and one not easy to explain except to those to whom it needs no explanation. Each several cast is an act of no little skill, with many stages between complete success and total failure; and each cast well made in good water is the beginning of a new and vivid hope of that surging swirl upon the water, or that heavy unseen pull, which marks the supreme moment of salmon fishing.

Of the pleasure of success in fishing I need say nothing. We all know it; and we all have felt it. Why do we look back upon that first quivering salmon and recall every detail of the scene? Many triumphs of every kind we can forget, but never that one. You may have a wife than whom no man has a dearer; you may have triumphed in endless ways; but not wedding days, nor schoolboy triumphs, nor student hopes fulfilled, nor snowy peaks, nor the hunter's fiercer joy will have so many cells in the honeycomb of memory as your first spring salmon. The eleventh of March seldom finds me near a river without my seeing that day well over twenty years ago when, as a boy, I stepped into the water and lifted out by the tail my first salmon—a little fish, as I know now, of $9\frac{1}{2}$ lbs., but then I thought it the most beautiful fish that ever was seen.

But even success has its limits; the fish is caught, the thing is done. It is our lost fish that I believe stay longest in our memory, and seize upon our thoughts whenever we look back to fishing days. The most gallant fish when eaten is forgotten, but the fish that, after a mad, glorious battle, has beaten us and left us quivering with excitement and vexation, is hooked and lost again in many a year to come.

I

THE ROD, LINE, AND GUT

MY DEAR BOYS,—'A large demonstration of words' is not the best way of teaching salmon fishing. Actual fishing in the company of a good salmon fisher is the best way, and, indeed, it is the only really good way; but I have myself found a great deal of help in reading books on fishing, and a great deal of pleasure, more especially when fish have been taking badly, in trying the various ways in which their authors advise you to proceed. From a book you cannot learn the whole art of salmon fishing, but you can learn to avoid many disastrous mistakes, and you can learn endless 'wrinkles' which make your fishing more finished and much more effectual than before.

We most of us begin as trout fishers, and after a season or two of salmon fishing we feel that we know all about it, and that there is really not much to be learnt by any decent trout fisher. But a larger experience brings doubts. We find that in low waters and in the worst conditions some few men can regularly catch fish, whilst everybody else on the river is doing nothing. When salmon are taking freely almost any one who can throw a fly may catch a salmon, but at other times the difference between a really good and a merely ordinary fisher is just as great in salmon fishing as it is in trouting, or as it is between the good and the ordinary performer in every other sport. In really bad conditions the good fisher alone will catch fish and the other will consistently catch nothing. Moreover, I am convinced that your really skilful salmon fisher is a much rarer bird than the really good trout fisher. It may be that the opportunities of gaining great experience of salmon fishing are not so common, and perhaps fall too often to somewhat luxurious and idle sportsmen who leave the whole direction in the hands of the gillie or keeper, whilst the good trout fisher does his own thinking, and becomes a far better performer. But certainly, whatever be the reason, great skill is not so common in salmon fishing.

Most books on fishing begin with a chapter on the natural history of the salmon and of his cousins the bull-trout and the sea-trout. Next they go on to deal at very great length with the rods and reels and flies, and the tackle of every sort, with which you may hope to catch him. As to the life-history of the salmon, our knowledge of it, thanks to systematic marking of fish, is only just now beginning to be worth anything at all; but this knowledge has hardly any bearing upon the actual catching of the fish with rod and line, and I shall keep for a later letter what little I have to say about the habits and food of the fish and about its deadly enemies at every stage of its life.

I shall deal also with rods and tackle in a separate letter. As to the tackle I will here only say this: as the prize is large, powerful, and greatly valued, so the tackle should in every detail be sound and strong and the best of its kind. I do not mean that the gut, for instance, should be of the stoutest, nor that the rod or reel need be very costly. Far from it. Many people use gut that is far too thick; so thick that it spoils the working of any small fly, and actually helps to prevent its users from ever hooking the fish that they have provided such strength to hold.

So also with flies. Many of the costly shop flies are so overloaded with feathers that when in the water they are only a sodden lump, and all life and movement is destroyed. These flies only begin to kill fish when they get old and knocked to bits with use. Their confiding owner, too, usually has a great tin box, or else a giant book, full of similar glories; and he spends a large part of his time, when he ought to be fishing, in inspecting these flies in order to decide which he shall use next, and then in tying it on in place of the one which he had last preferred. This extravagance in gut and flies, just as in rods or reels, does not help you one bit. Any sound rod, whether of greenheart or of cane, will do well;

but it ought not to be so long or so heavy as to overtax your strength in any way. Personally I generally use rods of split cane with steel centres, and I do that because they have been given to me; but I am inclined to think that the steel centre, though ensuring its long life, does not make the rod so quick and lively or so 'sweet' to fish with as is a simple split cane rod by an equally good maker. By this time I think that there are many satisfactory makers of such rods, but it is not my business to advertise them.

So with reels. Any sound reel will do, but I prefer to have a reel as small as possible—say four inches, or even three and a half inches, across the whole side—and to get the right length of line by using very thin and strong undressed 'backing' of plaited silk or hemp. If you have, as for years I had, only one rod—let us say a strong rod of seventeen feet, for that is about the size most generally useful—it is well worth while to have both a heavy and a light line for it. When the water is low, or when the weather is not very windy, the lighter line is the means of fishing with much less effort and very much more lightly and more pleasantly than you could do with the heavier one. In very windy weather the heavy line will fish better and will save you endless vexation and effort. Even if one keeps only a single reel to serve for both of these lines, the trouble of tying on a different line is very small, and changes need not usually be frequent, as one fishes with the lighter line always except in big waters or blustering winds. You keep each line whipped on to its own 60 to 100 yards of backing, and you reel off the whole together and then tie on the other line to the core or drum of the empty reel.

Although it will be rather costly, yet it is true economy to buy a really good line, and then to keep it sound by seeing that it is invariably put out and dried after use, even though you intend to fish the next day. For the heavier line I do not think it by any means necessary that it should be tapered, though it is pleasanter so; but the lighter one should be the softest and the most pliable double-tapered line that you can get.

As to gut, it need not be at all expensive if you make up your own casts; which is one of the simplest things in the world, almost as easy as falling off the proverbial log, as soon as you know the proper knot to use for strong gut.[1] Yet at the present time not one angler in fifty knows how to tie that knot, and it is used only by one or two fishing-tackle makers, who jealously keep the secret. For the strongest fish you may use quite thin gut if you in the first place select the gut and tie it properly, and then are always alert to watch it and to remove any weakened strand, and to re-tie any injured or 'necked' knot. The first sign of weakening may be seen by taking the cast by short lengths in both hands and bending it at

[1] See Chap. XIX. for this knot.

each knot, when any unsound or necked strand will at once show itself by a sharp uneven bend usually close to the knot. This is a much more searching test than a mere pull at the gut cast; and a cast that when soaked will stand a moderate, but firm, pull, and will show no weakness when bent at every knot, as I have just described, is quite sound and fit to stand the strain of any fish.

No more about tackle at present. Let us begin straightway to fish.

Yours,
A. H. C.

II

ON CASTING THE FLY

My dear Sons,—Every one can tell you that you cast a fly by using a rod in the same manner as you would a whip. That is correct enough, but when first you begin to put that advice into practice you will find it vague and unsatisfying to the last degree. Then you find that the only thing that you do not do with the fly is to send it out as you wish. You may know quite well how to handle a whip, but the strong salmon rod seems quite incapable of any similar movements, and the line persists in splashing into the water 'all in a heap,' whilst the gut ties itself into tangled knots. The fact is that the easy whip-like motion is only to be had in perfection with a long line, and the beginner, for obvious reasons, has not started with a long line.

The vital fault with most beginners is that they fail to bend the rod; they use it not as a whip but as if it were a stiff pole. In their effort to send the line back behind them they throw the point of the rod too far back. They *wave* the rod back, instead of first raising the line to the surface of the water, by lifting the rod top gently, and then sharply throwing the line back, and up into the air behind them, with a *flip* of the top of the rod.

CASTING

You should always start your learner in a swift, even-running stream, where his line will be pulled out taut for him by the current before each new cast is made. The act of casting with a salmon rod is, for the beginner, a straight overhead *flip-flip*, that is, a strong flip back and upwards; then a sharp and firm stopping of the rod whilst you may count steadily 'one,' 'two'; then a much easier flip forward and upward.

That is the cast; the essential acts of casting.

For the benefit of any learner without a present coach I will try to describe accurately in detail the method of casting with a salmon rod. Such a minute description is necessarily tedious to any one but the beginner, and should be skipped by every one else, except, perhaps, the paragraph on page 15, in which is pointed out the way of recovering one's form when, through being tired or out of practice, one is casting badly and spoiling half the pleasure of one's fishing. I ought to add that I have never been in the habit of using a Castle Connell rod or any rod of that type, and that I do not think my directions very appropriate for an exceedingly whippy or top-heavy rod. And one must remember that almost every rod varies slightly in the period, that is to say in the timing, of its action.

The Detail of Casting

Before the cast begins the rod must be raised, usually to an angle of about 45° from the water, in order to bring the line to the surface before you try to throw it back behind you. No rod can throw back a line which is still left sunk deeply in the water, except as a very occasional effort and in the hands of a skilled fisher.

For ordinary fishing the line must be brought as near the surface as possible before every cast.

Again, when the *flip-flip* has been given, the rod point is still high in the air and is allowed to sink almost in one movement to an easy position in which it may be held whilst the fly swings round. The novice often fails to see that the force is all put into the very beginning of the forward flip, and he firmly waves the rod forward down to the fishing position. His line follows the downward direction and falls in a heap.

Consider by itself the act of throwing the line forward. As you want a line, at that moment stretching back from the rod top, to be thrown straight forward over the water, it is easy to see that the impetus must be given at the highest part of the curve made by the rod, for that alone can give the line a forward pull parallel to the water level. Similarly, after making the backward flip, which is to lift the line, the rod should instantly be stopped firmly with the butt piece very little past the perpendicular—of course the top will bend back rather more. Even so, the line is falling as it runs out behind you, but if the rod is waved far back, as beginners almost always do, the line is dragged downwards and cannot extend behind you, as it is essential, for a beginner, that it should do in order to prepare for a clean and easy cast forward.

In describing the cast both back and forward again you may notice that I say that it should be a flip backwards *and upwards,* or forwards and *slightly upwards.* This is the great key to good casting. As the flip back is made, the wrists and elbows are raised, so that the lower of your two wrists is almost shoulder high. Then as the line runs back the rod, almost unconsciously, is allowed to sink six or eight inches perpendicularly, and as the forward flip is given the elbows are again raised, and the point of the rod, as it were, pushed out forward and upward, with a much slower and slighter flip than the backward one.

Even when you can cast well you will often, at the beginning of the season, or when getting tired, find that your casting is not pleasing you, is not so straight and easy as it should be, and that the fly is not falling at the full stretch of the gut. Then is the time to remember to use your wrists and raise them high, and as it were to *lift* the flip back and push out *and up* the cast forward, and I will undertake that you shall instantly find that all your old skill and lightness has returned.

A cast, then, is made thus (beginning from the fishing position at the end of the former cast) :—

    1. Raise the rod slowly to bring the line to the surface, then (without any pause)

    2. A sharp *flip* back and up, raising the arms

and stopping the rod sharply when the butt is just beyond the upright.
3. A pause of about a second, then an easy flip forward and upward. (During the pause the rod sinks perpendicularly a few inches, and at the end of the cast the arms are fully outstretched and level with the shoulders.)
4. Then the rod, without a pause, gently sinks to the fishing position, and the arms are drawn in to the sides.

The chief difficulty with a beginner is to get the time of the cast. He will hardly ever give the line time to run out behind him before making the cast forward. With an average length of line, say about three to four rod lengths out from the reel to the fly, the time is this:—(spoken slowly)—(*lift*, then) FLIP—one—two—*flip*—(and lower).

I need hardly say that when you become skilful you can choose amongst many styles of casting, and in each style can fish with much variation; but when once you have mastered the simple 'overhead' cast, as it is called, you can fish almost any pool perfectly well, and soon other ways of casting will come to you naturally and easily. For myself I almost always use another cast which consists in throwing the line not overhead, but to one side of you, and always up the stream, no matter from which side you are fishing. Then, chiefly with a turn of the wrists, you switch it forward and across in the line that you wish it to take in order to cover the stream for the next cast.

Casting against a high wind blowing almost straight in his face is a severe trial to a beginner. His fly will persist in falling back in a muddle just when the gut seemed about to uncurl and fall at its full stretch. He puts more and more force into the cast and quickly gets tired and disheartened. He should go at it not violently but more quietly, should throw the line rather on to the surface of the water than over it as usual, and should finish his cast with the rod top actually touching the water. He should cast quietly but cast, as it were, *at* the water, and he will soon find that he can cast even against such a wind quite comfortably and quite well. But a good rod is a great help to him.

Where to Cast

Now as to the direction of your cast. Your books will tell you to cast down and across the stream and at an angle of about 45°; and so you should do in straightforward, simple streams, where such a cast will enable you to put your fly well beyond the lie of the fish. But never hesitate to vary the angle to suit any pool. Especially in swirling pot holes or in any pool where there is a strong eddy on one or both sides, a cast made straight across or even slightly up-stream, and fished by raising the rod point slowly as the fly comes into the main current, appears to be particularly attractive to the fish. It is not only to salmon that this cast is deadly, for I have constantly found that large trout will snatch the salmon fly as it is just on the point of being towed out of the eddy into which it fell.

Such swirling pools are generally deep, and the fish usually take best at and below the point where the heavy boil ends and where the violent surging water begins to grow shallow and to run fan-wise, swift and glassy to all sides. There it is well to make two kinds of casts at each stand, one thrown well across to take fish lying in the eddy or on the farther edge of the heavy water, the other barely clearing the heavy water to hang well over fish lying on the nearer edge of the heavy water. Cast thus the fly will not be swept over these fish as quickly as you will find that in the former cast it is swept away when once the swirling current catches it.

On the other hand, when the water is dead low and the fish shy, you will often find that the quicker the fly can be made to sweep over them the better is your chance of a rise. At such times I have over and over again for weeks together caught almost all my fish by casting a small fly straight across the stream, keeping the fly near the surface by raising the rod point in a series of small, steady lifts, and ending by pulling in some yards

CASTING LIGHTLY

of line by hand as the fly fishes the nearer edge of the stream. Then, of course, one must 'shoot' that slack line through the rings as the next cast is made. Indeed, you are almost compelled to draw in line by hand in such slow waters in order to prevent the line from sinking too deep for you to make the next cast, and also in order to ensure that the fly shall fall softly on the water.

The soft falling of the fly on the water is not so important when waters are high or coloured, but is a very vital matter in low and 'gin' clear streams. People will tell you that it is of no practical importance to cast a salmon fly lightly and without any splash. Pay no attention to them. When the water gets low and clear, light casting—and light tackle too—becomes of cardinal importance. I have, hundreds of times, in low water seen fish bolt off the shallows into deep water when a clumsy cast, of my own or of some other's making, has fallen near them. Many times, also, I have seen the wave made by a fish moving off, though more quietly, at the sight of the finest tackle lightly cast, and when, from the place in which they were lying, it was almost certain that they could not have seen the fisher. If they can thus be so alarmed as to move off, how often must they, one would suppose, in a higher water, detect the gut or the splash when either they are not so much frightened as to move away, or by reason of the greater volume of water we are unable to see that they have done so.

Moving between the Casts

There is no hard-and-fast rule to be laid down as to the pace at which you should cover the water when salmon fishing. Speaking generally, one moves about a yard after each cast, but when your fly is covering the very best part of the pool or some place where you know that a good fish is lying, you may well move less than a yard at a time, or, still better, may make a second cast, placed rather less across the stream, before you move from each stand. There is one great error to be avoided which is a fault very common with beginners and one into which older fishers often fall; you must avoid moving down the pool whilst the fly is being swept over the fish. Take your step or steps down the pool before you cast the fly, and do not move again until that cast is fished out. To move down whilst the fly is fishing, unless perhaps in a very swift bit of water, obviously slackens the line and spoils the fishing of the fly. The chief object in striving to cast well is to have the line always stretched taut to the fly, partly in order that the fly, by stemming the current, may appear to the fish a living thing, partly that the fish, if he takes the fly, may not escape being hooked. Both these ends are lost if you move down-stream whilst the fly is fishing. You should try to move down whilst you are slowly lifting the fly as it hangs on the nearer edge of the stream after the cast is over, but if

AVOID DISTURBING FISH

the bank is rough or the wading difficult you have to move down as best you can, but always after the fly has done its journey across the pool.

Do not wade near the place where the fish lie unless neither you nor any one else is to fish that water again. Salmon are not very shy in big waters, but in low, clear water you may easily prevent them taking altogether. Indeed, I think that perhaps one of the chief reasons why fishing straight across the stream so often pays in low waters is that this method keeps the angler and his gleaming rod well away from the fish. For in sunlight the rod gleams brightly, and our absurd aluminium reels and nickelled gaffs flash in the sunlight, and the net is spread in vain in the sight of any bird.

Yet fishers constantly wade too far in and spoil their own sport. The fact is that one watches the place where the fly is fishing, forgetting the water that one has just passed.

There is a strong craving, too, in all of us, even the oldest, to cover just a yard or two more water than we comfortably can reach. It is a mistake from all points of view, but it has to be reckoned with, and you should constantly look at the water opposite to the place at which you are standing in order to see that you are not getting too far in.

If you have plenty of water to fish, do not allow yourself to become a slow, pottering fisher. Except at the best spots fish quickly, move rather more than a yard, even up to two yards, between the casts, and rather leave time to come back and try the pools again than consume your time in slowly going over them once. The fish that is not willing to take now may very well do so after noon or as the evening closes in. Two of the soundest pieces of advice that I know came down to me from an arrant old North Yorkshire poacher who had fished all his life in the river Tees, and who, about the year 1820, used to teach your great-grandfather to fish. This old rascal had two constant maxims. The first was, 'Keep stirring your foot,' by which, of course, he meant keep moving on, so as to cover new water, a most essential point in trout fishing with the wet fly, and hardly less valuable to the salmon fisher. His second maxim was intended solely for the salmon fisher, and it was this, 'You 've allers a chance of a daft 'un or a blind 'un.' This uncouth phrase was intended to express the fact that on the very worst day and at the least expected time and place you may well catch a salmon. On many and many a hopeless day I have persevered, with that in mind, and have not missed the reward. I still have a salmon fly of that old man's making, inherited from his pupil of 1820, together with much quaint old tackle. The fly is tied upon a big 2½-inch hook of the old 'Sproat' bend. The body is a huge caterpillar of coarse red wool as thick as a lead pencil, with a fibre of gold tinsel from an old epaulette twisted round it. There is a stubby tail made of a few barred strands from a jay's wing, and the fly is winged with two tail feathers of the wren, tied so as to lie almost flat along the body, like the wings of a stone-fly. It has no hackle, throat, cheeks, butt, tag, horns, or topping, none of the nonsense dear to the modern salmon fisher, but I have often been assured by my grandfather that with this fly the old man caught as many salmon as those fishers who could command the best flies of that day, and that except in very low waters he used no other fly but this.

How to Hold the Salmon Rod

The friendly scoffer thinks that all fishing is a gentle and restful method of enjoying the fresh air and the beauties of nature, and that as a manly exercise it is a mere nothing, perhaps something more vigorous than billiards. Tell him that salmon fishing is hard, bodily labour, and he cannot believe that you are serious. It looks so easy. But if you can only decoy him into a pair of long waders, and put him in a strong water and with a big rod in his hands, to attempt a day's salmon fishing, you will hear no more criticism of that kind. Even hardened salmon fishers, after a cold, rough day in heavy water, I have known to come in almost too tired to eat, and I have more than once seen a teasing hostess take a malicious pleasure in putting them, after dinner, into a comfortable arm-chair near a hot fire in order to enjoy seeing their heroic efforts to avoid the awful crime of falling asleep in the drawing-room. It is not only that the casting is hard work and finds out all the untrained muscles in your back, but the common way of holding a salmon rod when the cast is over is very tiring also. After the cast, and when the fly is fishing, the butt of the rod is usually placed against the hip or flank of the angler, and its weight is supported by one hand or the other, which holds the rod some eighteen inches beyond the reel. But owing to the leverage of the long, heavy rod the position is a strained one, and even to strong arms, not hardened by incessant fishing, becomes, in time, very tiring.

Before a long day is over your forearm and elbow can literally ache with the stiffness of this position, added to the exertion of much casting, and you long for some change, to rest the muscles on which the strain falls. Well, there is another and a much easier way of holding the rod either as a change from or as a substitute for the more common mode. The method is this:—As you make the cast, one hand, of course, is below the reel and the other is holding the rod about eighteen inches above it—about the top of the cork handle, if there is one. As the cast ends, you retain the grasp of this upper hand only, and you draw back the rod until the reel passes your side, placing your other hand on the rod just below the place where the lowest ring usually stands. You will find that the seventeen-foot or eighteen-foot rod is almost, though not quite, balanced in your hands, and further, that you can feel the pull of the line much better, and that you can strike with great quickness, yet without excessive force. My own firm belief is that from the time when I learned to hold the rod in this way I have hooked a much greater proportion of the fish which have touched my fly, and have hardly lost any by hard striking. Of course there is no mystery about this way of holding the rod: it is known to many old fishers and to not so many young ones, who are apt to regard it as not quite so taking in appearance as the commoner way. But I have the very highest opinion of it, not only for its ease and comfort, but as a great help to quick and certain hooking of the fish. I think that the mere drawing back of the rod involved is valuable as tightening the line after every cast, but the greatest point is the quickness with which you get in touch with your fish, and the freedom from the risk of breaking the gut by too sudden a stroke on feeling the pull of a salmon. I first began using this way of holding the rod from observing it practised by two of the best and most experienced fishers that I know, and one of them when fishing with me has in three days taken fourteen salmon on the same fly from successive rises and without missing one single rise. Years ago I used to think that an average of one fish landed for every three rises was fairly good fishing, but now I think that one ought to kill on an average well over two fish out of every three decent pulls or rises.

Holding the rod in this way is not difficult to learn, but you can bungle it. Some men never can keep the reel away from their bodies or clothing, or they manage to hold the line so that it cannot go free when a fish takes, but a very little practice will make this easy. It will be found, too, that the most easy position with a heavy rod is that where the right elbow is placed upon the rod above the reel, and the upward pressure of the butt is checked against the right forearm. Even a very big and heavy rod held in this way seems altogether lighter and livelier.

One hint or two upon carrying your rod whilst walking from place to place on the bank, and especially through woods or bushes. The top seems to flip about much less if the rod is carried almost horizontal and with the reel uppermost, and whilst going through trees it is advisable to carry it butt foremost. If carried over your shoulder, you will find that the closer you hold your hand to the point where the rod is resting on your shoulder the less the rod will flip about behind you. These things may seem trifles to tell you, but when you are carrying a heavy load of fish it is intensely annoying to have your rod constantly slashing against or catching in the trees as you pass them, and it is anything but easy to prevent it.

III

HOW TO FISH

My dear Boys,—When you have learnt to cast a fly tolerably, you then begin to tackle the real craft. That is, how to fish; how best to make use of your power of casting so that salmon may be induced to take the fly you throw for them.

There are few subjects in sport upon which more theories are held, or about which more nonsense is talked. These theories are held almost as articles of faith and are stated with angry conviction. Gillies and fishing-keepers are proverbial for their ignorant omniscience. Nearly all of them believe that there is only one way—and that, of course, is their way—to do everything, and the moment that they see a newcomer fish otherwise, they regard him as little better than a fool, and if he does not speedily conform to their ways, he will receive neither information nor help from them—and you want their information as to where the fish lie and where they take. The truth is that there are many ways to fish well, and no one way is the best in all cases. You may fish either deep or on the surface, with flies large or small, plain or gaudy, working the fly or bringing the rod round perfectly steady, and in general you may do well with each method.

The fact that different styles of fishing do hold their ground amongst good fishers suggests—as I believe is the case—that no one style should be adhered to slavishly, and that to fish with the greatest effect one should vary the methods of fishing with the varying waters fished. And not only do salmon pools differ greatly in character, but the same pool often requires fishing in a totally different place and manner according as the river is high or low. Personally I was taught to hold the rod almost level over the water and to fish a long line, letting the fly sink deep, and fishing without the least lifting motion of the rod point. A fine fisher, then always fishing near me, used the opposite method. With rod held high, as in trouting, and with a rather short line, cast lightly upon the water, he kept a much larger fly always skimming near the surface with a constant lifting motion intended to give the fly a lifelike play. Over our first five years of fishing together he maintained a slight but distinct lead in the number of salmon caught, but in every single year the fish taken in the same water by the deeper fishing of a small fly averaged from 1 to 3 lbs. heavier than those taken by the larger fly played near the surface. Other results we noticed. One method succeeded constantly in places where the other fisher used to fail, and in a big dark water the surface method was greatly inferior to the other.

TWO STYLES OF FISHING

So we came to vary the style of fishing to suit, as we judged, the different pools and waters. The result is that now in the rough stream of a medium-sized river, or in deep, strong waters, we fish with a long line cast well down-stream, and allowed to come round as deep in the water as possible without any playing of the rod, which is held with the tip only two or three feet above the water. But in low water, and in quiet streams or glassy swirling pools, unless very strong indeed, the fly is cast much more across the stream and worked round by a series of short lifts until the rod is almost upright, and often line is drawn in by hand before making the next cast.

The clearer the water, and the more shy the fish, the more I find myself fishing on the surface and playing the fly quickly. There are many tricks and variations. Across a glassy swirl one constantly casts at right angles to the central stream or even somewhat up-stream. After almost every deeply fished cast one allows a slight hang to the fly and then slowly draws it up with a series of short lifts. In fishing from the inner side of a curving stream a quite exaggerated hang, after the fly *appears* to have swung below you, and then a slow, jerky lifting, with rod stretched out far over the stream, has constantly produced fine fish just as the fly was about to be taken from the water. They seem either to follow it, or—as I have seen them do—to rush at it out of the part already fished, as they see the fly being drawn past them up the edge of the stream. Often the heaviest fish will thus take the fly, and take it so late that the only way to strike the hook home—as you must do with the line just about to leave the water and the rod nearly upright—is to jerk the top violently backward so that the weight of the line may jerk the hook hard into the fish. Often when a pool has been fished down blank in the ordinary style you may get a fish or two at once by fishing it over again, either by starting to fish from the bottom and backing upwards, or by fishing from the top downwards, and in either case casting straight across the stream and keeping the rod top well up-stream as the fly comes round. I have even seen a fish that in a dead low water had been pricked, and would not rise again, taken by the fisher standing at the head of the shrunken stream, holding out his rod over the current and letting down the same fly to his fish.

One more caution to you. Be most careful not to bring round the rod point faster than the line is being brought round by the current. This is a very common fault, especially when one is impatient or pressed for time, but it is a bad fault, for it keeps the line slack instead of taut to the fly. Rather do the opposite and keep the point of your rod out over the stream, particularly if the fly has to swing close in below you. When fishing from the inside of a curving stream you should be most careful to do this.

I would not have any one think that any of these

methods are stated as being necessarily the best, still less as the only good ways of fishing. The more you can vary your fishing with the water the better you will fish, but some idea of the ways that others find to succeed may help you when no mentor is at hand and the fish utterly decline your offers.

In quick, narrow rushes, when the river is dead low, a way that often succeeds is this: with a sea-trout fly or a big March brown on a light line and thin gut, make your cast straight across the rush, then with outstretched rod let the fly sink as deep as possible into the centre of the current, then with a short, jerky motion begin towing it up-stream as it approaches the side on which you stand. Constantly the fish will grab the fly just after the jerks begin.

On one, as I thought, quite hopeless afternoon in September 1904, hot, hazy, and windless, with a glaring sun, in a dead low water, in one short stream, I took in this way, with a double-handed trout rod and a small green-bodied, heckam-peckam fly, three fish of 13, 12, and 5 lbs., and lost a fourth. Many and many a time the odd fish that has saved a blank day in August or September has come by this method when the ordinary salmon fly and its manœuvres were quite useless. Again on two days in the season of 1907, in the dead low September waters of that year, I took four salmon each day with the same trout rod and tiny fly. For this kind of fishing I use a thin sea-trout cast ended off with three feet of ordinary trout worming gut, but gut always new and sound, and watched most carefully to detect the least sign of weakening. Such gut costs only a couple of shillings or so for a hundred strands, and one must simply throw away the cast so soon as it becomes frayed or weakened and make up a new one in its place. It sounds alarming to hook large salmon upon such thin gut, but if sound and new, such gut is very strong indeed, and with a light rod you need have no fear of a break unless the fish can get round some rock or snag. These things, of course, are generally more dangerous than ever in low waters, and of them you must take your chance, and must, when broken on them—as I constantly have been broken in low summer waters—reflect that you might easily have fared no better with the strongest gut, and that with it you would probably never have hooked the fish at all, nor had the fun of his fight and loss.

But for very low, clear water a very light line is almost as important as thin gut. Not only is the splash of its fall much less, but the feebler current can float a light line and give the fly a lively motion when the ordinary salmon line is almost useless except in the rush of the streams. However, when in despair you have taken to your small flies and trout tackle, it is worth while occasionally to try a big salmon fly in the streams. Occasionally a fish that has not seen a big fly for some time will seize one in the very smallest water.

When you have risen a fish and failed to hook him, you may be in doubt as to what is the best thing to do. If he has been pricked he may come again, but he is not likely to do so. But the mere fact that you have had a hard pull is nothing against the fish taking the fly again. I have taken a fish at the fourth offer which had taken my fly hard three times within as many minutes. Sometimes they will again take the fly cast to them instantly, and some people advise a long wait, but personally I almost always remain where I am, pull in three or four yards of line at the reel, and from the same stand fish down to the fish by letting out at each cast about a yard of the line drawn in. If that fails, and I do not want to fish on, I go out of the stream and begin twenty yards higher up and fish down to him again.

IV

ON FLIES

MY DEAR BOYS,—Many fishers, after learning to make a cast, think that the flies are everything. There are some even who think that success is to be had only with double hooks, or with some spinning head or some fanciful 'short rising' hook of monstrous shape. Still more salmon fishers, however, pin their faith to an endless variety of gorgeous flies with charming names—names that plainly speak their real use and object, that is, to catch the fisher, not the fish. These names are themselves a comedy.

Some are truculent, as Butcher, Bull-dog, Thunder and Lightning, Black Dose—carrying in their names the idea of triumphant compulsion brought to bear upon the unfortunate salmon. Others are romantic, as Fairy, Silver Grey, Green Highlander, Golden Eagle, Snowfly, Kate. Others recall the deeds of legendary heroes, such as Jock Scott, Popham, Wilkinson. Their varieties, or supposed varieties, run into thousands, and the whole lot show plainly that the fisher is quite as gullible as the fish.

In a recent book on Salmon Fishing, there are some really beautiful coloured plates of seventy-two of the best-known salmon flies. For any one who is fond of salmon flies these wonderful plates make the book a delightful possession. But the author, Mr. Hodgson, excuses himself for confining his list to so small a number of patterns, and he 'ventures to hope' that these flies would be a sufficient outfit to enable one to fish on any ordinary river in the United Kingdom. But just imagine the fisher hunting through a box containing half a dozen flies of each pattern—or of a quarter of the patterns. And any one who looks at these beautifully coloured flies must see that most of them are of precisely similar type, and dozens of them are for all practical fishing purposes identical—all dressed with the same general type of heavy mixed wing, with its yellow topping of golden pheasant, and a golden yellow tail, and the bodies shrouded by a thick and heavy hackle varying only in shades.

In shape and general design the professional fly tier commonly makes but little variation, and his numberless patterns differ from one another only in a few minor details of their multi-coloured gaudiness. In truth, a good fisher with only half a dozen patterns of really varied flies is, so far as catching salmon goes, not one whit behind the man who arms himself with every fly and angling 'requisite' that Hardy or Farlow or Malloch will so cheerfully sell to him.

But I do not wish to sneer at the possessor of many flies. There are plenty of keen fishers to whom the making or collecting of workmanlike flies is in itself a labour of love, but I think it is generally true that the better the fisher and the greater his opportunities of fishing, the fewer are the flies that you shall find him using—certainly it is so with the most skilful fishers that I have known.

The Choice of Flies

In my own opinion, if a fly is neat and workmanlike, well shaped, and with wing and hackle dressed sufficiently lightly to play freely in the water, it is of comparatively small importance after what pattern or of what colours the various parts are composed. There are, of course, points upon which some variety is obviously desirable. In big waters, or in waters stained with mud or with peat from moorland streams, one instinctively feels that the fly should be large and bright in order that it may be seen by as many fish as possible. Salmon have wonderfully good sight at all times of the day and night, and even in stained or muddy water they can see the fly in an astonishing way. Still, if fish are ever to be tempted to take the fly, the first essential is that they should see it; and so one demands some flies that shall be good to see. For this purpose I use either a Jock Scott or a sort of Silver Wilkinson, a silver body dressed with a white or pale blue hackle, and having a turkey wing with two large, bright jungle cocks over it. Then one wants some dark, sober fly as a

THE THROAT OF A POOL

A SALMON POOL.

contrast to the former ones in order to make a change—rather for the fisher than for the fish—when the bright flies have been well tried and have proved for the time being unable to attract the fish. For this purpose I generally use a fly with a rather rough body of claret wool, and with a claret hackle and a mallard wing, or else a very similar fly with a smooth body of port-wine coloured silk and a 'pigeon's blood' hackle, with brown or dun turkey wings. With a few flies of each type—Jock Scott, Silver body, and Claret—I should be well content to tackle a day's fishing, ay, or a week's or a month's fishing on any river whatever, unless it were very low and clear. Then I should like to have the choice of about three more flies—the port fly described above, a sober little fly with dun turkey wing and rough black and orange-brown body, known to me as a 'Gipps,' and a green heckam-peckam.

In the matter of flies I am therefore a heretic who thinks nothing of fishing through a long day without changing the fly more than once, and who would almost equally value his chances of taking fish with any well-dressed fly not excessive in size and gaudiness. But salmon, even on the good days, do not take every five minutes, and it is more satisfactory to be using a fly in which you have full confidence. If the fish will not take a fly with which you have lately done well, you feel confident that it is because they are not in taking humour. But with a new and untried pattern of fly hope soon gives place to doubt, and doubt quickly leads to dismissal—in favour, as Mr. Dooley said of the anti-Dreyfus witnesses, of some 'thried and thrusted perjurer.'

You will soon, and often, go through the stage when after some lucky day you pin your faith to, and for long catch nearly all your fish upon, some one fly which later on you have given up, and which now is rarely used and lightly valued. Even now looking at one's fishing-books, one sees that for long periods, or even for a whole season, one fly has been by far the most successful. Then another old favourite has a lucky turn, and for weeks together nearly everything is caught upon that pattern, and for the same reason as before, namely, that you have given it the first trial every day, and have never changed it for another unless the fish were not taking.[1]

I should advise you not to pay overmuch attention to the maxims current among salmon fishers as to what fly you should use or what you should do in this event or in that. For instance, you will be told, 'Always use big flies in spring, small flies in summer and autumn'; 'Never cast again over a risen or pricked fish until you have given him five minutes' rest,' or 'have smoked a pipe,' or 'have changed your fly for a smaller one,' or what not; 'Always use bright flies on a bright day, dark flies on a dark day,' and so on. Now

---

[1] I see that in the season of 1897 all my salmon were caught on four flies only; Jock Scott, claret, white and silver, and Gipps.

FISHING MAXIMS

these maxims, and many more like them, are all very well. They are well known and deeply revered amongst anglers, but I often wonder whether the poor misguided salmon is always quite sure of the path of duty thus laid down for him. They remind me of the story of the French visitor who showed some alarm at the prospect of passing a savage-looking dog that stood in the way, barking furiously. 'It's all right,' said his host; 'don't you know the proverb "Barking dogs don't bite"?' 'Ah, yes!' says the Frenchman, 'I know ze proverbe, and you know ze proverbe, but ze question is does ze dog know ze proverbe?' Such maxims may be good rough working rules, but one thing you may be sure of about a salmon, you never can tell either what he will do, or when he will do it, and if the fish doesn't come when invited in what you consider the orthodox manner, don't give him up, but try him in the most unorthodox way that you can think of, and I should suggest, to begin with, an absurdly small fly and fine tackle, and keep your very small flies, unless they have metal eyes, ready on a strand of gut, carefully tied before you go out, so that they may be well tied on and changed the more easily.

V

STRIKING THE FISH

My dear Boys,—All kinds of views are held as to the necessity or otherwise of striking, that is to say, of intentionally jerking the rod so that the point and barb of the hook may be buried in the fish's jaw.

One school of fishers holds that you must never strike when salmon fishing, that the salmon hooks himself. Another, that you should always strike 'from the reel,' as they express it; that is to say, leaving the line loose and free to run off the reel as you strike. Others hold that you should always strike a salmon just as you would strike in trout fishing, although not so quickly.

These differences, like so many other of our disputes, exist to a large extent upon confusion of terms. The disputants are often referring to different methods of fishing, and they mean different things by the word 'strike.' The man who fishes deep with his rod almost horizontal, and so with the point low, will rarely see the fish rise. His first knowledge of the fish is the pull on the line, and if he has had the skill to keep a good taut line, nothing more will be needed to drive his hook home than simply to raise the rod point. This

WHEN FISHING DEEP

should be done quickly, but anything like a jerk would, in a strong water, probably result in the fisher breaking the gut and leaving his fly in the fish's mouth. The effect of a sudden jerk upward given to a heavy salmon rod held almost horizontal is to pull up the butt, but at first to depress the rod point, which then flies up, putting on a far greater strain than the excited fisher either intends or realises. You, my boys, will strike thus with a violent jerk often enough, and will lose your fly many times before your nerves are always steady when they feel the savage snatch of an unexpected salmon.

By the prompt, firm raising of the rod point the fisher in this style has struck sufficiently; he has driven the hook home into the struggling fish, and he needs no sharp stroke like that given by the trout fisher with his quick turn of the wrist. But on the few occasions when the young angler in this style does actually see the great boil of a rising salmon, he will generally strike instinctively and—as I have both seen and done—will very often strike too soon.

The man, on the other hand, who fishes with rod point raised and fly near the surface as in trouting (a very good way, too, in clear water), will constantly see the rise; see the salmon like a great trout boiling up at his fly, and indeed he will often see the wave caused by the fish coming to or following his fly. In order to drive the hook home when fishing thus, with rod-top raised, a sharp, quick stroke is needed owing to the strain falling upon the thin and yielding top of the rod. But the beginner in this style will very quickly find that if he strikes the moment that he sees the boil, he will often fail to hook the fish, or even to feel any touch at all. If, however, he waits until the fish has begun to go down again, he will very rarely fail to strike the hook in firmly. He should wait perhaps two seconds. The best idea that I can give you of the time is this. You see the boil and then you count quietly, one—two—*strike*. The fish appears to be then about two feet below the surface, as you can often judge by the gut, as your strike lifts it partly out of the water. You will very rarely fail to hook him if he has ever touched the fly. But in swift water, and more especially in quick, glassy runs, the fish seem to take the fly more firmly, and you can safely strike more quickly.

The course that you, my boys, should take, until you see reason to think that you know a better one, is this :—

When fishing deep, in strong water, the moment you feel the pull, tighten firmly on the fish. If in rather slow water, give a much sharper pull, especially if the hook is a large one.

If fishing in low water—or indeed in any but the swiftest water—with the fly kept near the surface, then, when you see the rise, count ' one—two,' and then (at ' three ') strike sharply. But if your first knowledge of the rise is a pull, or a stopping of the line, then strike instantly.

LARGE HOOKS

In all cases, even when fishing deep, if the fish takes the fly after the top is raised in order to make the backward cast, then strike sharply on the touch.

When fishing with large hooks or with double hooks it is advisable, unless the fly has been taken savagely with a violent pull, to make sure that a marked and heavy pull is given to the fly as soon as possible after you have felt the fish. This is in order to ensure driving the hooks home. A few trials with a fly placed in the mouth of a dead salmon freshly caught will soon convince you that a good deal of force is required to drive a large hook into the firmer parts of the jaw even if the gut be held near the fly. Still more is it so if about twenty-five yards of line is let out and the effect of a pull made with the rod is tested upon the dead fish's mouth. It will be found that often the barb has not been buried in the fish, and if alive and thrashing about with open mouth, he very probably would have twisted out the point and would have escaped.

That fish, in the effort to get rid of the fly in their mouths, do—as one would expect—struggle and twist about with mouth wide open, I have myself seen several times when a bright sun shining into a clear water below a high bank has enabled the early struggles of the hooked fish to be seen with great distinctness.

In experimenting with a dead fish one curious thing will be noticed. The fly, if hooked into the tongue—the very thing which one would expect the downward-hanging hook to pierce—will rather easily tear out, splitting the tongue as it does so. No doubt it is for this reason that one so rarely lands a fish hooked in the tongue. I never remember doing so on a salmon rod unless the hook has been fixed right at the root or back of the tongue. This splitting of the tongue probably explains some of those vexatious losses of fish apparently well hooked, which nevertheless escape, after a few violent struggles.

Another thing that you must remember, my boys, is this: Never use a blunt hook. Always keep in your pocket or in your fly-case a small slip of hard whetstone to keep the point of your hooks as keen as it is possible to have them. The skin within a salmon's mouth is smooth and slippery, and the hook should have a needle point.

I advise you not to practise striking from the reel unless you find your nerves so 'jumpy' that you cannot trust yourself to hold the line. But you should so hold the line that as soon as the pull or strike is over, or even before, if the fish should give a sudden savage snatch, the line may be taken off the reel. And that is done by holding one or—when you are more experienced and hold the rod as I do—both forefingers over the line in the following way. You grasp the rod firmly as if to cast, leaving the line quite free. Then detach the forefinger and hook it over the line, closing it again beside the other fingers closely upon the rod, so that now the line goes under the forefinger and over the three others. Then on a sudden or heavy pull the line will easily and instinctively be allowed to lift the forefinger and thus permit the reel to run. Never under any circumstances have the line twisted round a finger —unless you want it broken.

I believe that both in harling and in trolling for salmon it is the practice to strike violently on awaking to the discovery that a fish has at last come to break the peaceful monotony of those cold and dreary pursuits.

VI

ON PLAYING A SALMON

My dear Boys,—I want to give you some advice on the playing of a salmon when you have hooked him, and there are several points that you must be careful to attend to.

Hold the rod up.—This, above all other things, is what you must remember to do. From the moment after the fish is hooked until the moment he is gaffed you should never, unless the fish is in the act of leaping out of the water, cease to hold the rod well up, the butt at or near the perpendicular. For when the rod is lowered towards the fish the lightness of play of the top joints is gone, and the gut is very apt to be broken. A much shorter yielding on the part of the fish permits the top to straighten and releases the pull of the rod altogether, whilst a very short rush passes from the stage where the rod is exerting no strain at all to the point where the pull, coming mainly upon the butt and middle joints, is the very heaviest that the rod can give.

Next, *watch the fish most carefully.*—If you see him leap out of the water, drop your point instantly, and raise it as soon as he has fallen into the water again. I was inclined, once, to neglect this traditional piece of advice as unnecessary, but paid the penalty in several broken hooks and lost fish, and soon returned to it again. If you feel a sudden quick rush, look out for a leap to follow it.

Never let the fish rest.—When the fish is rushing about and fighting hard, put no strain on it, but keep the line taut, and keep as near as possible to your fish. Always, too, keep the line well reeled up so as to have as little line dragging in the water as possible. When he makes a rush, let him go— even give him line pulled off the reel by your hand. But the very *moment* he slackens his efforts, pull him and worry him into action, and in a very short time he will be yours. Of the many hundreds of fish that I have caught I have never had one fish sulk, and this I believe to be due almost entirely to a habit of never allowing the fish to rest until the fight is done. When the tired fish attempts a run you may easily turn him by putting the rod down-stream and holding it low, and thus pulling his head from the down-stream side, when he will almost always circle round and come nearer to the fisherman, and will very soon lose his courage at such treatment. By this particular manœuvre you can bring in a slow, sluggish fish in very quick time. In the old days when men caught salmon on the 'loop' rod, without a reel, they used to make a great point of keeping rather below the fish, and there is little doubt that that is the most advantageous place for the angler. As I have said, you should do everything you can to keep near the fish and to prevent him having a very long line out if it can be helped. But at the same time you must take care not to have him on a very short line until he is ready to come to the gaff. If he is within anything like a rod's length of the top ring, he is too close. If he is swimming deep, this does not matter, but to have a fish reeled up close that is splashing and struggling near the surface is to invite a break and to deserve one. Similarly, when the fish is tired and you have to reel him up short in order to use the gaff or net, never hold his head out of the water. Never let the rod point be directly above the fish to be lifting him out of the water, but keep it either down-stream or up-stream of the fish, so that the pull of the gut is not a lifting pull. If the fish is being lifted, and he begins to kick and splash, as he will do—to jigger, as it is called—the jerking on the line is very sudden, and constantly snaps either the line, the hook, or else the hold that the hook had in the fish. Enormous numbers of grilse and small, active salmon are lost in this way every season. If you hook a very active fish on fine tackle when fishing with a big rod, his wild leaps and rushes will make you tremble for the safety of your gut, especially if the fish takes a lot of line. A great deal may be done to ease the strain by keeping as near as possible to the fish, even by wading into the water again, and holding the rod very high and very close to the butt with both hands. I have caught large salmon on an eighteen-foot-six rod with a cast tipped with three feet of plain trout gut, but then, when using such gut, I put the button of the rod in one palm and hold the rod close above the reel with my other hand, playing the fish almost entirely upon the top joint, and if the trout gut is sound the rod will manage it perfectly.

If you do hook a big fish he may take hours to land if you don't worry him enough. But if you *have* to leave him, don't cut your line; put down your rod and haul him in by hand. Some monks who have a house on Loch Ness have a stuffed salmon that they netted in 1907 which weighed $37\frac{1}{2}$ lbs. In his mouth was a minnow attached to over thirty yards of line, and on inquiry they heard that, a few days before, an old gentleman had hooked this fish and played it for several hours, and then, cold and tired out, had cut his line and gone home. Some of the lost fish really are big, you see.

A still more grievous loss happened to a distinguished barrister now in a high official position. Fishing one afternoon in the Förde River in Norway he hooked a great salmon, and twice he had the fish almost within reach of the gaff. Twice the gaffer went out, and with a longer gaff would probably have got him. As it was, he just failed to reach the fish, and it never again allowed itself to be brought near the shore. The rod was a light one and the tackle fine, and the fight lasted for six mortal hours, but at last in the darkness the gut was broken by the weight of the exhausted fish swept down by the strong stream, and half a mile below where he was hooked. The next day the angler went home, and the day after that the Norwegian boatmen netted the pool where he had been hooked, and there caught the fish. It weighed over fifty pounds and still carried the fly, which they returned to its owner.

When wading, if you hook a fish, do not, as a rule, begin to move towards the shore until the fish has had his first few plunges and begins to steady himself. But if he begins to tear off line and gets far away from you, go after him as promptly as you can. Never let him have a long line out if that can be avoided.

After playing should come gaffing, but fish without number are lost every year in the attempt to gaff them. An inexplicable nervousness attacks the beginner, he approaches the fish quietly and confidently, but then he bungles the job most horribly, and in a moment he is making wild rakes at the fish which often end in his gaffing the line and losing the salmon on the spot. The only good advice I can give you is this: Keep the point of the gaff sharp as a needle. Quietly stretch it over the middle of the back of your salmon, and touch his farther side with the point: then give a firm pull—not a wild jerk—and instantly draw him in, lifting the handle of your gaff as you do it, so that the fish hangs perpendicularly below it.[1] As you gaff him, drop

[1] See Appendix, Note 1.

your rod forward so as to slacken the gut to the fish's head, or he may break the cast or the rod top. Don't be flurried, and the thing can hardly go wrong. When gaffing for a friend, keep still while he brings the fish to a position where the stroke is a certainty; take no risks, and when you gaff, do it quietly.

Andrew Young, in his *Angler's Guide to the Rivers and Lochs of the North of Scotland* (published in 1857), besides describing minutely all the principal rivers and lakes, has some delightful advice to give as to the best methods of fishing, and his advice, or at any rate some of his advice, shows that we have learnt very little that is new since his day.

' I could easily,' he says, ' give a list of the flies likely to kill on these rivers; but of what use would it be, when we don't see two on the same river use the same kind of flies? The fact is that the fly that killed the last fish is always considered best, whatever be its shape, size or colour, until some one supersedes it with another.

' But I would seriously warn anglers against " striking the fish," and " pulling hard." Striking the fish means giving the rod a sudden upward jerk, as soon as the fish breaks the water to catch the fly. This is a vile practice that has crept in among anglers of late years.'

Old Andrew, you see, like many other arguers, begins by stating the ' vile practice ' out of court. In salmon fishing no one could defend striking ' as soon as the fish breaks the water.' Striking at a rise that you see, but after waiting a couple of seconds to allow the fish to turn with the fly, is a very different matter. He goes on :—

'And when the fish is hooked be sure that you don't pull hard, for that is a most dangerous practice, by which many a hook and many a fish is lost. . . .

'There is some excuse for a young angler losing his first fish in that manner from agitation, and want of the proper weight of his hand ; but when anglers of twenty years' standing, who are considered first-rate casters and hookers of fish, play the fool in that way, they are inexcusable. I have known one good caster and hooker in one month lose ninety fish, all of which were hooked so well that at least eighty would have been landed by any cautious fisher.' Great heavens, one thinks, how many fish were landed in that month by this furious Jehu of the salmon rod. But he goes on : 'I never like to hear of this foolish brag of having landed an eighteen-pound fish in ten minutes, and an eight-pound grilse in five minutes—that's the work of a butcher and not of an angler ; for giving a fish fair play, and an angler fair sport, from thirty to thirty-five minutes is little enough time to play a fish of eighteen pounds. Some may take more, but few less, with fair play, and from fifteen to twenty minutes for a grilse.'

Again, 'We would also warn the young angler against endeavouring to cast a long line, for that is a besetting fault in new beginners. They see a long-practised hand spin the fly almost across the river, and they think that doing the same would constitute them anglers all at once. But in that they are grossly mistaken; for with a long slack line fish can never be hooked, for the current forces the unbent middle of the line down the stream, dragging the fly down after it, and entirely preventing the proper working of the line.'

It is curious to see that already in 1857 he can recommend playing the fly a little as it hangs after coming out of the current, and can also say that 'Some are in the habit of commencing near the lower end of the pool and fishing backwards against the stream.' Quite lately we have heard this method extolled, and proclaimed as a wonderful new-found Haliday. I believe that it is quite a sensible experiment to make on a hopeless day, but Andrew viewed it—very justly—as 'a reprehensible practice, for it exhibits the splash of the line to the fish when they should only see the fly.' He insists most vigorously that the only proper way to fish a salmon pool is 'to remove never more than a yard at one time, always giving three offers of the fly at each removal.' If you raise no fish he tells you to 'rest ten minutes, change your fly for one of a quite opposite colour, and fish over the pool a second time with the same care.' 'Some anglers,' he says, after an exhortation against haste, 'run over the best pools with only a few casts and then declare that there are no fish in the pool; but the patient angler finds fish there as soon as Mr. Short-Temper leaves it.'

His 'concluding advice to the young angler' is quite delightful. After telling him to be sure at night to dry his flies and his line, and to examine both line and gut carefully, he adds this: 'Send the gilly early to bed, and be sure not to drink that stuff that they compound of whisky, sugar, and boiling water. It is bad for muddling the brain, and angling requires a clear brain.'

You will see that Andrew and I do not see eye to eye on a good many points. He is horrified at the very thought of killing a fish quickly, although that is not done by 'pulling hard,' but by never allowing the fish to take a moment's rest.

VII

THE SENSE OF PAIN IN FISH

MY DEAR BOYS,—You will often hear fishermen debating the question whether fish feel pain. It is not that anybody, so far as I know, thinks that fish are wholly proof against the feeling of pain, but many people believe that fish are much less sensible of pain than are warm-blooded animals such as we are. Seeing a long and frantic struggle for life on the part of a beautiful creature which has never given the smallest cause of offence to mankind, a humane fisher is forced to consider whether he is being guilty of wanton cruelty; whether, if he must take fish in order to eat them, he is justified in taking them with the rod, instead of by some means that is either painless—such as stunning them by the use of dynamite or shooting them—or whereby death at least is quickly over, such as spearing them or taking them with a draft net. No doubt the angler puts himself upon his trial with every intention of securing his own acquittal if it be possible. But is he really guilty?

The very thought of using, against a salmon, such devices as dynamite, nets, traps, or spears, is revolting to a man who loves, or perhaps thinks that he loves, the salmon, and who feels angry and disgusted every time that he sees one of those pictures of their wholesale slaughter in such places as the salmon canneries of British Columbia. Why ? Is it merely a selfish desire to capture the fish ourselves, or is it that we feel that a noble fish, even when we need him for food, should have the much greater chance of escape that the rod gives him as compared with the murderous bars of the salmon trap or the toils of the deadly net ? It is not merely that the rod gives him a fair chance of escape after he has been hooked ; it does not, like the net or the fish trap, sweep the fish off wholesale from the pools or from the narrows through which they are compelled to pass. The rod can take only such fish as are disposed to seize the fly or bait, and we all know that at times such fish are rare indeed, and at no time do they form, I believe, any large proportion of the fish present in the pools.

Anglers are not, as a rule, men given to cruelty in the affairs of life, and yet the fear of possible cruelty in fishing does not impress them as a real one. Some cruelty must be involved in causing the death of any creature, and so long as humane men and women desire to eat slaughtered sheep, cattle, poultry, game, and fish, the angler need not much concern himself beyond proving that his sport involves no greater cruelty than this. A great accumulation of instances in which fish seem to have shown an almost complete indifference to wounds or injuries that would cause extreme agony to warm-blooded animals, seems to establish as a

ACTUAL INSTANCES

fact that fish are comparatively insensible to pain.

I have myself hooked a fine spring salmon of about 18 lbs., which, after taking the fly with a firm pull, merely sank with it to the bottom of the river, and gave no sign of feeling anything unusual. As I was wading in deep and difficult water, the first thing was to get into the shallows and shorten the line, and then I gave a good sharp pull at the fish. Nothing happened. I gave another and a more severe pull, now almost doubting whether the fish was still on, or whether by any chance it had left the fly in some new and uncharted snag. That doubt did not last long. At the third pull the fish bolted past me up the deep stream, then turned and dashed slanting across to the far side of the river, repeatedly rising to the surface and wallowing along half out of the water at every few yards. Off ran the forty yards of casting line, but still the fish held on for some rocky shallows, whilst the thin silk backing cut the forefinger that was trying to check it. He won. No sooner did he get amongst the boulders than he got the line round one of them, and, with a few splashing plunges, he broke me and departed. Luckily the line came free, and with it came back the large claret fly that he had taken, but with the hook now snapped off just at the tail of the fly. It must have gone firmly into some pretty tough spot to break at such a place.

From his behaviour it is hard to think that this

fish felt much pain from the hook, and his vigorous and effective line of action after the third pull was given to him may have been due quite as much to realising that some fisher had got hold of him, as to any feeling of pain from the extra pull at the hook, when he had shown none at the first or the second pull.

A similar thing happened to me on September 30, 1905, when fishing with a phantom minnow on a falling flood in a heavy black water with a good deal of mud still in it. On the shallow edge at the far side of some very heavy water I hooked what I felt sure was a good fish. I thought that I had felt the quiver of life, but a full minute's tugging convinced me that I must have been mistaken, and I had actually taken the line in my hand to drag the hooks off the bottom or to break away, when the line calmly moved off into deep water. This time also, as luck would have it, I lost the fish, as he succeeded about ten minutes later in getting round a point some distance below, where it was not possible to follow him. But he was a strong one, and he was a very heavy one.

Another instance I know of, which happened to an angler who was fishing some water below me. He hooked a fish which went straightway back to his lying-place on the bottom and sulked there for an hour before he could be induced to move. Then, in due time, he was landed and was found to weigh 28 lbs. He was hooked in the point of the lower jaw. One cannot imagine any warm-blooded animal, hooked in the nose or mouth or ear or in any other place, however gristly, which could without a single preliminary struggle calmly stay where he was and allow his captor to tug and pull at him to his heart's content. One would suppose that ' sulking ' would be almost impossible if the salmon felt acute pain from the repeated tugging at the hook. Yet fish do sulk often enough—although, in fact, it has never happened to me to have one do so. And people who, in clear water, have been able to see the sulking fish, say that he may be seen poised head downwards, with his nose on the gravel and his tail gently waving to keep him down against the pull of the rod. Such conduct does not suggest any acute pain.

One knows, too, that a salmon will frequently take a fly several times, and sometimes even after he has had a very sharp prick. Once in the month of August 1890 I was fishing a quiet glassy pool, bent on catching a large fish weighing, as I judged, close on 30 lbs., that I had seen and tried so often that I knew his position almost to a yard. The river was low and clear, and I had to wade out with great care to avoid making a ripple. Just as I got to the place from which I had hoped to cover him, I saw a wasp fall into the river and go drifting down, buzzing upon the surface of the water straight over the salmon. As I watched it in the bright sunshine, a big shoulder rose quietly out of the water, followed by a black tail, and down went my friend the wasp, and he certainly did not come to the surface again. Thereupon I changed my tiny silver fly for a small black and orange fly with dun turkey wings known as a 'Gipps,' and with it at once hooked my friend. Now that fish had no fear of a wasp. Of course he may have crushed it instantly in his jaws, but it is an experiment that no warm-blooded animal cares to try twice, although every puppy has generally tried it once. And wasps are abundant by the river-side in August, and it is not likely that this was the first that my friend had ever taken. I wish I had been able to cut him open and so perhaps prove that he had swallowed this wasp, but I did not succeed in landing him.

I have only once taken a salmon that had any tackle upon him; and then it was merely some trout fisher's March brown, with a foot of gut attached to it and left in the mouth of a 15-lb. fish; but there have been endless well-proved instances of fish being taken with not only flies but even worm-hooks and spinning traces still about or inside them, as witnesses of some former escape. And, with a worm, I have taken a large trout of about 2 lbs. weight, which had six inches of gut hanging out of his mouth, and had in his stomach a big hook with a worm still upon it that had been lost not twenty minutes previously by a schoolboy—one of your uncles—who had hooked and lost the trout before asking me to try him. Some twenty or more times I have seen salmon taken upon a fly notwithstanding that they had frightful raw wounds upon their bodies caused by seals or porpoises. Now it is pretty clearly proved that a fish whilst in the river does not take food because it must eat to live, but, at the most, from greed only, or possibly from curiosity or destructiveness. Well, just imagine a man, not starving, not even hungry, and with a dreadful, unhealed wound in his body, yet ready to leap up or to rush about to get a single cherry.

Nearly every one who considers the matter is forced to the conclusion that the salmon suffers very little direct pain, and that the distress of its struggles to escape capture is not very serious when compared with its drowning, held fast by the gills in a stake net, or its savage mauling by seals or porpoises. Some men go further and point out that the salmon himself is the savage and relentless foe of the herring and the smaller fry, and even of the young of his own species, and that he is captured in the very act of trying to kill what he thinks is some beautiful creature swimming through the pool. The *locus classicus* is a well-known passage in the *Days and Nights of Salmon Fishing*,[1] which I will quote again in order that you may be induced to read the whole book.

Scrope says at the beginning of Chapter IV: ' Let us see how the case stands. I take a little

---

[1] Published in 1835. Reprinted with only two plates in 1854 (the edition which we have), but a very good and cheap reprint was published in 1885.

wool and feather, and, tying it in a particular manner upon a hook, make an imitation of a fly; then I throw it across the river and let it sweep round the stream with a lively motion. This I have an undoubted right to do, for the river belongs to me or my friend; but mark what follows. Up starts a monster fish with his murderous jaws, and makes a dash at my little Andromeda. Thus he is the aggressor, not I; his intention is evidently to commit murder. He is caught in the act of putting that intention into execution. Having wantonly intruded himself on my hook, which I contend he had no right to do, he darts about in various directions, evidently surprised to find that the fly, which he hoped to make an easy conquest of, is much stronger than himself. I naturally attempt to regain this fly, unjustly withheld from me. The fish gets tired and weak in his lawless endeavours to deprive me of it. I take advantage of his weakness, I own, and drag him, somewhat loth, to the shore, where one rap on his head ends him in an instant.'

VIII

SPRING FISHING

MY DEAR BOYS,—One good day's salmon fishing in spring is worth a week in the late autumn, and I would not exchange one brilliant glittering spring salmon for half a dozen autumn fish, or for half a score of the hideous red sharks that one often catches at the end of October, not to speak of the month of November, where November fishing is lawful. The spring fish is quite a different creature, and he can be inexpressibly more brilliant and more beautiful than the average autumn fish, although there are, of course, spring fish long up from the sea that are by no means so glittering as the best fish are.

Then you are fishing for the spring salmon in a time of hope and joy, and of budding leaves and singing birds, and at the beginning of a new salmon season when the mere casting of the fly again is a perfect holiday. But though you máy get then some of the fairest days of the whole year, you may equally, in spring, get some of the foulest, so far as weather goes. I will tell you of a week's spring fishing.

The Easter of 1908 was a late one, but in weather it was much more like Christmas. On the

Saturday after Easter they had a foot of snow in Oxford, and in Hampshire there was even more. I went north with a friend for seven days' fishing, and we had blustering north or north-east winds and repeated snow showers every day. But the salmon seemed to like it; and four or five were taken in the very worst moments, whilst we fought our way down the pools against blinding showers of snow and sleet. At such times a savage snatch often finds you unprepared. I was using some gut, stout enough, but bought ten years ago, and during that week I left four flies in fish— whether in kelts or in spring fish I cannot tell, but one always hopes that a very violent tug comes from a good, clean fish. In very stormy winds, when you are using your heaviest line, it is worth while to remember that the force of the strike upon the gut is much more sudden and more violent than it is with a lighter and more springy line, and unless care and sound tackle be used you will often be left, as I was, to grieve over the loss of both fish and fly.

However, this Easter, the only fly that the fish seemed ready to take was a large, blood-coloured claret with a thick, rough body, a broad silver rib and a plain turkey or mallard wing set on low like the wings of a bee or a stone-fly. With this fly I began to fish early on the Saturday in a bitter grey north wind. At the third pool I was just picking my steps through some willows growing among the rocks on the bank when, in the thin

FIRST DAY OF THE SEASON

glassy slide at the tail of the pool there was a swirl, a pull, and a few rolling plunges, and my first fish of 1908 had come and gone. . . . Well, this is black luck, but it shows that there's one good fish up, and there may be more; so on to the next pool. There, near the top of it, just as the fly swings out of the current and is carefully see-sawed alongside a ragged mass of logs sunk in the water, there comes a slight draw—so slight that it might easily pass unnoticed. A quick stroke, however, reveals the unmistakable quiver of life, and after a few deep struggles, which just show as oily swirls upon the quieter water beside the stream, a great fish dashes into the heavy current and goes down on the top of it, walloping over and over, and tearing the line with short screeches off the reel. This, at any rate, is no kelt. After a stubborn sporting run in the course of which he twice goes up into the pool above only to dash back down the rapids, and in which he repeatedly tries to take refuge amongst the snags which line the steep bank, he gives a chance and is gaffed. Sure enough he is a clean fish of 17, 18, or 19 lbs.;[1] but it is the first day of the season and the scales have been left at home. I go over all these pools again with the same fly, but nothing moves. Then I try a silver-bodied fly with bright jungle cock over dark turkey wings.

It is now past one o'clock, so slinging the fish by head and tail with a couple of yards of thick

[1] The fish weighed $18\frac{1}{2}$ lbs.

string, I carry it down to the fishing hut to meet my friend and your friend, Professor S. Though a learned man, and certainly the greatest master in England of his own particular subject, yet for salmon fishing he has the heart of a boy. When he is on a fishing holiday his keenness might be that of a certain tribe of pagan gentlemen of the Tartar race who in Siberia inhabit—or did inhabit, until the Russians massacred most of them—the banks of the river Amur. They are clothed in salmon skins, and they live in tents made of salmon skins. Of them it is said : ' The Golde have only one idea in the world, and that is " salmon." They catch it, they eat it, they talk of it, and they dream of it.' I feel sure that on a fishing holiday S., who is a fine fisher, nightly dreams of salmon.

Well, here he is, more than waist deep in the stream : a strong pair of arms and shoulders clothed in sand-coloured Harris tweed being so close to the water that it looks as if another inch deeper must float him off. He has got no spring fish yet, though he has landed several kelts. After lunch I begin on a lower pool and land a kelt—a thing that some anglers affect to despise, but it is a thing that I, for one, am very glad to do on the first day of the new season, when a pull of any kind gives you a jump of pleasure. Next comes a savage tug, and a perfect spring battle begins. Straight off goes the fish, down and across the broad river, whilst I hurry along the bank hoping that the tackle will stand these repeated mad dashes. Suddenly he swings round and dashes back to my bank, the long line, as he comes, cutting the water many yards behind where the wave shows the travelling fish. Then turning upwards he dashes past, almost under my feet, and flings himself twice out of the water. Reeling up as fast as possible, and backing away from the water to get the line taut, I find him still on, only to have the same tactics repeated again and again, except that each time he keeps a little deeper; then, getting tired, he doggedly bores his way right across the pool and into the shallows opposite. There he splashes about with his back out of the water, and, though I hold the rod butt over my head in order to gain as much height as possible, yet there is eighty yards of line out, and at any moment he may catch it round a stone. But he does not; and, keeping below him, I steadily coax him back, first into the deep water and soon under my bank. After a time he is almost done, and the gaff is got ready; but the whole bank at my feet is fringed with dwarf willows, and I have to gaff him over these. Suddenly he turns and bolts into them. I can see his tail, and it is within reach. If I try to pull him back out of the willows he may foul the gut and break it, so I decide to gaff him where he is. Leaning over, I gaff him as far up as I can do, but it is two hand-breadths only from the tail. Splashing and struggling, he is hauled up the bank, but the gut is caught on the willows, and will not pull through them. I give a violent pull, intending to break the gut, but, somehow or other, as the gut breaks the fish comes off the gaff, falls again into the willows, kicks through them, and is free.

I walk down the bank, gaff in hand, peering into the water, for I know that he is sorely wounded, but no sign of him do I see. Two village lads who saw the fight that he made loudly express their grief, but I find no words. I never do when I lose a fish. As a parent I ought to be ashamed to confess that at small annoyances I do, sometimes, swear; but I have not yet felt as if any mere words could mitigate the loss of any salmon, much less of a beautiful spring fish. At any rate, one hopes that the fish may live to fight such a battle again. But it is not so. Next day come the two lads to say that they can see the fish with a fly in its mouth lying dead in the water a hundred yards lower down, and with a boat we get him out and take my fly from his jaws. The gaff had struck him full in the side and had not torn out, but apparently had jerked out on the breaking of the gut, because the point had stuck in the backbone of the fish. The fish, which weighed 16 lbs., I gave to the boys who had found him for me, and the fly I still have. It took two more spring fish during the week.

On Easter Monday I got two fish, 6 lbs. and 20 lbs., both caught during snow showers, and both on the claret. From the second fish I had an exceptionally long and lively run. On Tuesday

A HIGHLAND RIVER

A 25 LBS. FISH ON A SPINNING ROD

FISHING IN SNOW

evening S. was to go home, and we hoped for a great day before he left; but the water rose and spoilt the fishing. Not even the kelts would take. At five o'clock we were wet and cold and had almost abandoned hope, when a fish, at the same spot as my first on Saturday, pulled heavily at my fly. He was carefully tried again, but without result, and as a last chance in the big water S. went over him with a phantom minnow. Instantly he took it, and after tugging and fighting for twenty minutes in the deepest part of the stream, he was gaffed out, a hard, glittering cock fish of 18 lbs.; and he went South that evening with his captor.

On Wednesday, fishing alone, I got two fish of $14\frac{1}{2}$ and 23 lbs., both caught in showers of snow. On Thursday, in miserable weather, I had a total blank, losing two flies in fish and landing only a couple of kelts. The next day furnished such a 'fishing yarn' that perhaps I had better copy out for you the letter I wrote to S. to give him an account of it.

26/4/1908.

MY DEAR S.,—On Friday morning the snow lay thick on the ground and a bitter N.E. gale was blowing. I went rather late to the river, and tried chiefly for three fish that I had moved the day before. About 3.30 one of them threw himself out of the water opposite the clump of willows in the Boat pool, and I saw that he was a good spring fish. I had already fished over him once, but a blinding snow shower came on and I tried him again there and then. He rose at once, but after five or six plunges, when I thought him pretty safe, the hook came away. I fished on with very small hope until five o'clock, and then got warm by driving in the posts, with an iron maul, for the new railing at the fishing hut. Before going home I tried a fish lying in the tail of the heavy stream below the hut. He had already taken the claret fly the day before, and he took it again—hard—but the hook came away. He could not be induced to look at the fly any more, so I put up a spinning rod and tried him with a small minnow, just as a snow shower was passing off. He took the minnow after two or three offers and played strongly for five minutes, when he contrived to get the line round the end of a long, thin larch pole that lay under the bank deep in the water. No poking of the top of the rod down to the pole would get the line off, although it ran quite freely under the pole to the fish, so I let out a lot of slack line and then jumped in and gaffed up the pole, getting wet pretty nearly up to the neck. Tom Falshaw stood on the bank below me, and on raising the pole I swung it round to him and he released the line, which had lodged behind a small branch near the end of it. Luckily the line had continued to run freely and the fish was still on. For another five or six minutes he kept playing in the heavy water, but then he came to the surface a few yards above me and rolled

A LUCKY FLUKE

over on his side, and the minnow instantly flew up into the air. At first the fish did not seem to realise that he was free. Whilst you might count five or six he floated down on his side in the centre of the current, but when just opposite to us he righted himself and slowly dived into the stream. There was little more than a rod's length of line out, and I had been preparing to drop the minnow over him, as he floated by, and then to try to strike it into him. But seeing him dive and disappear I thought all hope was gone. Still, I judged that he would allow himself to go down with the current, so I swung the minnow over and dropped it in well beyond and below him, and after counting five, to allow time for it to sink, I struck hard up-stream, but with only the very faintest hope of any result. I could hardly believe my senses when I felt that it had struck him—deep in the water, so that not even any of the six-foot long spinning trace was visible. However, he left no doubt about it, for he promptly bolted down the heavy stream and bored away across the river until he got into two feet of water. There he kept splashing about, always pulling straight away from me and going down-stream, so that, knowing him to be hooked foul, I guessed that he must be hooked in the tail. After a time he came slowly walloping to the surface and continued to roll about on the top whilst I towed him tail first and very slowly—for I was uncommonly fearful and gentle with him—across to my side, where I gaffed him. He was a beautiful, clean-run fish of 15 lbs., and the minnow was holding by one triangle at the base of the upper ray of his tail, and it fell out as I carried him up the bank.

It really is such a preposterous fluke that I can hardly ask to be believed in telling it. However, I had two 'lawful men of the vicinage' as witnesses, Tom Falshaw, and Alick, too, who had arrived just as the fish was released from the snag on which he had hung up the line.

After such miracle-working as this, yesterday—which was my last day—was tame enough, though it was an almost exact repetition of your day on Tuesday. There were at least two inches of fresh snow, and Dorothy and I spent the morning in building a huge kneeling snow man for the two boys, with lumps of coal for eyes, and adorned like a scarecrow with pipe, stick, and an old fishing hat. I went up to fish at 12.30, and at one o'clock landed a big kelt from the far side of the Stakes. A bitter, black east wind came on, and about five I went up to try the more sheltered water of No. 4 pool. There, exactly as you had done on Tuesday, but about a long cast lower down the pool, I got a very strong cock fish of 20 lbs.—a very wild, jumping fighter, and the best for shape and colour that I have got this spring. I do not think that I ever had a better, or at any rate a much better, fish.

This ended the stormiest and coldest fishing,

ANOTHER SPRING DAY

but the best for steady sport, that I ever remember at Easter.—Yours, A. C.

And, my boys, I believe that that letter, which I wrote in the train to S., by no means exaggerates the extraordinary fluke that had occurred.

MY DEAR BOYS,—I will begin with another letter to S.

Train going South,
Monday Evening, 4*th May* 1908.

MY DEAR S.,—I had to go North for a good sportsman's burying to-day—my cousin Bill. On Friday evening I found myself free, so after wiring to know what the river was doing, I started off by the night train to get one day at the salmon.

On Saturday morning I found the river still in flood and very high—a foot above the rails,[1] but reported to be clearing and falling quickly. There was a wretched, foggy east wind, but on a one-day fishing, if only the water will let me fish, I shall never waste time in grumbling at the weather.

In the fourth pool I got a good yellow trout of 2 lbs. I saw a fresh fish in the level dub of the A. pool opposite the stone jetty, and in the evening saw a second lying above him by the fence. Twenty yards above the railings in the Thorns stream there was another fish splashing every now

[1] These 'rails' were the mark of very high fishing water on that river.

and then in the heavy stream, but none of them would take a fly, or even a minnow, though I pegged away at them until about four o'clock. Then I went to the hut and fished down. The stream below that was far too heavy to fish, but when I got to the pool below the Stakes it grew suddenly dark. About five o'clock a gentle, misty rain began, and just below the neck of the stream, to my surprise—for the Devil's Water coming in just above was still in muddy flood—a good fish took on the edge of the stream and almost under my bank. First he rushed me about and then I hustled him about, but took the very greatest care in doing so, as I felt sure that it was my only chance of the day, and I was anxious to get him thoroughly 'done' before bringing him up to that ugly, bushy bank, in the high water that was running. Even when he got tired he kept out of reach for some time, but at last he swirled round just above me and began boring under some willows. He was swimming almost straight downwards in deep water with his head out of sight, but against the roots of the willows, and his tail slowly waving in the dark red water about six inches below the surface. I reached over the willows below him and, to lessen the great risk of gaffing the line, I gaffed him in the 'tummy,' near the tail—greatly fearing another bungle such as that by which I lost a fish in the same place when we were last fishing together. This time all went well, and he proved to be a clinking good fish,

THE ONLY RISE

a perfect little pig in shape, and he weighed 18 lbs.

I fished that pool over again and then hurried off to give a last trial to my friends of the morning, but though the water was clearing and looked quite good enough for them, yet my eighteen-pounder remained the only taker of the day.—Yours,

A. C.

That, my dear boys, is spring fishing all over. Pool after pool, looking perfect, and certain, as you feel, to hold fish, you fish over without a sign. Your high hopes are growing faint or have gone altogether, when, often at the most unlikely place, jump in your arm goes an electric thrill, and the one rise of the day has come and the fish is gone: or else, hardly knowing how it has happened, your nerves are found watching, and the half-raised rod is twitching and quivering with the line tight upon a plunging, splashing, rolling salmon, beginning a battle of anxious, growing hope, ending with a noble, glittering prize.

As far as catching fish goes, you may now go home. Unless your lines are, indeed, cast in pleasant places you have had your only fish of the day, and you will catch no more. The memories of many days of spring fishing tell us so, and in our hearts we know it as we admire this shapely, shining fish. But, go home! do you say? Hang it, man, the day is only just begun. Go home! Don't you know that every cast that I make after this I shall feel certain that I am going to take another fish. I shall be fishing better than I have ever fished to-day. I 've got one; nothing can make it a blank day now, and, with a little luck, I shall certainly get another.

Well, this is called patience by those who don't know. But it is nothing at all like patience. It is hope, undying, unquenchable, the heart and soul of salmon fishing.

To a Salmon River in Spring

> Springing in the moorlands
> In a thousand rills,
> Each a tiny torrent
> That the rain-storm fills,
> Here a mighty river
> Pouring from the hills.
>
> Brown rushing river
> Swirling round our knees,
> Running here so broadly
> Through the lowland leas,
> But hiding lusty salmon
> Fresh from wintry seas!

Yield up these monarchs of thy peat-stained streams!
Show us each fastness where a salmon gleams!
Make us the dreamers of thy fairest dreams!

IX

A WEEK-END IN OCTOBER

MY DEAR BOYS,—This is Monday evening, and as I rush back to London in the fastest train that runs from Scotland, I am passing the time by writing an account for you of the last three days' fishing.

I travelled North last Thursday night and had a very early breakfast on Friday. Then I hastened off to the river and was ready to make my first cast at five minutes to nine.

Just look at the day! It is dull and foggy, and the wind is from the east. The water is fairly clear, but is still very high and is stained with peat, for it was news of a sudden flood just before the season closed that had brought me up.

What fly shall we begin with? I think I shall start in that long, rough stream, and shall begin with the very biggest fly that I have, this great clumsy Jock Scott, a full two and a half inches long. Very often in a big black water the fish have taken such a fly when they would not look at anything smaller, however bright it might be.

With the river as high as this we will skip the first forty yards, the swiftest and roughest of the water, for it is only where the stream begins to spread out and to run less turbulently that we shall take a fish to-day. So the first cast is made abreast of a broken fence that stands amongst the bushes on the opposite bank. For one, two, five, ten, fifteen minutes, nothing happens, though every sense is on the alert as the fly comes round in the very best water that we ever fish. Can the fish be going to sulk on the first fly day after an October flood?

It almost seems so. A fresh cast is made almost square across the water, and the line at once begins to 'belly' in the rushing current. 'Phist' goes the slacking line, up goes the rod, and almost before I know what has happened or how it happened, the line is tightened hard and the thudding, heavy plunges of a good fish come plain and unmistakable. In a moment he breaks the surface and then, whilst one may count ten, he thrashes about to get rid of this terrifying restraint. Lash—lash—lash—lash; then a second of quiet and again the thrashing begins. There is no mistaking a good fish when he does this, however little you may be able to see of him. Presently he settles down and begins trying short dashes about the pool, then a resolute boring up to the head of the stream and a sudden dash down again. Then the end begins; he comes out into the quieter water and presently his sullen plunges begin to break the surface of the water again, and in a few minutes more he rolls over on his side and is brought out with a long gaff. Well, he is a clinker; a short, thick and hard, though reddish, cock fish of four-and-twenty pounds.

I start the pool again. This time only a few casts down it the line suddenly tightens and three or four heavy kicks tell of a good fish. But he is gone; and he refuses, of course, to come again. Another ten minutes and just off the end of the fence, where the first fish took, a thumping rise is followed by the slow, heavy thrashing of another big fish. Five seconds, ten seconds pass—a long time they seem—and one is just feeling sure that the fish is well hooked when up flies the top of the quivering rod and the long line hangs loose. He must have broken me. With a sickening feeling of disappointment I pull in the line. No! the fly is there. The point of the hook is not blunted, and the hook itself is firm and rigid and is not 'sprung.' It must have got only a slight hold, or else I think that its point must have been resting against a bone. But they are getting off the hook in a most unaccountable way. Perhaps this hook is too big; at any rate the point is sharp and the fish are coming to this fly, so we will try it again in the deepest water. Presently a gallant fish comes, and he makes such a wild, dashing, tearing fight that, failing to break the gut, he is soon 'dead beat,' turns on his back, and is taken out within five minutes of his hooking, a short, bright fish of 17 lbs.

Gemini! what a day! It is only just past ten o'clock and we have taken two good fish and lost two more, both of which, with ordinary luck, should have been landed. But the next hour and a half brings no more rises though we fish the entire pool again with the big Jock Scott, then with a big claret and mallard, and finally go over the best of it with a smaller Jock Scott.

Then we go to the slower stream above, a deep, still pool ending with a big, strong-running dub, which itself ends in a glassy suck past big stones to the rapids. It is fished from a broad gravel bed, making very easy wading. As the rod is being lifted to recover the line after the very first cast, a fish follows the fly and snatches it. It is not a big fish, and, in this open water it gets little mercy, and a very lively five minutes sees it also on the gravel bank—a hen fish of 13 lbs.

For the rest of that long pool, a good hour of most careful fishing, not one fish moved. But at the very end a fish showed himself. He was above me, just breaking the surface at the far side of the glassy run, and lying so far over that the fly had not covered him, so I worked myself back a few yards and let out line cast by cast until he saw the fly and took it. A jolly, stout-hearted fish he proved to be, and after thrashing about until he got right into the rapids, he came steadily up-stream and explored his own pool in every direction, grubbed amongst the rocks under the opposite bank, and sailed round and round the great boulder in the stream. Then he turned again for the rapids and splashed and raced down them into the pool below. There the game ended in favour of the rod, and he was duly weighed out at 22 lbs.

It was now one o'clock, so I sent Tom off to the fishing hut to boil the kettle whilst I went down the rough stream once more with a large white and silver fly. This time I began a little higher up, and when I had come just opposite the fence as the fly—which fell in the slack water—was being towed by the current into the rush, there was a splashing rise like that of a great trout. A big belly of line tore out of the stream as the rod was raised, and a few yards higher up a red cock fish flung himself out with the line trailing behind him. His way of fighting was most unusual. It was to make long, dogged runs down and across the stream. Then under the other bank he would begin jig-jig-jiggering, and keep this up until I had got him near my bank again, when he would once more dash off for the other side and repeat the same performance. He had contrived to get the gut caught round the bony cartilage at the corner of his mouth on the farther side from me, and possibly that may have been the reason why he preferred to make all his runs down-stream. However, all things come to an end, and he soon ended on the bank—$14\frac{1}{2}$ lbs.

It was now half-past one, but before going down to luncheon I finished out the pool and hooked and lost a very heavy fish. How big he was I cannot say, for though he kept splashing on the surface of the water he never showed himself clear of it, and he was only on for a few minutes. Certainly he was not less than 20 lbs.—my hopes put him at not less than five-and-twenty.

And so to lunch. Past two o'clock and I had got five fish and lost three. I found your 'Uncle' Clervaux, who had only begun to fish at twelve o'clock, with a white and silver fly that I had made for him ten days before, had got three good fish, $14\frac{1}{2}$, $14\frac{1}{2}$, and 12 lbs. The day was getting darker and more foggy, and when we went on again the fish were much more shy. At the tail of my first stream I hooked, and after a few minutes lost, a heavy fish, and also had another rise and held for a few splashes a little fish of 6 or 7 lbs. From then until dusk not a fish would look at the fly, but then in a swift, smooth run a nice fish boiled up and just touched the fly. At the next cast he again came up and followed the fly across the pool, but after that he would not move, although I tried him with several flies. As a last resort as darkness set in he was tried and killed on a small phantom minnow. He weighed 11 lbs. So ended my day. Six fish, 24, 17, 13, 22, $14\frac{1}{2}$, and 11 lbs., and five fish lost. Uncle Clervaux got one more fish, a fine hen fish of 25 lbs.

On Saturday we began early. S. arrived by a train early enough to permit of breakfast at 7.15, and by eight o'clock we were off to the river. A gusty wind, strong and bitterly cold, blew up-stream and made fishing very hard work indeed. I went to the water that I had fished on Friday. In the dub, at 9.15, a fish swirled up just after the fly had fallen on the water, but he missed it. At the next cast he followed the fly for six or seven yards, and at the third cast he did the same, but this time he ended by taking it with a rush and a fine swirl. Then he bolted down through the rapids into the next pool, where in due time he was landed, a cock fish of 19 lbs. This fish had received at some time what must have been a most terrible wound. The vent and a large part of the left side above it for a distance of five or six inches had been torn or bitten out. The wound in the side had healed perfectly, though still showing a great hollow, but the vent was altogether gone, and in its place, though rather to one side, was a great round hole into which one could have thrust a half-crown piece.

I then fished the lower pool with a white and silver fly. In the heaviest water a big fish took the fly with a glorious snatch. He seemed to be firmly hooked, and he gave a great run for ten minutes, but then I lost him by a piece of gross carelessness—by shifting the rod to my right hand and with it holding rod and line together just as the fish made a dash down-stream, splashing along the surface and tearing out the hold.

Immediately after losing this fish I got a vicious pull from another, and a few minutes later a third fish came twice to the fly, but was not hooked. From that time, about ten o'clock, until four, though I slaved hard and fished the very best I knew, I got no rise at all.

At four o'clock a good fish followed the fly twice, but would not touch it, and shortly afterwards, fishing above our boat-house, a big fish lying in very quiet water snatched the fly, and throwing himself over and over, broke the gut. I suppose it had been weakened by casting in the rough wind, but still a break like that is entirely the fault of the fisher. It is inexcusable not to test the gut often, and more frequently than ever should one try it on a windy day, when one ought to know that gut runs great risk of becoming weakened. S., I was told, had got four good fish, and my bag looked very poor beside his. But luck came, as it does so often, with the dusk. The sun had come out and had shone brightly during the afternoon, and just as it was setting I saw a heavy fish rising near the point of a jetty. The place is a favourite and most deadly cast if the fly is allowed to hang beside the current; and I fished it most carefully now with a small Jock Scott. No sooner had I finished it than the same fish began to rise again and again. So I put on a large white and silver fly [1] and began the pool anew. As the fly covered him he rose with a quick flicker of the tail that made me feel sure that he had taken it. He had not, but at the

[1] This fly, called a 'white and silver,' has a perfectly plain body of oval silver, a rather long white hackle, and wings of dark turkey, with a large jungle-cock's feather over each wing. No tail, tag, butt, head, or any other adornment.

next cast he made no mistake and took the fly hard, under water.

At first he kept deep in the water, but as soon as he got thoroughly frightened he bolted down the stream for twenty or thirty yards and then flung himself clear out of the water, falling in with a mighty splash and then tearing off down-stream again. Up to that moment I had no idea that he was more than a decent twenty-pounder, but my heart jumped as I realised that he must be at least 30 lbs., and that we were to fight it out in growing darkness on the worst piece of bank and in the most risky piece of water on the river, the whole bank being lined with snags and sunken logs, and one fine snag lying right in midstream about ten yards below him.

There is not much to be said about the next twenty minutes, but a great deal was done in it, and there was much water splashed about and much running up and down of banks and struggling and tumbling through willows and bushes on my part, but it all ended right, in a fine cock fish of 33 lbs., though a very red one, with the most enormous ' gib ' that I have ever seen. As I lifted him up the bank the fly fell out of his mouth, and we found that at some time during the fight he had snapped the hook off behind the barb. It was a bit of luck to land him, and all the more welcome because this was the heaviest fish that I had ever landed on the fly. The fly itself I shall keep in my museum box of treasures.

To-day, Monday, was my last day. I had to leave the water by two o'clock—absolutely the last moment if I would catch this train that I am now in. We began to fish at a quarter-past nine. The day was wretched, with constant showers and a cold north-east wind, and by eleven o'clock I had had three feeble rises and had got no fish, so I put up a spinning rod and at the first cast took a sea-trout of 3 lbs. A few minutes later I got a salmon of 19 lbs., and shortly afterwards lost a big fish on the minnow. The fish contrived to get the line foul on a rock and tore itself away, taking with it both of the triangles from my minnow. Then I took to the fly again, a small port-wine coloured fly, and landed a beautiful bright cock fish of 17 lbs.—an exceptionally good fish for so late in the year. Then I moved to an upper pool and had another pull, and presently amongst the boulders at the far side of the pool a fish boiled up at the fly, and after a little coaxing came again and was hooked and landed—a female fish, short and thick, of 16 or 17 lbs. However, as October was nearly out and female fish are poor to eat, but precious for spawning, she was gently unhooked and slipped in again, though looking rather sorry for herself. By this time it is nearly two o'clock, and I go up and have five minutes' fishing at the place where I took the thirty-three pounder last Saturday. Then I try a few last casts with the minnow rod before taking it down, and in making my very longest throw for the very last cast of the

THE LAST CAST OF THE SEASON

season the minnow sticks fast on the gravelly shallows opposite. I take hold of the line, point the rod at the water and pull heavily, meaning to break the line; but the strain drags away the minnow, no doubt turning over the stone on which it had caught. The minnow swings into the heavy water, and as I reel up some fish snatches it and begins to splash in all directions. Just after two o'clock he is landed, a sea-trout of 5 lbs., and in ten minutes more I am in the dogcart with two out of three salmon and two sea-trout, and my week-end and my season are both over.

Not a bad week-end either—eleven salmon, weighing 205 lbs., an average of over $18\frac{1}{2}$ lbs. apiece, besides two sea-trout. Nor a bad season either that is ended by this week-end. Seventy-three salmon it has found for me in one place or another, including my heaviest fish—$40\frac{1}{2}$ lbs.

X

MINNOW FISHING

My dear Boys,—Avoid minnow fishing for salmon as a canker that will eat into some of the very best days of your fly fishing.

Before the introduction of the 'Silex' casting reel, minnow fishing was a tedious and clumsy process, and there was little to tempt any good fly fisher to use a minnow beyond the period for which alone, as I think, it is fitted or is really justifiable. That is during the rise or fall of a flood when the water is more or less muddy and inky black, and the fly is useless or very nearly useless. Then, without doubt, the artificial minnow can kill fish well, and as the water clears can do great execution amongst the very largest fish.

But it is a dangerous thing for you to begin its use. As soon as one has mastered the knack of casting from the reel, one can fish a minnow tolerably, and can drag out in the most summary way three or four large fish on a day when one's fly fishing is quite fruitless. The next day the river has cleared and has become perfect for the fly. It ought to be a tip-top day. But you are tempted of the devil to try just for an hour the phantom minnow that you know proved so deadly the day before. You take a fish or two and then you go on with the minnow all day long, making a big bag perhaps, but dragging out the fish with a trace made of steel wire, and armed with two or three triangle hooks, and at the end of the day feeling that you have been rather a butcher than a fisherman, and that you might almost as well have used a net; and conscious also that your comrade, who has kept on with the fly and has had but a couple of good fish, is a better sportsman than you have been, and has had a far more enjoyable day.

Still more fatally tempting is the relapse to minnow when, after a good day minnowing, you find next morning that the water is right for the fly, and you resolve to make it a day of fly only. You put on your best fly and you begin full of hope. For an hour or two you cover much water without a single rise, and you begin to doubt whether the fish mean to take at all to-day. Soon, just to see whether they will move at all, you put up the spinning rod, resolved merely to have one try down the pool. A fish takes the accursed thing, and you are lost. Abandoning all sense of decency, you pursue the horrible craft, and at dusk you stagger back to the fishing hut with half a dozen great fish upon your back and with your conscience hanging about the neck of your heart, which keeps on protesting in vain that this was really no day for the fly.

Fortunately, when the water really clears, you must throw aside your wretched spinning tackle, for—except, perhaps, in the early spring—it then becomes almost useless, and the fly is greatly superior to it.

However, in a cold, wet season, when the river is in flood for weeks together, with only odd days when fishing is possible, the minnow can be really and legitimately useful. Then in big, dark waters, stained or muddy from the floods, you should cast well across the stream and let your minnow swing as deep in the water as possible, winding in the line very slowly, just fast enough to enable you to keep touch with your bait, in order to keep it off the bottom and to feel the least sign of any attack upon it.

A fish often takes the minnow with a savage grab, but sometimes he takes it so quietly that you may think it was merely some floating leaf that has touched your line. Only when you make a second cast and at the same spot take a salmon do you know what caused this tiny check to the minnow.

One spring morning only a few seasons ago, some idlers were hanging over the parapet of the bridge that you know very well over our lowest pool, and were watching an angler spinning a big phantom minnow in the pool below their feet. Suddenly a big fish of four- or five-and-twenty pounds appeared out of the black depths, followed the minnow out of the strong current, then seized it and slowly began to sink, plainly holding the minnow in his jaws. To their amazement the fisher gave no sign of having perceived anything, although they knew that he was fishing for that very fish. They shouted to him, 'You've got him!' and he struck violently, but too late. The fish had discovered the fraud and had already let go the minnow.

That incident was only an extreme case, luckily not unseen, of an attack by a salmon upon a phantom minnow which conveyed but the faintest impression, if any, to the angler. I am convinced that in every kind of fishing, whether with fly or bait, such things are much commoner than most fishers suppose. A quick eye will, especially in windy weather, often see the flash of a turning salmon which has followed the minnow into shallow water and has not seized it in time. A second cast brought round more slowly will often result in a savage grab just before the minnow reaches the same place, or just before it is to be lifted out of the water.

In spring, especially on sunny and frosty mornings, a small and fast-spinning minnow fished through the most rapid streams will frequently kill fish in the very lowest and clearest water. But when fishing in clear water the minnow, if you are to do well, must spin fast, and if the water is not only clear but low, the faster the minnow moves through the pool the better is your chance of taking fish. And even in low—

dead low—waters a minnow, as darkness sets in, may take the shyest and the wariest salmon.

Tackle for Spinning

For spinning the artificial minnow or for fishing with prawn or any other bait, the best rod that I know is an eleven-foot six-inch spinning rod. If made of cane it will be unbreakable, and will also be lighter and easier to fish with, holding it, as you have to do, in one hand, whilst the other hand is busy with the reel. A split cane rod, built especially for spinning, is, of course, the best, but a cheap sixteen-foot fly rod of whole cane, costing about twenty or twenty-five shillings, does very well indeed as a bait casting or spinning rod if it is cut down to a length of about fourteen feet to fourteen feet six inches, and it is a job that any one can do for himself. One has only to cut off about eighteen or twenty inches from the top, and tie on the top ring again.

Then for the reel, a 'Silex' reel (which is really only the old Nottingham reel, but made of metal instead of wood, and fitted with an ingenious brake and check) is better than anything else that I know. A newer reel of the same type is being sold now, but I do not like it so well. As soon as you learn the gentle upward swish that is required in fishing with such a reel, you can cast a great distance with much ease and great accuracy.

At first you will be much bothered by the awful tangles caused by the reel overrunning. Generally this has been caused by your using too much force in the throw, but a sudden and jerky start is very apt to produce overrunning. The cast should be more a sweep than a jerk, and the less you attempt to guide the line on to the drum of the reel the better. But if, as you wind it in, you find the line piling up on one side of the drum, that is due—unless you are allowing something to touch the line—to the reel not being set on perfectly straight, and a reel set even slightly crooked will give immense trouble, and the true cause is very often not noticed.

There is one tip with a badly overrun line. If you try to pull off the line you generally end in making things worse. Take the drum bodily out of the reel with the tangle untouched, and you can then very quickly throw off the whole of the tangled line and wind it again on the drum. And if you don't know it already it is worth remembering that if you hold the line, first with one hand and then with the other--winding on, say, twenty or thirty turns with the right hand, then keeping the drum in the same position and winding on about the same number of turns with the left, and so on—you will counteract the twist that is given with each turn if you wind on a string or line over the end of a reel (or of anything else) that is not revolving. *Never pull a tangle.*

As a spinning line, forty yards of ordinary dressed silk trout line, costing a penny a yard or less, is far better and cheaper than the thick and costly lines in sixty or eighty yard lengths sold by the fishing-tackle shops as spinning lines for salmon. The trout line has ample strength. With it you may, when using a steel wire trace, smash your hooks in order to free the minnow when hung up on a rock or a stake ; and the thinness of the line is a great advantage both for ease in casting a light bait and as being less visible to the fish.

One thing is vital, with every spinning line. Every few hours, unless your line is quite new, you must test, by a fair pull between your hands, the last ten feet or so of the line next the trace, in order to see if it has yet become dangerously worn by the friction upon the rings of the rod. If the line breaks on a fair pull between the hands, you must ruthlessly continue to break pieces off until you have got rid of the whole of the weakened part. Any shirking or neglect in this respect may cost you dear, for you will probably lose, not merely the trace and minnow, but a good fish as well. Yet I will make bold to prophesy that you will neglect to test it, and will more than once pay the penalty and then realise full well why you have done so.

In this matter the strong, thick spinning line is even more dangerous than the thin trout line. The latter looks thin and fragile and invites constant testing. The former takes a longer time to wear, in the first instance, but when badly worn, still looks thick and strong, and that causes you to forget the need of frequent tests.

Behind the spinning line you want some backing

TROUT LINES FOR SPINNING

—forty to eighty yards, according to the nature of the rivers you are likely to fish—of thin, strong silk or hemp. Undressed silk plait is by far the strongest and the best for backing, if you wish to have a very long line upon your spinning reel, but a hundred yards of immensely strong, thin plaited hemp line can be bought for ninepence or a shilling.

As to minnows : I always use a phantom or else a Devon minnow. Natural bait of any kind, if kept alive, is messy and a nuisance, and if kept dead it soon becomes a stinking abomination. The best phantom for dark water, so far as my experience goes, is Brown's silk phantom, painted with a blue back and an ivory belly, but either silver or gold colour does well enough in place of the ivory, although neither is so conspicuous in a dark water as the ivory colour appears to be. For big waters I use a three and a half inch minnow (that is, three and a half inches from the snout to the tip of the tail), and for lower waters a minnow of three inches, two and three-quarter inches, or even less. The minnow should be leaded up to the total weight of half an ounce or thereabouts, but the smallest sizes cannot very well be brought up to this weight, and the largest sizes may well be a trifle heavier. But a weight of half an ounce is heavy enough to enable one to throw the minnow easily, and it also is enough to ensure its sinking pretty deeply in the water. Do not buy your phantoms leaded, but buy a pound of lead wire ; and buy it at an ironmonger's shop and not from a fishing-tackle maker, who will charge you many times the price for it. Then cut the lead wire into lengths and insert them into your phantom either through the mouth, beside the swivel, or else through a small hole cut with a knife point in the back near the metal head. You must cut your hole in the back of the phantom rather to one side of the centre line, or you will cut the stitches which sew up the silken body, and will spoil your minnow. The most useful size of lead wire is about No. 17 British wire gauge, but if your wire is too thick it can very easily be made thinner by taking a steady pull on the length which you are going to cut up, when the ductile metal will stretch and reduce its thickness to any degree that you may desire.

In order to keep the loose leads from wearing or breaking through the silken body of your phantom in which the lead is contained, it is a good thing to tie round the body, after the lead is put into it, a few turns of stout thread or thin twine at a point about half an inch above the neck of the tail. The tail itself I always cut off. Neither the tail nor the fins of a swimming fish are visible, and the phantom seems to last longer without its imitation tail, which gets much knocked about by the violent splash with which the heavy leaded minnow falls into the water at each cast. The metal fins also are a weak point in the design of the minnow as you buy it. One side of them is dark, and that is right enough, but the lower side is always painted a brilliant silver or ivory colour to match the belly. This does well enough in black or thick waters, but in moderate waters it is a great mistake. The fin of the living minnow, when swimming, is not visible. That of the artificial copy is needed to make the body spin so as to hide the fraud as much as possible, but the fins should be made as inconspicuous as possible. You will find it a great advantage to take the point of your knife and scrape off all the paint or silvering from the lower side of the fins so as to leave them as little obtrusive in colour as may be.

Several tackle-makers have a good, small phantom with an olive-coloured or dark-greenish back and a yellowish or ivory belly—perhaps rather more like a loach than a minnow. These kill well in low, clear water whenever a minnow will kill at all in such water—that is, chiefly in the spring or at the fall of dusk.

A small minnow, mounted as usual with three triangles, is much improved by removing the triangle nearest to the head and slightly increasing the length of the gut by which the middle triangle is attached. Usually both the flying triangles are tied to the same piece of twisted gut, so care must be taken, when removing one triangle, to see that the other is left securely knotted.

In any case the spin of the artificial minnow is improved and the life of the twisted gut holding the flying triangle is increased by tying a turn of thin string or a few turns of stout thread tightly behind the metal fins to prevent the flying triangles from swinging forward during the cast, and so catching the trace or chafing their gut mounts against the metal fins.

As a spinning trace gut is well enough for trout, and it, of course, will do for salmon, but it is not from any point of view to be compared with steel wire as a trace for spinning for salmon. It is, as I think, better not to use either twisted wire traces or the blackened steel wire now usually sold in the tackle shops. Plain piano wire, as sold by any ironmonger who deals in piano wire, at the price of about sevenpence a hank, is far the best thing that can be got. Though of white, unlacquered metal, yet it is so thin that in use it alarms the fish less than the gut does, even in a clear water, and its strength is far beyond all gut and beyond all needs. Each hank contains several dozen yards, and the traces are so cheap and so quickly made that one need never hesitate to throw away any piece of wire that, in the course of playing a fish, has become, as wire sometimes does become, twisted corkscrew fashion or rendered uneven and unsightly by many sharp bends.[1]

For clear, low water it is worth while, I think, to use as much as six to eight feet of wire as a trace, but in heavy or in stained water four or five feet of wire is enough. To make a trace you have

---

[1] As a piano wire seller may not be easy to find, I will give you the address of one. I have bought mine for many years as No. 3 music wire from Goddard of 68 Tottenham Court Road.

WIRE TRACES

only to cut off the required length of wire and then to fasten one end to a stout double swivel and the other end to the swivel in the head of your phantom. To attach the reel line to this trace you pass the end of the line through the other ring of the top swivel—through the ring twice if the swivel is big enough—then knot the loose end of the line once round the upper line above the swivel, draw this knot tight and then pull the sort of running noose thus formed firmly home upon the swivel ring. This knot, well tied, will stand any strain and will never slip.[1]

To fasten the wire to the swivels one need only put the wire once through the ring and then, bending the end back, twist it neatly four or five times round the trace and then break or cut off the loose end with a pair of pliers.

This leaves a neat little loop like the bottom of the figure 6, as that figure is usually written by hand, and in order to prevent this loop, on receiving a strong pull, running up like a slip knot and jamming hard on the swivel ring, you should, with your pliers, take hold of the twisted roll above this loop and as close to it as possible, and then with a slight turn of the pliers bend the junction of the trace and loop so that the loop ceases to resemble the written figure 6 and becomes pear-shaped—the trace representing the stalk of the pear and pointing into the centre of the loop, and no longer in line with one side of it. Then the loop will never slip. A small pair of

[1] See Appendix, Note 2.

cutting pliers suitable for making up and cutting off this steel wire can be got for two shillings and sixpence from Buck of Tottenham Court Road, or of Holtzapfel, or any of the lathe tool makers; but to cut piano wire the pliers must be of the very best quality. With any plain pair of small pliers, costing only a few pence, the wire can be broken easily and neatly by a little sharp twisting to and fro. *Never use rusted wire.*

It is worth knowing also, as a quick and simple means of cutting off from the swivels, in order to throw away, a damaged trace, that without any tool you can cut this thin wire by purposely making a complete kink and pulling it tight. Then, upon opening out the kink again, the wire will break without the least effort. You would think that anything that can be broken in such a simple fashion must be utterly unreliable for salmon fishing. I thought so too at one time, yet, notwithstanding this facility of breaking, I have never had and have never heard of one single break in actual fishing with this wire, although I have used it for years and have taken with it at the very least a hundred salmon. I have tried wire, too, as a trace for fly fishing, using flies with eyes of metal instead of loops of gut or of fiddle-string. In heavy waters, where one wants to use a very big fly, the wire trace is tolerable, and I dare say that if one got accustomed to it one would fish with nothing else, but it seems rather to slash the fly into the water, it whistles as it flies through the air, and one misses the softness of the fall given by the uncurling gut cast. So much of the pleasure of a day's salmon fishing consists in the clean, easy stretching of your cast upon the water, consists in everything going 'sweetly,' as they say of machinery that is running perfectly, that I do not think that wire will, for a long time to come, supersede gut for fly fishing. However, he is a rash man who in these days will prophesy.

Two Simple Tackles for Natural Minnow

My dear Boys,—Sometimes you may wish to fish a natural bait with a fly rod. There are two very good tackles for doing so. The one is merely a triangle (or two triangles) whipped to a strand of stout gut which has a loop made at the other end. You must insert a baiting needle (an ordinary thin steel crochet hook would do very well, or a big darning needle with one side of the eye filed out) into the natural minnow or loach either at the vent, or, still better, at the back opposite the vent, and you must bring the needle out at the mouth or the point of the nose, drawing the gut through after it until the shank of the triangle is buried in the bait. You then weight the bait by thrusting down its throat either a few loose shot or else a lead sinker attached by a loop to the cast, so as to slide down into the bait. Though not necessary, it is an advantage, also, to close the mouth of the bait, either with a twist of fine wire put through the lips or by a stitch or two with a needle and thread. The bait is then cast very gently with the fly rod and allowed to sink rather deep, and is then played slowly by raising and lowering the rod point.

You must remember that this is not a spinning bait. At the most it slowly wobbles. I have never caught a salmon on natural minnow myself, but I have often seen the natural minnow, mounted in this way, and used by a certain old fisherman, prove very killing in the lowest and clearest water in spring and early summer. Except for the careful and gentle casting needed, and the slowness with which it is worked, the minnow is fished exactly like a fly. The bait is not swung out, but is cast as a fly is cast. In order to avoid injury to the bait it is wise to use a very slow recovery and backward cast, and to avoid any jerk when the forward cast is made, by waiting until you can feel the pull of the bait behind you before you begin the forward throw. You will find this care imperative if you wish to cast anything heavy, whether it is a bait or an artificial minnow or any other lure with a fly rod. Unless you delay making the cast forward until you can feel the pull of the weight upon the line behind you, a violent jerk or crack will be given to the cast which no tackle will stand for long. Not only will there be a violent jerk, but the cast that you make will be a very poor one. If you wait until this pull is felt the line is then at full stretch behind you, and a fairly easy forward throw makes the cast smoothly and without a jerk, and covers a great deal more water. Also when casting a minnow or any weighted bait with a fly rod you should always 'shoot' a certain amount of line just before the minnow is about to fall upon the water. Thus you gain a double advantage. By pulling in your line before each cast you shorten the line and lessen the risk of cracking off your bait, and the act of shooting the line in making the forward throw ensures a much softer fall of your line and its burden upon the water.

The other method of baiting is that used by David Webster, who wrote *The Angler and the Loop Rod*, one of the most delightful and instructive books ever written about fishing. His minnow tackle, a very ancient one in the North Country, requires no baiting needle, and is therefore much more quickly and more easily adjusted to the bait. It is simply three round bend hooks lashed to a strand of gut exactly like a Stewart tackle, one below the other, with the middle one pointing in the opposite direction to the other two—back to back, as it were.

You put the top hook through the head of the bait, passing it through the sockets of both eyes, by which means it has a firm hold even in a very delicate bait. The middle hook you pass through the back fin, and the end one you pass through the skin at the tail or near it. The points of the hooks are all left projecting, and the minnow should then be slightly weighted as described for the last tackle. The pull of the line being from one eye, the bait, which should be left perfectly straight, will slowly wobble over and over in a most attractive manner, and a swivel is, of course, needed upon the trace. The hooks, though they lie very close to the bait, and are not easy to see, yet will readily hook any fish that may attack the bait. This tackle is a most excellent one for trout fishing, and it has the advantage of being one that any angler can make for himself who has a few hooks and some waxed thread. A small sinker of lead or some turns of lead wire a few feet away helps to keep the bait deep in the water, but in case of need a few small stones pushed down its throat are enough to sink the minnow sufficiently. The tackle is all the better if the uppermost hook has the shank shortened by snapping it off either with a pair of pincers or by inserting the point of it in some crack. Both of these tackles are quite as good for trout as for salmon. But the great trouble about natural minnow as a bait is the difficulty of getting minnows when they are wanted. We have not all got the advantages in that way of a certain famous parson in the Yorkshire dales. His clerk, having refused to fix a christening for Tuesday, the mother is said to have replied, ' T' christening must be Tuesday because t' cakes is made for Tuesday.' ' Nay! nay! ' says the clerk, ' t' christening can't be Tuesday, for parson's going fishing Wednesday, and he's got his minnads in t' font.'

XI

WORMING

My dear Boys,—The worm is not a thing that at all times, and in all places, is effectual as a means of killing salmon. Its utility as a bait seems to differ in an extraordinary way upon various rivers. In Norway, in bright, low water, the worm often kills when nothing else except a prawn is of the least use. And in many British and Irish rivers the worm is used with success when other methods fail. Still, I have only once caught any salmon upon a worm. On September 6, 1902, I reached the river-side about nine o'clock in the morning, and found that a dead low water had given place to a small but exceedingly muddy flood. Heavy thunderstorms higher up the valley had washed the dusty roads and had swept the mud into the river. So muddy was it that when the upper part of one's brogues were just under water the toes could not be seen at all through the four or five inches of yellow water that covered them. The dogcart that brought me had already gone home before I saw the river or I should have gone home in it; as it was, I lit a pipe and stayed to watch the flood before getting off my waders in order to walk back. The flood slowly increased, but a fish began rising again and again near the bank and in a place where I knew that the water could not be more than about three feet deep. I determined that he should be offered a worm if one could be got. Some men working in a field close by lent me a spade, and with it four large lobworms were soon dug up in a damp, grassy hollow. They were then bunched on a large hook and fastened to the gut cast. A good-sized pebble was tied to the gut about eighteen inches above the worms, in order to serve as a sinker, and the whole was then carefully dropped into the stream about twenty feet above the fish, which was lying within a rod's length of the bank. As soon as the bait reached the place where the fish had been rising the line stopped, trembled for a few moments, and then began to move slowly up-stream in the way that no fisher can possibly mistake. I had always heard that the salmon should have ample time to gorge the worm, and so he had it. It was not until a series of little tugs began that I struck firmly and sent him flying wildly round the pool—which was a little one. A very few minutes of the maddest rushes and splashings left me with a beautiful little 9 lbs. grilse upon the bank. Looking into his mouth, the gut disappears down his throat, and no hook is visible, and no worm either except a bit two inches long and still threaded upon the gut, but about two feet away from his mouth, my pebble having gone long ago. So I cut him open in the middle and I find, struck firmly into his stomach, the naked hook. When it went there one cannot doubt that it had the four worms still upon it. Now there is not one scrap of worm to be found inside him. Where and how have they gone? You may solve that question for yourselves with the aid of the bit of worm still remaining on the cast. It was certainly not there when the salmon ate it. It seems pretty clear that the fish has vomited out the worms on feeling the hook, and that it has been able to eject them notwithstanding that they were partly threaded upon the hook. Once ejected out of the salmon's mouth, any bit of worm still threaded upon the gut will soon get washed along the cast as the fish tears up-stream, dragging the gut and line behind him. But there are some—let us say, the extreme blue water school of salmon theorists—who believe that a salmon in fresh water never eats anything at all, but merely takes flies and other food into his mouth from curiosity or rage, or, perhaps they will say, for the mere pleasure of spitting it out again. However that may be, this fish so far forgot himself as to swallow those worms.

Well, having succeeded beyond my hopes in this muddy water, some more worms were soon dug up and put into a broken bottle, and I began to fish the likeliest spots with a big bunch of lobworms. In about an hour, when hope was almost gone, I noticed a wave beginning ten to fifteen feet below and coming up-stream to the place where I had just pitched in my worms. The wave advanced to meet the worms, and then there was a swirl under water, about where the worms must be, and, forgetting all my wise advice, I struck instantly. The hook caught in the point of the jaw of a fish just about the same size as the last, and in another five minutes he was duly landed. But in this case the worms, though somewhat knocked about, were all still upon the hook.

More than once since then I have tried the worm, and in bright, clear water as well as in the yellowest mud, but so far I have never caught another fish upon it, nor have I had a single nibble from a salmon. I have caught a sea-trout or two, and sundry eels; and once a 'dab' or river flounder, about eight inches in length, contrived to get the lobworm which was on the point of the salmon hook into his mouth, and was tossed ashore, where he was promptly eaten by my dog.

Still there can be no doubt whatever that in many rivers worm is a deadly bait, and especially in the lowest state of the water. Henderson, for instance, in *My Life as an Angler*, tells (at p. 198) of his taking with the worm seven salmon in a single stream of the Tweed one autumn morning in the year 1856. He was, as his delightful book shows, a most expert fisher of the clear water worm for trout in the heat of midsummer, and in his opinion the only worms that, as he puts it, ' have power to captivate the fancy of a salmon ' are ' the green sickly-looking dew-worms.' I don't know how that may be, but the way to get such worms in unlimited quantities, if you want them either for salmon or, as I used to do as a small boy, for eel fishing, is to take out a lighted candle after dark, and on every lawn hundreds of this kind of worm will be seen on any dewy night disporting themselves together. But although they are stretched out at full length, each has his tail still in the mouth of his hole, and can flick himself back out of danger with the most surprising quickness. He moves more like a piece of stretched elastic than like a slow-moving worm. At first you will fail to catch two out of every three that you touch. All you have to do, however, is to put your foot lightly upon him before trying to pick him up. You can then pull his tail out of his hole, and once that is done you may remove your foot, for he will make no further effort to escape. He seems to know that escape is hopeless.

As I have said, I cannot tell you from any personal success what is the best way to fish with a worm for salmon—if you have to come down to that. But I know how it is done with much success by the Norwegian in low, clear water. He takes his stand at the head of a good running stream, facing directly down-stream, and with the rod held across his body and pointing away from the stream. He has about a rod's length of line out with a large bunch of worms at the end of it, and if he has a reel he often keeps a good many yards loose at the reel. Then he swings his rod right round in front of him, finally releasing the loose line at the reel and throwing the bunch of worms as far up-stream as he can. As they are washed down the stream he raises the rod point to keep the line taut and thus keep the worms rolling along the bottom, and he walks down beside the stream until his worms get swept out of the main current. Then he pulls in his line and repeats the cast again.

The Norwegian often uses no sinker of any sort, but I understand that in strong water it is advisable to have a sinker about fourteen to eighteen inches from the worms, and the best sinker is a round bullet of lead at least as big as a boiled pea, and for heavy waters it must be larger than that. The bullet should be split, like a big split-shot, and should be attached to the salmon cast by six inches of horse-hair or of cotton or of gut much thinner than the main cast. Then if the sinker catches fast in the stones you can break it off and save the rest of your tackle. The worms, if a good bunch be used, will not often catch in the stones if you keep the line fairly taut, just feeling the lead rolling along the bottom. It is surprising how seldom, if you do this, a good round lead will catch even upon a rocky bottom.

In fishing with worm for trout—and I suppose it is the same for salmon—next to keeping out of the fish's sight, the most important thing that you have to attend to is to keep the line taut and stretched evenly from the rod top to the bait, and not to let the worm be washed down the stream 'anyhow' with slack line in the water.

I first learnt that lesson in 1886 when sent out as a boy to fish a brook called the Linburn at Witton in the county of Durham, belonging to an uncle, with whom I was living, and in the charge of a truculent black-bearded keeper of his, known as 'Black Tom.' You never saw Tom. He stood over six feet in height, had a voice like a bull, a short curly beard of raven blackness, a big mouth full of gleaming teeth, and an aspect of swarthy, brawny fierceness that might remind you of some giant in Grimm, or of one of those ferocious guardians of the way who opposed Christian in the *Pilgrim's Progress*. I hope that the sight of him impressed the local poachers, but I fear that it didn't, for under this fierce exterior Tom had a very kindly heart. He was a nailing good shot, the best that I ever saw at a rabbit in covert ; he seemed to snap at the mere quiver of a leaf, but somehow you always found a rabbit lying near. At winged game Tom was no great performer, and as to his fishing, it was confined to worming the streams after a flood. I have known him to confess without a blush that some shot found at table in a salmon that he had sent up to the house were due to his having 'had to' slaughter it with a shot-gun as it passed under a bridge. However, when the burn came down in flood, Tom would take down an old string-mended trout rod, get a bag of worms, and sally out to a game that he thoroughly knew, and a very heavy creel of trout was certain to be the result. Well, on this day we fished up the stream on opposite sides, I being generally rather ahead of Tom. The water was quite cloudy, and no skill seemed to be required. From the first Tom took fish much faster than I did. I said I thought it must be the worms, but he threw me over his bag and took mine, and of course it made no difference whatever. I caught only a fish here and there, but Tom seemed to find a trout behind every stone. At last we came to a pool below a waterfall, and into this Tom cast his worm four times and each time took a good trout. I was busily fishing opposite him and getting never a nibble. I said, ' Tom, I 'm coming round to try your side.' ' Ay, do,' said he, ' but ye 'll tak nowt till I tell ye.' I did go over, and got nothing except a wretched little misery that I threw in again. Then Tom showed me what was the matter. It was that I was fishing with a slack line, and he assured me that if I kept the line taut, as he did, I should catch them just as easily as he. Tom's remedy, like the washing in Jordan, seemed too simple for anything, but I tried it and caught fish after fish. Then I went back to my side of the pool where I had found no takers and immediately caught four or five good trout. When Tom showed me the way to do it I had got six fish and he had got thirty-five. Before we left that pool I had taken nine good trout out of it, and for the rest of the day managed to get

A TAUT LINE

about half as many as Tom did of these chubby, lively, brook trout, averaging about five or six to the pound.

It is a lesson that I have never forgotten, and it applies to every kind of fishing. With a slack line you neither bring the fish to your hook, nor do you strike such as do unwarily come there.

ON PRAWNING. See Appendix.

XII

ONE OF OUR BEST DAYS

My dear Boys,—Now away with all this teaching: come with me to the fishing, and let us go again over one of our very best days. And so that the details may be fresh, we will take a day that is not only one of our best, but is also, at this present moment, only two days old.

Yesterday, September 6, 1908, a flood stopped all fishing. This morning the river is very high, and is black as ink with the stained water coming off the peat that lies away up on the moorlands forty miles away. It is still above fishing height, although it has already fallen many feet.

There is a good deal of dirt in the water, but we hope that it will run down into good order before evening. It is of no use to make an early start, but there may be a chance during the morning with a big minnow.

About ten o'clock Godfrey and I go up to the fishing hut. When we get there a drizzling rain is falling, the wind is from the south-east, and everything looks miserable. We each begin to fish with a big five-inch phantom minnow well stuffed with bits of lead wire to make it sink as deeply as possible. We each fish the quietest water that we can find, going in opposite ways, and you two shall come with me.

For a long time we see nothing. Then suddenly in an eddy, just as the minnow is being lifted out, there is a slight swirl and a little flicking splash, and some fish has got the minnow and has bolted out into the current. Only a bull-trout, I expect. No! a good fish it is; look at that determined, vicious tugging and at the short, steel-centred rod doubling up, yet without bringing the fish to the surface even in that strong water.

Off he goes for the other side of the river, and we will take this opportunity of pulling him down-stream past that great mass of snags at the next point, so that we may land him on the sandy spit where the Devil's Water comes into the main stream. Again and again he refuses to come down, and fights his way up past the snags and broken weiring, but at last he is got past the point and is soon landed on the sand, a cock fish with many sea-lice, but already showing a faint reddish autumn colour, and weighing 13 lbs.

That eddy is a find. We will try it again. At the very tail of it, close under the bank, 'jug' goes the rod and we are fast in another fish. This fellow makes no trouble whatever about going down past the snags to reach a landing-place. He, like the famous wife of Jack Spratt, prefers exactly the opposite course to his fellow, and he straightway bolts down-stream and keeps on tearing off the line in repeated rushes as we run down the high, rough bank and scramble over a fence. Soon he has reached and passed the Devil's Water foot and is nearing the rapids which are some seventy yards below it. He means going through these rapids into the next pool, but to-day we cannot cross the Devil's Water anywhere near its mouth, and so at all costs he must not go down. Already he has taken more than sixty yards of line, and is out beyond some formidable stakes just above the rapids. The fish must break rather than be allowed to go any farther, so the line is seized and held fast. A fierce splashing struggle in the glassy water above the rapid ends in favour of steel wire and sound tackle, and slowly the fish comes up and out of danger. His one great run has finished him, and within little more than five minutes of the hooking he is gaffed and weighed—14 lbs.—a cock fish, and as bright as new-minted silver.

We now put on long waders and go up the Devil's Water to cross it and fish the pool below. The river is very broad, and the Devil's Water, though high, is clear, so it looks as if the fish might see a fly below the junction. We go over the pool with a huge fly—a Jock Scott—and then with a great flaring yellow turkey. When that has proved vain we return to the spinning rod. The very first cast yields a most beautifully shaped cock fish of 24 lbs., which must have been lying in only a foot or two of water at the throat of the rush.

There he grabs the minnow when it has been wound up to within ten feet of the rod point. Did you see me strike hard and firmly, keeping the rod low, and then raise the rod, letting the line fly off the reel almost unchecked? When a big fish takes on a very short line like this you must keep cool and strike firmly, and then instantly and freely let him have line, even at the risk of the reel overrunning, or of the line being slack for a second or two. If you try to hold the fish on this short line you will almost certainly lose him, and you will probably damage your rod as well.

A few casts lower down the pool a fish of 14 lbs. seizes the minnow and is landed, and then after a long trial at the very tail of the pool a fish snatches the bait and goes off on a tremendous expedition. First he dashes madly round the pool, just breaking the surface with his tail, then he sets his face for the sea and hustles us down-stream, at a run, for just short of half a mile, gradually getting near the opposite bank a hundred yards away, but all the time, or nearly so, keeping close to the surface in a most unusual way. He simply must be foul hooked. Finally he stops running, and after a long, wearisome jiggering is brought to shore and gaffed. He has the tail triangle in the corner of his mouth, but the other triangle is firmly fixed in his right pectoral fin, taking the whole pull of the line, and that seems to explain his activity and the power that he had in the strong stream, though he was by no means a large fish, weighing only 12 lbs.

It is now two o'clock, the rain is still falling, and wet through we get back to the fishing hut to find that Godfrey, though using a precisely similar minnow, has been so unlucky as to have had no fish, not even a run from any fish.

We are both sick of minnowing, and we have kept the quietest and best pool till the afternoon in order to fish it with the fly. But this wind, now nearly due east, and the cold rain are disheartening, and it is past three o'clock when we begin again. Godfrey goes first with a very big Dusty Miller, and we follow with a small Jock Scott. In a moment a fish snatches the Dusty Miller, but the hook—badly tempered or perhaps lodging on a bone—opens out and lets him go. A big Popham is put on. Five minutes later a fish grabs it, and this time takes both the Popham and also half Godfrey's cast. Standing out in the stream with hands trembling with excitement, he ties on another Popham at the end of his remaining two feet of single gut, and, resolving not to strike again in such a stream, he begins anew, and after another twenty casts, hooks a good fish. This time all goes well, and in due season we gaff this fish, a real beauty of 18 lbs., and the biggest that he has caught so far. But better is to come for him. Again he begins the pool—a very strong dub—at the deepest part, and almost immediately hooks and presently lands a clinking good fish, weighing

A LOST FISH

20 lbs. Meanwhile, fishing with a small fly, we have not had even one rise, but on making an extra long cast to a shallow ledge in midstream, there is a big boiling rise, and the fly is snatched almost as it touches the water. The fish—of 17 or 18 lbs.—immediately begins flinging himself about—out of the water and head over heels in all directions. After a few minutes he changes his tactics and bores across the river, over many great boulders which, in a lower water, stand clear out, until he finds himself right under the willows that fringe the bank. Once he is safely got back into the stream, but he repeats the move, and this time he works his way for eight or ten yards up-stream under the fringe of willows, his tail breaking the surface as he goes. Though the eighteen-foot rod is being held high, indeed with the reel overhead, yet there is a great length of line out, seventy or eighty yards, and a good deal is sagging in the water behind the fish. Presently he turns down again, we feel the line grate and catch, then we see the fish splash, and the line comes back loose with the twisted gut of the cast broken about eight inches from the reel line.

He is gone, and I really think we do not much grudge him his freedom; he has been such a gallant fighter. At least we say so on the spot, and try to think that we mean it.

Godfrey, who had come down to ply the gaff for us, goes back and instantly hooks and lands a grilse of 7 lbs. This is reversing the fortunes of the morning with a vengeance. Since luncheon he has got three fish and lost two, and we have not landed one. So up goes a big Jock Scott in place of the lost small one, and in a very few minutes a heavy pull under water announces that the change has worked. Godfrey comes down and presently gaffs for us a good fish of 20 lbs. Then he himself begins to fish, and no sooner is his line out than a fish quite close inshore snatches his last Popham and breaks it off. Immediately he puts on the nearest fly that he has to the lost one, and at once gets hold of an exceedingly lively fourteen-pounder at the very same spot, and we hurry up the gravel bed to watch the fun and to gaff the fish for him, anxiously expecting to find the lost Popham in his jaws. He is landed right enough, but the other fly is not to be found, though we both feel perfectly certain that it is the same fish that took the first fly. We then return and begin casting again at the spot where we had taken the last fish, and twenty yards lower down there comes a slight touch. The cast is repeated and the touch becomes a violent pull, and we are fast in another good fish. He flings himself out once—twice—thrice, and then bolts down the long rapids into the next pool. There he wastes much precious time in a backwater, refusing either to fight hard or to come near the gaff. However, Godfrey, seeing the fight so long, comes down in time to gaff him for me. He proves to be just over 20 lbs., and he has taken quite twenty-five minutes to land. When we begin again the darkness is fast coming on, and we both fish down our big pool without a rise. Then, as a last chance, we rush off to try the tail of a pool higher up. Precious time is wasted in getting there, but the chance turns out trumps, and we hook and safely land a nice fish of 18 lbs. It is now past seven o'clock and almost pitch dark, though the rain, which we hardly noticed in the keenness of our fishing, has stopped. The dogcart was to meet us at the crossroads at a quarter to seven, and it is hopeless to think of taking all these fish so far, so we must be content to get them to the fishing hut and leave them there for the night. But here are eight fish averaging about 16 lbs. apiece, and we are half a mile above the hut. Well, Godfrey carries down the rods and baskets and I tie a stout cord through the jaw of one fish, then string the other seven upon the cord and simply wade down the half-mile of water, towing the fish behind me. The night is very dark, and as one wades down, most of the time waist deep in the dark river under the wooded banks, it is difficult to believe that these eight big fish are still upon the string. In the water they weigh, of course, absolutely nothing, though out of it they weigh together a good deal more than a hundredweight. Time and again one pulls them to the surface to convince oneself that they are really there, and yet in a few minutes the same curious conviction returns upon you that most of them must have slipped off by some means. It makes one realise a little better the folly of holding up a tired salmon—as one so often sees people do—in such a way that his head and shoulders are practically lifted out of the water. Many a fish, and more especially many a grilse and small salmon, have we lost in this way. To you, my boys, I would say, Never hold the head of any salmon or large fish out of the water, however tired he may be. When reeled up short, if the fish is on the surface, don't hold the rod point above him, but hold it sideways or down-stream, so that it does not lift him upwards. If the rod is lifting any part of the fish's weight—that can only be so if some part of the fish is being held above water—then every kick that the fish gives, makes, as he falls back, a very sudden twanging jerk on the line and on the rod top, and if the hold is at all weakened by the fight it will almost certainly give way. After the first few struggles that follow the taking of the fly there is no stage of the fight at which so many fish are lost as that in which the tired fish is resisting the final efforts to bring him to shore, and the cause of loss is almost always a plain and preventible want of care. One forgets that on a very short line the jerks are ten times more sudden and more severe than they are when there is a fair length of line out and the rod is not doubled up like half a hoop.

Well, to return to our catch. Here we are at the fishing hut. Candle-ends are lighted, the fish are laid out on the floor, waders are taken off and rods taken down, and we hasten off to the dog-cart and so home to mulled claret and hot baths, and a dinner that we are almost too tired to eat.

It has rained and blown all day, and next morning a flood in the river greets our earliest waking eyes. So the fish are sent for and brought home and are carefully weighed, and there being nothing to do at the river we pass the time away by laying out the whole catch upon a grassy bank and taking a photograph of them.

We have rather blessed that flood since then, as without it we should not have had the photograph by which to remember that day. You may see it next this page. Godfrey's fish weighed 20, 18, 14, and 7 lbs.; ours 24, 20, 20, 18, 16, 14, 14, 13, and 12 lbs. His four weighed 59 lbs.; our nine 151 lbs., an average of just upon 17 lbs. apiece.

Before this we had once taken nine salmon and two bull-trout in a day, but the salmon were not such good fish as these, and the bull-trout hardly count. These fish were all beauties. Just look at them! I think that fish of 24 lbs., which you see near the middle of the picture, is as well shaped and as hog-backed as you could wish any salmon, and so are the three twenty-pounders on the right of him.

For real joy of success I do not think that this day could compare at all with my best spring day with five salmon landed on the fly and two more fish lost, or even with four fish taken on a day in March or April, but still it was a great day, and there was one glorious hour in it, for I have never known fish take the fly more madly than these did during a part of that miserably cold afternoon, although most of the rises did not come my way. The rain pelted steadily, and the wind, veering from south-east to east and then to north-east, blew more or less in our faces all day; the river was, as we usually think, too high for the fly, yet the fish that afternoon would not be denied. It was a glorious piece of luck, and all the more so because it was wholly unexpected. I hope that you may both be lucky enough to find such days, but they will not be many, so fish hard, and put on a good big fly after a flood. One other thing I have to say, don't be discouraged by rain or by an east wind—why, perhaps the very best day's salmon fishing of which we have any record was the 9th of April 1795, when the tenth Lord Home, fishing on the Dee, took thirty-eight salmon, of weights ranging from 6 to 36 lbs., on his own fifteen-foot rod. One has read of catching grilse on the Grimersta, like troutlets, by the score, but Lord Home's day, even allowing for a large number of kelts, which were all lawful fish in those days, is, to my mind, a far greater performance. And that 9th of April of the year 1795 was a rainy day, with an east wind blowing. I wonder what salmon fisher's mind fails to bridge that hundred years. Can't you see the rain pattering on the grey water, ruffled by a cold wind, and a stout-hearted angler, long ago crumbled into dust, yet still, with his short rod and his thick hair line, fishing envied of us all? I think that it is the matter-of-fact description of ill weather on that long-past day that brings it so vividly to the eye.

XIII

ON OTTERS AND OTHER POACHERS

My dear Boys,—There are two kinds of otters that come or may come within the range of an angler's vision. Both are notorious as poachers, but the one otter is a living thing, the other is an inanimate device of wood and lead. The use of the latter in this country is illegal, though it is far from being unknown, but in Norway and Sweden you may find one or more of them by the side of every lake that has fish in it—or at least, if you don't find them, it will not be because the otters are not there.

This otter is simply a piece of board about eighteen inches to two feet long and six to eight inches deep, with a keel of lead fastened along one side of the board to make it ride in the water upright on that edge. Then the line is fastened to the board just as the string is fastened to a kite. The thing is, in fact, nothing but a water kite, and by walking along the shore and towing the line the 'otter' is made to run out on the surface of the lake and to travel along nearly parallel to the shore, whilst the flies, which are tied to the line at intervals, bob and dribble along the surface of the

AN 'OTTER' BOARD

water in a way that is most tempting and most fatal to the fish. The first time that I saw an otter at work was on my earliest visit to Norway over ten years ago. On the strength of reports of trout many and big to be had in a certain lake among the mountains on the edge of the Hardanger Vidde, I and another had taken our rods and made a toilsome journey into the hills along the vilest track that you can conceive. No one but a Norseman would have called it a path at all. At last we sighted our El Dorado, a lonely pool, very narrow and about a mile long, with the left-hand edge lying against the foot of a rocky cliff, whilst the other bank was formed by a gentle slope of moorland covered with patches of cloudberries. One solitary native was to be seen close to the lake. Presently we sighted this wretched little board sailing merrily along abreast of him. Our disgust was great, but was tempered with the hope of actually seeing for ourselves the exceeding destructiveness of this famous poaching dodge. We approached the native and tried our whole stock of Norsk upon him. I will spare you the details of it, but the end of it was that the native said something unintelligible, then clapped his breeches-pocket, thrust in his hand, and drew out a wet and bleeding trout weighing about three-quarters of a pound. Then, chiefly by signs, we learnt that he lived in a saeter close by, that there were very few fish in the lake, and that this was an unusually big one, and that he would be very glad to see us catch something. We tried hard to oblige him, but could only produce two sizeable trout, and it was small wonder, for we saw that our friend had made quite a path along the edge of the lake by his daily tramping to and fro with his infernal engine. The day, however, was not quite a failure, for we took our revenge upon his cloudberries (multa baer), and, whilst I think of it, my boys, let me tell you never to accept —at least without the most careful questioning— a Norseman's report of good trout fishing to be had in any lake or river. He has no idea of misleading you, but it only means that he has heard of some one who, possibly with a net or perhaps a dozen night lines, has once caught a good basket of trout in that water. But if you ask him in detail whether he himself has seen fish caught there, whether it was with the fly or with 'sleuk' (minnow), how many the fish were and how long, and how often he has known such catches made and in what months, he will try to answer you quite truthfully, and you can then divide the result by two and hope for the best. But as for the Norseman himself, if he looks a good fellow, take him with you fishing, or climbing, or stalking the reindeer—or what you will—and, taking him, treat him like a brother, and you will gain a friend who will never flatter you and will never forget you, and, what is more, a friend whose staunch loyalty and frank, uncringing manliness you will never forget. At least that has been many times my good fortune with them, and I believe it to be in no way unusual.

And now, my boys, whilst I am speaking of Norway, let me give you one piece of advice. When you go amongst people who are poor and who live simply, as they do in Norway, always be on the watch to see that you are not trespassing on their kindness, and are not expecting them to do things for you that they would never think of doing for one another. Remember that the customs of one country are not those of another, and be careful to see that you give no unnecessary trouble, and do everything for yourself. Never forget the truth that was once expressed in his own way by a Maori chief when he said, after he had known Bishop Selwyn, 'Gentleman gentleman not mind what he do; piggy gentleman always very particular.' You may talk about 'manners makyth man'; I think that savage chief got a great deal nearer to the true heart of things when he picked out this as *his* test of the real and the pinchbeck article in gentlemen.

And it is not only in Norway that you'll find this useful. Nothing has caused more misunderstanding—on both sides—in our Colonies and in all new countries than the perfectly innocent and unwitting assumption that you will have everything done for you just as it is in England. Many a man has found to his vexation that his host or his host's daughters were cleaning his boots for him because he was obviously expecting or even asking for them to be done, and the servants, following the custom of the country, absolutely declined to touch them. Even in the hotels you may put your boots outside your door, but no one cleans them. You just take brown boots and clean them yourself, and you keep your eyes open for other little things of the same kind, and very difficult it is to see them.

However, to return to the otter, we have learnt since then that its evil reputation does not belie it and that it can kill fish. We were again together in Norway last year, and coming over the fjeld we saw a man carrying, in loops of string, what we at first took to be two large bunches of grey ptarmigan. When we got nearer we saw that his burden was nothing but fish. There were some eight or ten fine trout, the least weighing a pound and a half, four weighing about 4 lbs. apiece, and one that must have been well over 5 lbs. He told us that he had caught them with the otter which he was carrying and in a lake a few miles away, across the mountains, and, as you may believe, we took down its name and address pretty carefully. He said that he had caught them all in a very short time, and then had to stop fishing because he had already got more fish than he could carry.

And now of our English otters. I have said that they are notorious as poachers, but I believe that their ill-fame, so far as salmon goes, is largely undeserved. Stories about finding brilliant new-run salmon on the river-bank with a small piece bitten out of the shoulder by an otter are common in books on fishing, but I have fished for twenty years in rivers where otters were abundant, where one saw them constantly, and where one may see their fresh seal in the sand every day, and I entirely disbelieve that they do any serious harm to salmon. Perhaps in a small stream, or in the spawning season when fish are weak, the otters may catch and devour a weak or dying fish or a badly mended kelt. Even that is not, I think, very common, though it is always dangerous to make positive generalisations from one's own limited experience. I have known one case where several otters had eaten and, from the fresh blood and scales lying about, seemed also to have killed a big salmon. Once I saw the fresh body of a bull-trout kelt of 6 or 7 lbs. which for some days, and once before my eyes, was visited and partly eaten by an otter, but whether he had killed it or not I cannot say. He had certainly not either killed or found it where it lay, on a grassy bank some eight feet above the river. Several times I have known them to eat the carcasses of dead kelts which they had certainly not killed, and once—in September 1908—I marked the daily eating of a salmon of about 16 lbs. weight which I saw to be a stale, dead fish the day the otter ate the first small piece of him. After three days the carcass, still with only some 5 or 6 lbs. eaten away, was carried straight across a swift pool and left half out of the water on the opposite side whence two days later it was washed away by a flood.

The first of these occasions, when I think that the otters had really killed their salmon, was in 1902, a season of great drought. The river was very low, and disease began to appear amongst the fish in the shape of whitish spots of fungus, like the mould that grows upon jam, which appeared on the head or gill covers of the fish. That autumn I found by the water the bodies of four fish on which otters had certainly been feeding, but I could see nothing to determine whether or no they had been taken whilst alive; certainly they all were diseased. But on October 3, beside the rush at the head of a very strong pool I came upon a mass of pellets of spawn, fresh blood and scales, together with the two pectoral fins of a big salmon. Several large stones had been displaced, the sand was much torn up, and I could see the marks of several otters. It looked as if a great battle had taken place there, and of the two fins left one had a large piece, the shape and size of an otter's mouth, bitten clean out of the end of it. The head, bones, and the rest of the carcass were nowhere to be found, though I made a careful search. However, some hundred and fifty yards above the place there is an otter's holt under the roots of a bunch of alders, and on some stones near that I found some more pellets of spawn, so I have little doubt that the body had been carried up there to feed the cubs. On comparing the pectoral fins with those of a

15-lb. salmon caught the same day it was plain that the fish killed by the otters had been considerably larger than this, if it also was a salmon, but the pectoral fin of a bull-trout is larger than that of a salmon of equal weight. I can hardly think that the fish could have been strong and well. The kill had taken place beside and near the head of a very strong stream where one would think that the fish would have every chance of escape, or at any rate would have carried the otters down the pool a very long way before they could have landed him.

In that year I saw more signs of otters eating salmon than in all the other twenty and more that I have fished, and I believe that to have been due to the weakness of the fish caused by disease, and that most of these fish were dead or dying when taken by the otters.

Being addicted to fishing both early in the morning and late in the evening, I have often had the good fortune to see the otters fishing. Once a fine dog otter swam up to me and landed almost at my feet, and on one October evening at sunset I had lifted my right foot to step upon what I took for a brown lump of wood lying amongst some rubbish beside a log, when the lump, which was an otter lying asleep there, suddenly sprang into the river—almost causing me to fall in after it. In 1889, on the Ure in the North Riding of Yorkshire, a pair of otters came up over a rapid and began fishing the shallows at the foot of the pool where I was. Luckily they did not see me, and by lying along the trunk of an overhanging tree I had a good view of their fishing for nearly a quarter of an hour. Then another fisherman appeared, and the otters both went down-stream. Again, on the river Tyne on June 14, 1905, with your Uncle D'Arcy, we saw an otter in broad sunlight about four o'clock in the afternoon busily fishing amongst the rocks opposite to us. He swam round each boulder, keeping his head poked under the edge of it; several times he found a hole big enough to allow him to dive right under the rock and come up on the other side. After some ten minutes he caught an eel about fourteen inches long and as thick as one's thumb. This he brought out on to a big flat rock and there he ate it. All this time we were in full view of him, and I was not twenty-five yards away, and the sound of his teeth tearing the eel to pieces was plainly audible to us. It seemed a remarkably tough and leathery morsel, too, for it sounded like tearing up an old boot. Next, the otter went up the stream, crossed it to our side and then came across the gravel bed to get to some willows, but finding D'Arcy in front of him he went back to the water and swam across and disappeared. A quarter of an hour later he came out from some bushes, crossed the river about sixty yards above us, and began fishing in the very shallow water on our side of it. I put down my salmon rod and began to stalk him. Every time he put his head under

CATCHING AN OTTER

water I pressed on, and when he thrust his head out to breathe I stood stock still. At last, much to my surprise, I got within ten feet of him and could see everything that he was doing, could see him dashing in among the tiny fry collected in the shallows. Then he poked his head under the edge of a flat stone. I advanced a couple of steps, and as he came up to breathe he saw me. I jumped forward and raked him ashore with the gaff, which had a cork on, but a quarter of an inch of steel projected through it. The point of the gaff caught in the loose skin of his flank, but the hide is so tough—as you know who have seen otters killed by hounds—that the gaff did not pierce it, but I was able to swing him off the ground and grab him by the tail. By that I carried him kicking, twisting up, and snapping to the bank and thence to the fishing hut, where we shut him up until the next day, when we brought up the ladies to see him released. On finding himself free again he ran in a great hurry to the water, but once there he seemed quite confident, swam steadily up the shallows and then landed and disappeared in a holt.

He was a small dog otter, weighing perhaps 12 to 15 lbs. At first we had thought he was either blind or else blinded by the sunlight, but when he was caught we could see nothing wrong with his eyes, and his extraordinary lack of caution must have been due either to the bright sun or, as I have since been inclined to think, he may possibly have been at some time tamed or made a pet of. But we could never hear of there being any tame otter in the district, still less of any such having been lost. However that may be, he gave us a most interesting and delightful view of an otter's methods of fishing. His methodical quartering of the ground was wonderful, and when he caught the eel it hardly wriggled at all; he seemed to have paralysed it at once with his bites.

XIV

SOME MORE POACHERS

MY DEAR BOYS,—I have said that otters are not a serious danger to a full-grown salmon. His real foes are seals and porpoises in the sea and netsmen on the coasts and in the rivers. But far worse than all these together are the scoundrels who, in defiance of the law and of the rights of their neighbours, openly or secretly discharge poison and pollution into our streams.

The seals and porpoises are a very real danger. In one season during which I was fishing in the river Tyne, one out of every five fish taken on the water was marked with more or less severe gashes and tooth marks, and in all the rivers on the north-east coast fish showing wounds from that cause are not uncommon. But the net fisher in the river itself is an even more deadly foe to the spring and early summer fish, for those are the slow-running fish, dawdling in the tideway and in the lower reaches, and the nets, where they are numerous, mop up the majority of such fish. It is quite certain that in many rivers which are not great 'spring' rivers, only a small proportion of the fish which spawn in them in winter come in at all as spring fish during the course of their lives.

Such as do run in spring are the very best fish of the whole lot, the best in condition and the boldest and strongest fighters of the whole year, yet we do our very utmost to kill them out by allowing netting which is practically continuous, in the lower reaches of the rivers. For the small weekly close time is not enough to let the slowly running spring fish get past all the netting stations. Those fish which habitually come into the rivers in September or later escape the river nets altogether, but we steadily do our best to eliminate all the fish which have the habit of running in spring or summer. Just consider how slowly these fish run and how they are exposed to the dangers of the nets in the lower reaches of a river. In the close time before the season of 1897 began, one hundred and fifty clean spring fish were marked in the river Spey. Of these sixty-seven were retaken after the season opened; thirty-four of them had moved up the river, twenty-five had dropped down, and eight were recaptured at or about the places at which they had been marked.

In most rivers, at any rate, I do not think that fair and ordinary rod fishing levies any very appreciable toll upon the salmon when compared with the numbers of fish coming into the river. On one lucky day a single net will not unfrequently take as many salmon as are taken with the rod in a whole season on some of the best rod fishings of the river, and in a single week, when fish are running, the various nets may, and often do, take as many fish as fall to rod and line in that river throughout the whole season. But perhaps it is not easy to be just when one sees fifteen or twenty beautiful spring fish struggling in the meshes of a net, or hears of twelve hundred salmon and seatrout as the total for a week's fishing at one netting station on one of our smaller rivers, or of from one to two thousand fish coming into the Tay Fishery Company's fish-houses in one day at certain times of the year.

Human poachers on the spawning beds and in the moorland streams still do a good deal of damage. In the Teviot, for instance, one party from Hawick was caught in November 1908 with over a hundred salmon in sacks on the bank, all taken out with the gaff. I have been told by a veteran poacher of the head-waters of the river Eden that the first fish arrive in the moorland streams as early as the end of September, and that during October and early November his sport with torch and cleek, or leister, is at its best, and the fish are good eating, at least if kippered; but that as soon as hard frost sets in the fish become soft and their flesh poor and sludgy, and that after that they are not worth taking. That may be the view of the superior craftsman, but the weaver or the miner or the youthful shepherd, who poaches mainly for the fun of it, cares little whether the fish that he catches are or are not fit for food. The excitement of the sport and the risk of being captured themselves make the fish caught taste at any rate tolerable, just as the vivid green apple does to the schoolboy who has 'bagged' it from an orchard long before the fruit is at all fit to eat.

Formerly the salmon spear or the clodding (throwing) leister were the usual weapon even of the solitary poacher, and there was something of wild dignity about their open defiance of the law, but now the more common poacher is a hero who sneaks about the river-banks carrying in his hand a stick, ostensibly a walking-stick or staff, and in his pocket a gaff hook and some stout string. Once a fish is spotted within his reach the harmless stick quickly becomes a gaff, and can as quickly resume its humbler form if any watcher or keeper should appear. The old hand, apprehensive of searching, takes care to hook the gaff-head into the lining of his coat or into part of his clothing. Quite recently an amusing letter in the *Field* related the conviction by Cumberland justices of an old poacher of eighty whose pockets had been twice carefully searched, but who still taunted the keeper to have another look. The third search did it. The hook with the string wet was found at the old rascal's back hanging from the fork of his braces.

A bullet from a Mannlicher or from a .303 rifle is a very effective instrument for poaching a salmon, and this is not unknown to some skylarking deerstalkers in the North of Scotland. But in the crystal clear rivers of Canada and of

A RIFLE BULLET

New Zealand many salmon or great trout die every year by shooting. The fish are not hit by the rifle bullet—that is quite unnecessary. They are generally picked up without a mark on their bodies, stunned apparently by the shock caused by the bullet striking the incompressible water in their direction. As a matter of fact, owing to the refraction of the rays of light on passing from water to air, the fish, when seen from the bank or from any position except one directly above him, is, as you know, not exactly in the place that he seems to your eye to occupy, but is really lying a little deeper in the water. You know that if you put a stick slanting into the water you see it appear to bend upward, though one knows that it must go straight. The bullet, too, on striking the water at an angle is deflected, and, unless you can shoot at the fish from directly above him, it is a matter of considerable difficulty to hit him. That, however, the sporting farmer in those two Dominions has found to be unnecessary, and so, in out-of-the-way districts, you may see him take down his rifle in the most matter-of-fact way to go out and shoot a fish for your supper.

Quis custodiet ipsos custodes? The temptations of river watchers to do a little poaching on their own account are great. They have to spend long days and longer nights on unfrequented river-banks, and when they see a salmon lying in some place where it would be the easiest thing in the world to take him, and where nobody's fishing would be injured, it is not much to be wondered at if they sometimes look the other way whilst a friend takes the salmon, or even if they take him themselves. A certain sporting parson that I know well lives in a house just above the end of an ancient high-pitched stone bridge that spans a famous salmon pool. One evening only two or three years ago, about midnight, he heard a tap on his study window, and a parishioner whispered to him that he thought the house was being watched by burglars as he had for a long time seen two men skulking under the shelter of a wall at the foot of the parson's garden. The parson went out with him and found that the men were gone, but saw a light on the water under one of the arches of the bridge. After a little time the light moved to the other side of the river and the parson went across the bridge to reconnoitre. On the way over whom should he meet but the river watcher employed by the Salmon Conservancy Board in company with the village policeman, and carrying with them a fine spring salmon. A very few days afterwards these two worthies found that a change of air was needed for the benefit of their health. This little incident is a trifle disquieting, but I believe that on the whole the police and the river watchers are men who do their duty often far away from all help and when the general feeling of the dwellers by the moorland streams is pretty strongly on the side of the poachers. Then it is due to the efforts of the police and the watchers alone that the salmon have any chance of spawning in safety.

But there is one form of poacher, and in my opinion about the worst of all, which no watcher deters and no law restrains, but which, on the contrary, is protected and encouraged by the law, I mean the seagull of every species. Ever since the Wild Birds Protection Acts have been extended to include them, the seagulls have increased by leaps and bounds. As late as 1889 your great-grandfather could write that on the Tees seagulls seldom came far inland. Now, on all the rivers of the east coast flocks of forty, fifty, or a hundred gulls are the commonest of sights at the time when the young parr or brandlings and the smolts are crowded in the shallows. Such a flock will hover over the shallows; the frightened little fishes dash hither and thither, quick enough perhaps to escape from one foe, but falling an easy prey to the multitude of their enemies. The small black-headed gull generally breeds on inland waters, and they, like the rest, have increased enormously in numbers. Every Londoner knows how they have increased upon the Thames and in the parks of late years. Uncounted thousands of these gulls are to be found nesting on the shores of the lakes and tarns near the upper waters of our salmon rivers, and thence they fly in great flocks and resort to the streams for food. Many times, when fishing in spring and early summer, I have seen a flock of these gulls pitch upon the shallows among a shoal of parr or of smolts, and have seen the little fish caught and eaten literally by hundreds, and I think it almost impossible to exaggerate the damage done by the operation of this foolish and misdirected law. Under its 'Orders' rare and beautiful birds were constantly, until very recent days, unprotected, yet the most mischievous and destructive of our commoner birds, and in particular the gulls, have, under its protection, increased ten-thousandfold.[1]

[1] See Appendix, Note 12.

XV

THE LAST DAY OF A SEASON

MY DEAR BOYS,—The last day of any season—
that is to say, the last that one can spend at the
river—is always a day full of great hopes, and, of
course, they are generally unfulfilled. But for
various reasons the last day that I could give to
the river in 1908 was a day without much hope for
an angler, but yet it proved a good day, marked
with a white stone, by reason of a lucky chance.
For the river was very low indeed, and the weather
hot, still, and misty. There were fish in plenty
in the pools, but on the Tuesday I had had but one
rise, and that on a trout fly, from a fish which was
weighed out nearly an hour later at 19 lbs. On the
Wednesday also I had one rise only and again on the
trout rod and some trout flies, which I had taken
to in despair of moving a fish with the salmon rod.
At the very tail of a long stream a big fish
rose and quietly sucked in the dropper, a tiny
black fly with a bright orange hackle. I suppose
that the gut was 'necked,' or else I held him too
hard, for I felt the hold break and he was gone.
No, he has taken it again—no doubt, really, it has
by some chance taken him. He flings himself
out, and then madly bolts down the stream, turns

up again and rushes past under the very point of the rod, the line swishing in the water, and the frail little rod quite helpless to check him in anything that he may choose to do. He chooses to bolt to the gravel bed behind me, then, finding himself upon the stones with his back out of water, he splashes round and starts for the opposite side. There is sixty yards of line on the reel and the trout gut is new and strong, but as he nears the other bank the reel has only fifteen, ten, five yards left, and now I can give him only a few turns. I try all the rod will bear to stop him, but he goes straight in among the lower branches of the willows growing on the opposite bank, and there he flounces about for a moment or two, and then the line comes back with both flies gone. I think that the fish must have had the gut cast across his jaws when the dropper broke off, and then the tail fly being pulled up towards his mouth must have caught in his eye or in some very tender spot. The way in which he rushed ashore first on one side of the water and then on the other seemed to show that he was blinded with pain or fright, and he was a good fish, too, of 16 or 17 lbs.

Well, a solitary and rather fluky rise on each of the two preceding days did not give much hope of success on the Thursday, especially as I had to leave the water at two o'clock to catch my train southwards.

I got all my packing done early and began to fish at ten o'clock in a swift run at the head of a long pool where I knew that a number of good fish were lying. About the tenth cast a large fish jumped just as the line was stretched out to fall upon the water, and I saw that the fish fell right across the line about twelve feet from the fly. At once I struck, as I have done dozens of times before when a fish has jumped or risen over the line. This time my luck was in, for I felt the drag on the line, and the fly, a half-inch-long green heckam-peckam, struck firmly in something that I felt sure must be the 'tummy' of that fish. Instantly he set all doubts at rest by flinging himself out, with a violent wriggle in the air, then falling back and bolting up and down and to and fro in the very swiftest and shallowest part of the stream, so that three or four times I thought that he had broken away, and that the loose line coming back to me had neither fish nor fly at the end of it. Then he decided to splash his way up the rocky rapids to the next pool, and no sooner had he got to it than round he came to my side of the stream and dropped down the edge with his back fin out of water, until, catching sight of Tom Falshaw on the bank waiting with the long gaff, he turned out into deeper water and bolted back to the place where he was hooked. There he stayed for a few minutes, slowly boring his way up the strong water, and then swinging back again with a dash, only to bore up again. Presently he seemed to decide that streams were doing him no good, and he dropped quickly down the pool to fight out the rest of this battle in quiet water. And a long, stubborn fight it is, in which he tries to rid himself of this accursed thorn in the flesh. Not a minute of it do I grudge on such a hopeless-looking day as this, and it is a full forty-five minutes before he is gaffed, a quarter of a mile lower down the river. He is a little red—for is it not October the 8th?—but a thick and handsome fish, and he weighs $19\frac{1}{2}$ lbs. The little fly is hooked into his left ventral fin. It has split the fin down for half an inch or more, but seems then to have got a firm hold.[1]

Back we go to fish the pool very carefully, but without a touch. Then again, with a gay salmon fly a full inch in length, and then we try a dull brown little fly with a dun turkey wing in a long stream above. Half-way down the pool a small fish of 7 lbs. takes it, and is safely landed after a brief splashing struggle. Then we fish the pool again from the top to the bottom without a rise. A good fish and a grilse have been throwing themselves out again and again in the quickest

---

[1] This was a lucky fluke, and I have told you of a still greater fluke in my letter on spring fishing (at page 71), but I once witnessed the capture of a salmon in a way even more astonishing. In the summer of 1896 I was fishing a pool down after another angler—Mr. Charles Liddell, of Warwick Hall, Cumberland—who was casting from the other side and wading far out in the stream. We both stopped fishing about the same moment and I began to walk up the bank, when I heard a shout and saw him picking up a fine grilse of 6 or 7 lbs. As he waded out of the stream the fish had risen in shallow water, and on his coming to the place it had rushed ashore. It was deeply marked by the meshes of a net through which it had obviously forced its way only a few days before.

rush at the throat of the pool. We will try them once more before we go, for two o'clock is now close at hand. Sure enough in the shallow, tumbling water one of them takes. Luckily it is the big one, and he puts up a great fight, rushing madly to every part of the pool, once even fouling the line round a rock close to the far bank. Fortunately this stone is mossy and the line runs freely round it, and presently the fish struggles on the surface, the line gives a flick and a twang, and we see it come free from the stone, bringing away with it a little tuft of moss, which for several minutes dangles in the air. After this he soon tires and in a few minutes is on the gravel dead beat with his wild struggle; it is not more than six or seven minutes from the hooking, I feel certain, yet he is a beautiful bright cock fish and weighs 16 lbs.

There remains only time for a few hasty casts in the best places as I go up the river to meet the dogcart, and in an hour or two—and at this very moment at which I write—I am flying southward with three good fish packed in cool ferns and bracken lying in the guard's van.

XVI

MY BEST FISH

MY DEAR BOYS,—My best fish—so far, may I say without touching wood—was no great monster. Four-and-twenty pounds it was for a long time, and then for some years a fish of 28 lbs. held the field. In 1904 it became 32 lbs., and now—this last week ' as ever was '—his place has been taken by a fish of 34 lbs. But he is nothing to feel very proud of, because he was taken on the minnow, with a trace of steel wire, and so his last gallant battle was but brief and brutal.

The twenty-four pounder was the best sportsman of the lot. He was a beautiful spring fish, his back blue-grey and his sides of burnished silver, and with that peach-coloured or rose-pink iridescence over the glistening under sides that you never see upon a late autumn fish. Yet he was taken on the 28th of October. A big flood had lasted for a week, and the river had begun to run clear, though it was still very high. On the 27th I had touched a fish on the fly, but had done nothing else. It was a perfect day for a minnow, but I used no minnow in those days. I began on the 28th at the same spot, and immediately got a

AN OCTOBER SPRING FISH

heavy pull from this fish, but the hook got no hold, and he could not be induced to come again. All day I fished blank, and about five o'clock I returned to give my friend another trial. When I reached him I felt the faintest draw on the line, yet it was a quite slow draw such as only a good fish can give. I made the same cast again, and this time with a snatch he made sure of his fly. The current ran strong, and the very butt seemed to creak as the top of the rod was dragged down to the water. Like so many strong fish that are well hooked, he didn't show himself at first, but kept deep down in the water, and after a few moments of heavy 'jagging' he began steadily to bore his way up the stream. In five-and-twenty minutes he showed himself but once, and then it was only one sudden leaping somersault about ten minutes after he had been hooked. At last his strength began to fail and I tried to strand him on the gravel bed, but every time that he touched the stones he turned and splashed out into deep water, and stubbornly refused to be coaxed to shore again. The rod was a most powerful steel-centred cane rod, and I knew that the tackle was strong, so I did not spare him in the least, and I can remember to this day how my left arm ached with the cramped strain of holding the rod so hard against him. However, at last, after five-and-thirty minutes of the severest treatment that I ever remember, he was safely stranded and lifted out by the tail. I had, of course, seen for some time that his whole colouring was very unusual, and each time that he had stranded upon the shallows I had noticed that his wet back showed as a sort of warm yellowish grey—like the wet back of a great trout, and entirely unlike the colour of the autumn fish, which, even at their brightest, show a dark and rather dull-looking back as they are drawn on to the shallows. But until I saw this fish out of the water I had never thought of the chance of taking a clean spring fish at that time of year, and I could hardly believe my eyes when I saw him shining before me with that unmistakable rosy pink bloom, and his fins and tail standing out in contrast almost as black as ink. Well, he was a cock fish, and, as I have told you, he weighed 24 lbs. He had taken a fly that I had made the night before—a silver body with a pale blue hackle and a plain dark mallard wing—and he was sent off to a very young lady who is now your mother; and I believe that she thought then that I caught fish just like that every day.

For a good many years 24 lbs. was my best. I caught fish of 22 lbs. and 23 lbs. often, I caught even several of 24 lbs., but I could go no higher. At length in the course of one season I rose first to $25\frac{1}{2}$, then to $26\frac{1}{2}$, and then to 28 lbs. The twenty-five pounder I caught as a small flood was rising. A week later, when it had fallen again, and the water had become dead low, so low that for days we had caught no salmon, I was fishing one evening with a very light double-handed sea-trout rod, a trout cast, and a small green heckampeckam fly, about the size of a large March brown, when I saw the flicker of a big tail in the shallow rushing water right at the throat of a pool. I got into the river well above the place and fished down to it almost inch by inch, for I knew that the fish must be lying just where the water deepened, and that the fly would almost touch his nose. Whatever it did he took it. There is little to be said about the next hour and five minutes. There never—or very rarely—is hard or quick fighting with a heavy salmon on a light rod in a big pool where the fish has plenty of sea-room. I was as gentle as possible, merely doing my best whenever he grew quiet to urge him to keep up his struggles. At the end of that time I floated him, dead beat and lying on his side, on to a sand-bank a quarter of a mile below the place where he was hooked, and there lifted him out. He was a cock fish and weighed 26½ lbs., and the hook of the little green fly had opened out a good deal, but I keep it as a pattern; many salmon have since died upon copies of it. The twenty-eight pounder was caught in September and upon the rising water of a flood. He had been fished for in vain for many days, but had been hooked and lost that same morning. Fortune must have been smiling that day, for the line was badly 'knuckled' above the cast, and though it was strained almost to breaking-point in turning the fish away from some logs, yet it held then, although it snapped like rotten thread when tested—as you must always do—after the big fish was landed.

It was several years before I got to 30 lbs. Then one day in a heavy, muddy flood, on a river on which we were guests, two of us had been fishing with fly and minnow all day on the only pool quiet enough to offer us any chance of a fish. At five o'clock we decided to give it one last turn with the phantom, and in that turn my big fish boiled up at the minnow on the shallow tail of the pool. He missed the minnow, but turned and rushed after it along the top of the water and seized it a few yards farther on. I was wading waist-deep, and as soon as I had got back on to the shallows the fish flung himself out of the water. None of your wild somersaults, but a stately dive, head first out and in again, like that which one sees done by each one of a school of porpoises as they dive into the air out of the side of a wave and pop in again in the trough. I saw, and said on the spot, that he must weigh 30 lbs., and, as you may suppose, I was very careful with him. But care does not mean easing the strain and playing gently; it means watching every move of the fish to be sure that if he gives a sudden dash or leap the rod and reel are ready to respond to it. Well, he made a fine fight; twice more he leaped clean out and repeatedly dropped down to the edge of the rapids and there lashed about on the surface. In one long run up the farther side of the river he caught the line upon a great round boulder, and it seemed as if he must break it, but after a few moments of horrible grating I felt a twang, and the line was released from the boulder and sprang into the air again taut upon the fish, some ten yards higher up the stream, but carrying fast upon it a lump of moss about the size of a cricket ball torn from the side of the boulder. The last effort of the fish was to bolt down the rapids into the pool below, where, after a stubborn fight, he was brought to the gravel and taken out, thirty-five minutes after he was hooked. Thirty-two pounds he weighed, and proud as Punch I was of him in those days, making an outline model of his tubby figure in strong drawing-paper and touching it up with ink, to fill in the eyes, fins, and other details, and the spots and shading of the back.

This remained the best fish until September 1908, when on the 18th I took six fish weighing as they came 15, 5, 15, 14, 18 and 34 lbs. The big one was caught upon a minnow in a quiet, slow-running pool where I had never dreamed of taking a very big fish.

But that pool must have been well suited for big fish, for seven days later—and since I wrote what you have just been reading—I was lucky enough to hook there and land a fish of 40½ lbs., my heaviest salmon up to the present, and one that I am not very likely to beat. During the morning three fish had touched my fly, two, weighing 14 and 16 lbs., had been landed and the other lost; but after midday not a rise could be got, so as a last chance before going home I went to try this pool. Whilst I took one turn over it with the fly I got Tom to put up the spinning rod, and then I mounted a small phantom minnow and at the second cast hooked the big fish. He fought and walloped and plunged on the surface for a long time, taking a great deal out of himself and also showing me that I had a very big fish to deal with. It was growing dark and the bank was fringed with willows, but luckily the fish kept to the open water and put up a very active plunging fight, so that in about fifteen minutes I was able, at a gap in the willows, to bring him near enough to use the gaff. Up to then I believed that he was a big fish, about 30 lbs. perhaps, but until, as I dragged him ashore, I saw his great length and his thick back, I had no idea that I was in for the long-coveted forty-pounder. But when I saw him come out of the water I hoped for even more than 40 lbs., and I am certain that if he had not been bitten, as he was, he must have weighed from 45 to 50 lbs. For he measured just over forty-eight inches from the snout to the centre of the tail, and these big fish usually weigh about a pound to the inch, or if in really fine condition, a little more than a pound to the inch. But my victim had lately received a frightful double wound from the teeth of some predatory beast—some seal or porpoise most probably—and although he showed no sign of autumn redness, in spite of a large 'gib' and a hooked jaw, yet he was not as deep as he ought to have been, and he must have lost many pounds in condition from this injury.

His would-be captor had quite obviously seized his salmon from underneath, for there were two great gashes on each side of his belly, and the scrapes of his captor's teeth backwards and downwards to the anal fin were quite plainly to be seen. What a meal he would have made for almost anything!

Well, we photographed him the next morning before going to fish, and his portrait (beside a little boy of six years that I think you know) is here at page 156. The wound on the side is not very clearly shown, but the scrape of the teeth from that wound just in front of the ventral fins, in a sort of half-moon, back to the torn anal fin, can be traced pretty plainly.

XVII

WHEN AND WHERE TO EXPECT SALMON

My dear Boys,—Cold winds and wretched weather, which send the trout fisher home empty-handed, seem often to make little or no difference to the salmon. The wind and the weather do affect success in salmon fishing, but it is in a very uncertain and capricious manner. No day and no weather is hopeless if there are salmon in the pools, but a fresh and even a strong wind is usually a good thing for the salmon fisher. Even bitter north and east winds do not prevent the fish from taking the fly, though they can make the fisher pretty miserable, and especially if on his water they happen to be foul winds, that is to say, winds blowing up-stream or in his face. But salmon seem to dislike haze and gloom, and they seldom take well either in hot and hazy weather or in dull gloom. But if the air is clear and without mist the day may be as hot or as cold, as sunny or as dark as you will, and still you may have a very fine day's salmon fishing.

In big, dark waters a bright sun is a positive advantage, as the fish seem to see the fly better in sunlight, or at any rate they take it much better. But in low, clear water most fishers prefer to have

TWILIGHT

no sunshine, although if the day is fresh and the horizon clear and bright, a sunny day often proves a very good day and especially in the spring. After a hot, glaring day in August or September the hour of sunset and twilight is never without hope and may prove most deadly. Many and many a time I have known two, three, and four fish to be taken in this hour by a rod that had moved nothing all day. But too often the fisher has gone home to dinner at the very time when he should be fishing hardest. The best chance lasts but a short time and comes after sunset, when the light has failed so much that the surface of the water seems to reflect it all, and you seem to be casting into a river of liquid metal. On such hopeless days you should keep one of your likeliest spots for the last few casts in the failing light, and should be careful to disturb the fish there as little as possible during the afternoon.

Rain is by no means against success in salmon fishing, rather the contrary, and fish often take well in slashing storms of rain. But in very late autumn, when fish are anxious to press on and ascend the river, rain and even showery weather seems to suggest floods, and the fish often become unsettled and take very badly in what seems to be almost perfect water. And often at other times when they appear to be expecting a flood, salmon take very badly, although the moment that the water begins to rise they may take savagely. On a quick, sudden rise of water it is well known that fish will take, but it is often said that they will not take in water that is rising slowly and steadily. This may be true in some rivers, but is not so in all, for I have a good many times known fish take very well in such water. Even in snowstorms and thunderstorms, and just before thunderstorms, I have known them to rise well, although far more often they refuse to rise at all.

Probably for the actual taking of salmon, apart from the joy and pleasure of fishing, the best day upon the whole, in spring or summer or early autumn fishing, is such a day as is described in the old ballad:

> 'The wind doth blow to-day, my love,
> And a few small drops of rain';

and the very worst days are—at all times of the year—warm, muggy days, when the air feels close and heavy and the river is covered with floating foam and bubbles. This foam is a very odd thing. On some days every stream and pool may be covered with flecks and lumps of foam, and every backwater and every eddy by the streams is covered with a blanket of hissing bubbles. Such days are more common in autumn than in spring and are always close and muggy days, and the almost soap-sud foam seems to be due to some peculiar state of air and water which delays the bursting of the bubbles formed in the splashing streams. If the day freshens the foam may disappear in a few minutes, but whilst this foam is on the water I have always, or almost always, found the fish take very badly—indeed on only one day in twenty years can I remember to have done well in such foam. On that day the salmon suddenly began to take, and between three and four o'clock I got four fish, but the whole day before and after it was a total blank without a rise.

This last season, 1909, was an example. For days together, when the water was in fine order, the foam floated everywhere and hardly a fish was taken. Why it should be so I cannot say. It may be that the endless flecks of foam floating over the fish tire his eye or distract his attention from the fly. However, on such days the best thing to do is to try the tails of long, quiet pools where the froth has had time to disappear. There you may get a rise.

Night fishing. Salmon take very well, just as trout do, when it is dark or almost dark—so dark that you cannot see the fly or the line—but I have seldom found them ready to take on a cold, raw night. On a warm, mild night they will take quite a small fly in the smooth, quiet streams and in glassy runs. In late evening fishing, too, smooth and swift-running water is the best to fish, and any small fly with a pair of large, bright jungle cock's feathers in the wings will kill the very biggest fish which earlier in the day were lying in the deep water. But in the heavy streams and in big waters at dusk, or when it has grown quite dark, you may use your very largest fly, and may take fish that would not look at anything during the day. But always—and whether you are fishing for trout or salmon—when you cannot clearly see the fly fall on the water you should draw in a few inches of line and 'shoot' it at each cast, and you will soon acquire a sense of touch which tells you with certainty whether the cast has been a clean one or not.

There are—or one gets to believe that there are—certain times of the day which seem to be critical times, when salmon take, if they are going to take at all. About nine o'clock, about one o'clock, about four, and at dusk are, I should say, the best times, and of them all I should put dusk first and midday second.

As to the places in which you may look for fish, there is no guide like experience and constant knowledge of the water. Even when you have fished a stretch of water for years you may find some place where in certain states of the water salmon take eagerly, and yet you may never before have thought of fishing there. I have had two most striking instances of that, and indeed I caught my only 40-lb. fish in a place where for years it had not been thought worth while to fish. If you do not know the water, and have nobody who knows it thoroughly to advise you, go out very early in the morning and be on the water late in the evening, and you will then see where the fish are lying, for all salmon, even spring fish, which generally show themselves very little, are

QUIET RUNS

apt to move and show themselves in the morning and evening. And keep a rough chart and mark upon it the exact position of every fish that you see.

Of course, when the river is very high, fish will lie and will take in quiet streams which they leave when the water has fallen to its normal level, and you should look out most carefully for such places. The ordinary gillie is amazingly ignorant as to the best places in which to look for fish in high water. Long before fish can be taken in the ordinary low-water pools they may rise in the quiet streams, where they stop first as the flood falls. And in big, dark waters on a falling flood try a very large fly in these quiet streams, and you will at times have a great day in places where you catch nothing later on. In spring, too, these quiet, gliding, high-water catches often hold the best spring fish. I remember one of a small syndicate of anglers asking a beginner to fish 'any day next week.' The visitor arrived on an inconvenient day, and after splashing over the best water was sent to a bit of quiet water where it was believed that he could do no harm, since nobody ever troubled to fish it. Yet in the evening he turned up beaming, carrying a beautiful spring fish of five-and-twenty pounds, and explaining that he had lost another almost as good.

It may be some help to you when fishing strange waters if I give you the kind of pools that usually fish best under different circumstances. But this, of course, is only a rough rule of thumb. One bit of shallow water in a deep pool may make that pool a fine high-water pool, and there may be nothing to tell you where that shallow is.

In high water after a flood.—The quiet ' dubs ' at the tails of long pools, and the thin, glassy water where the tail of any pool sucks down to a rapid below, are usually the most likely places. Also any narrower waist or stronger running place in pools which are, at ordinary level, long, still pools. These places are very deadly in early spring or late autumn, and you may find them by watching the surface of the river when a flood is rising or falling, and seeing where the stream runs strongest and boils most.

Occasionally in special places, and when fish are running, the shallow water at the edge of the strong streams rushing into the head of big pools holds good taking fish in high water.

In big waters on a rapid rise from normal.—Fish just where fish were lying before the rise came, but close in to the shallows. Also beside the runs at the head of the stream.

In dead low waters.—Try the very neck of the stream just where the water running into the pool becomes deep enough to hold a salmon—two or three feet deep—and fish down the rush so long as it is strong enough to swirl the fly about. Also try the strongest swirls of pot holes and broken water.

In the evening.—*In low water*, with fine tackle

SEPTEMBER 7TH, 1908

A FORTY-POUNDER

fish at the very tails of long dubs where the water slips over into the next pool.

At the tail of a deep swirling pool wherever the water shallows and begins to run out fan-wise.

On the shallowing water below any deep pool.

In the evening, in large or high waters, fish the big dubs and in strong streams running smoothly, rather than in water that is broken and rough.

In bright sun.—Fish the streams and in the very quickest part of the streams with bright and especially with glittering silver or gold-bodied flies. And in sunny weather remember, too, that you may take all the glitter off your gut by rubbing it with the rolled-up leaf of an alder.

In wild, rough, windy weather in low water.—Fish anywhere, but especially on the quieter flats where lately there has not been current enough to kill fish. Use a small, bright fly or a large, dark claret or black fly.

On a rise in the water.—Go at once to fish all the places where lately it was too low to fish.

XVIII

HINTS ON FLY TYING

My dear Boys,—It is of no use trying to tell you within the compass of any reasonable letter how to tie a salmon fly. You must have some one to show you how to do that, for all mere descriptions that I have ever seen are intensely tedious and boring, because the writer has to be minute in every detail if he is unable to assume that his reader knows such simple things as the usual position of the hands in tying a fly, how to hold the hook, how to set about tying on a wing, or a hackle—if he cannot assume that you know these things, which one practical lesson would show you through the eye in a few moments. But even so there are books which explain everything to the uttermost detail. Mr. Kelson's great book on the *Salmon Fly* is one of them, and there is a useful little booklet by Captain Hale, which is well worth having by you, and no doubt there are others. All that I intend to do is to give you some ' tips ' which I have found useful, tips that you will not find, so far as I know, in any of those books.

First—to take them more or less in the order in which you would tie a fly—for tying on the loop to the hook I always use, unless the hook is under an inch long, stout saddlers' twist, well waxed. It is a yellow silk thread (Pearsall's No. 14), immensely strong, and you can use any amount of force in the winding without risk of a break, whilst its thickness causes it to cover the hook in much fewer turns than does the fine silk ordinarily used.

Next, for the loops themselves, I always use fiddle-string—the thinnest E string of the violin, and, for the very small flies, banjo strings, which are thinner still. The great merit of these loops is that they soften instantly on being wetted, and you do not and cannot crack off the fly at the loop even in the highest wind. Of course it is possible to crack off the single gut above the fly, but even that feat of folly is rendered difficult, even for a beginner, by having the fly joined to the gut with a loop which is perfectly soft and flexible.

Next, having tied the loop to the hook, varnish the lapping well with celluloid varnish. That is merely celluloid dissolved in acetone or amyl acetate, two perfectly harmless and inexpensive drugs to be had of any good chemist. Celluloid is to be found nowadays in almost every country-house in the form of photographic films. You have only to soak some old films, used or unused, in hot water and then strip off the sensitised gelatine, and then the harder film may be cut up into strips and dissolved in your acetone or amyl acetate. A ready-made solution of celluloid in amyl acetate—the drug which smells so strongly of pear drops—is sold, under the name of Zapon, as a varnish or lacquer to keep silver and bright metal ornaments from tarnishing in the fogs of London. It costs about a shilling a bottle and can be got at the Stores, and no doubt elsewhere. It is rather too thin a solution for fly tying, but that can very easily be cured either by adding a little photographic film to the solution, or by leaving the cork out and allowing a little of the liquid to evaporate.

This celluloid varnish penetrates into anything, dries quickly, and never becomes hard or brittle as most other varnishes do in cold weather. It is immensely better for making flies, and every sort of fishing-tackle, than any other thing that I have ever come across in the way of varnishes. One's flies now last three or four times as long as they used to do, and, better still, one can wing one's flies without using cobbler's wax upon the silk, an advantage which I will explain presently.

Now, having got your hook with the loop tied securely to it, you want to dress a fly upon it. First fasten your tying silk to the hook, and be careful to begin the fly far enough back. The first lapping of the silk should be made exactly opposite the point of the barb of a hook of the ordinary Limerick shape. Apart from mere want of skill, three simple faults cause the beginner's flies to look so unattractive to the experienced fisher. They are, first, that the bodies are usually not begun nearly far enough back on the hook; secondly, that the bodies are carried too far forward, leaving too little space free to tie the hackle and wing; and, thirdly, that the beginner almost always makes the wings of his flies too long. The wings should not extend much, if at all, beyond the bend of the hook if the fly is to look a workmanlike and killing fly. And almost one-third of the shank of the hook next the loop should be left quite free of any body dressing, in order to give room for the hackle, or throat, and the wings and head. Both wings and hackle are then more easily and more firmly tied, and your fly will look better and will last better.

Well, to begin again, fasten your tying silk opposite to the barb point and at once tie on the end of your tinsel. The only tinsel worth using is that which is made up of a threadlike silver or gold wire wrapped round and round on a floss silk foundation. This tinsel cannot be broken by the teeth of a fish. If you fray out the end of this tinsel, by pulling off a few turns of the wire that enwraps it, and then tie the now fluffy end to your hook with a few turns of silk, and after that touch the fastening with a dab of celluloid varnish, the ends can be fastened so rigidly that the tinsel will never, or hardly ever, be torn loose, and will be a great support to the body of the fly. In spring more especially, when the salmon kelts and the bull-trout and sea-trout kelts, chew your best flies to pieces, you will find the benefit of tying and varnishing your tinsel, and indeed every part of your fly, in the best possible manner.

A good many things have to be tied on at the tail of a salmon fly, and it is not easy to keep this part neat. I begin a fly thus: I take a turn of waxed silk round the hook opposite the barb point, then lay on the end of the tinsel and take two or three turns and a half-hitch, then give a dab of varnish, then tie on the tail—if I mean to have one, but I now rarely do so—with three turns of silk; then, if the fly is to have a silver or gold body, begin straightway to wind on the body, turning the hook against the tinsel. When I say turning the hook against the tinsel, I mean that you hold with your right hand the shank of the hook, with the ribbon of tinsel projecting at right angles to it. Then holding the hook by the bend with your left hand you turn or roll the hook round and round, thus winding on the tinsel with a smoothness and regularity that is very difficult to attain by any other method.

But if your fly is not to have a tinsel body you must, after tying on the tail, tie on the strand of floss silk or of wool or of mohair that you mean to use for the body. I think that fish, when they take a fly, expect a juicy morsel. It is not the wings that they want to eat, and so I believe in having a fairly thick body; but as it approaches the forward end don't forget to leave, as I have said, a fourth to a third of the shank quite bare for the hackle and the wings, and, moreover, taper off your body somewhat at the shoulder end as well as at the tail.

MAKE FLIES STRONGLY

When you have wound on your body of wool and tied down the end of it, then wind on your tinsel and fasten it securely—and it is better to wind it the opposite way round. When done, take a turn or two round it with the silk, then snip off the tinsel with your scissors a quarter of an inch away and expose the silk foundation of this bit by pulling off the wire wrapping from it, and then take a few more turns with your tying silk over that end, give it a dab of celluloid, and you have finished your body. With decent luck it will be indestructible, and you may re-wing that body three or four times, and the more worn it gets the better the fish seem to like it. Never omit that dab of varnish upon the turns of tying silk; you need not wait for it to dry, it sinks in at once, but it will, as I say, make your fly almost indestructible.

Now you will want to tie on a hackle, and here I have a little tip for you to do it neatly and easily. First, of course, you spread the hackle so that every strand stands at right angles to the central line of the feather. This is the old-fashioned plan, and I think it is easier than rolling or doubling over the hackle. But for the beginner it is easier still to strip off one side of the hackle altogether. Then you wet the tip of the hackle to close that up and then tie it to the body. Then hold the hook in your left hand *point upwards*, take hold of the butt of your hackle with your spring pliers, and carefully make one or two turns of the hackle round the hook; then leaving the hackle to hang, kept down by the weight of the pliers, you press back the kind of frill of hackles that you have made, coaxing the side strands upwards so as to get as many strands as possible at the throat of the fly, where you want the hackle to show. You smooth all back with your right forefinger and thumb, and then hold the tips down close to the body with your left hand whilst you take up the pliers that are hanging on the hackle and wind on another frill of two or three turns, press this frill back as before, hold it down to the body in the same way, and so on until you have got enough hackle for your fancy. My fancy is for a very thin hackle; no fly has more than six legs.

Although I think that the fly would still in all probability kill as well as it did before, yet it is an annoying thing to find that the hackle has come off a killing fly. So, to prevent this, do not omit a dab of celluloid on the silk fastenings when you begin and when you end off the hackle.

Now for the wing :—

It is the wing that gives most trouble to the commencing fly tier. On some days the wing *will* not go right. Do what you can the feathers will roll up and stick out in all directions in the most exasperating way. The silk catches in the strips of feather as the beginner tries to fasten them down, pulling them all to one side and spoiling the whole thing in a moment. Now silk always is a little apt to catch in feather over which it is being drawn, but the troubles of the beginner are immensely increased by the fact that his silk is usually waxed with cobbler's wax for the very purpose of making it sticky. The penetrating power and strength of celluloid as a varnish now enables you to dispense with the waxing of the silk that you use for tying on the wings. If the beginner will start his wing with two rather narrow strips of some easily tied feather, such as that from the tail or wing of a turkey, will use unwaxed silk and give the fastening a dab of celluloid after each fresh layer of feather is bound on, he will not, I think, find the tying of a simple and workmanlike wing a matter of any particular difficulty.

The dark-barred mallard feather is one of the most tender as well as one of the most useful of the common feathers, and if your silk is unwaxed you can tie on broad strips of mallard without much risk at a stage when your skill is wholly unequal to controlling the same feather with waxed silk, when without rhyme or reason the strips go wrong time after time.

You should remember that feathers gathered when the bird is in fresh plumage are much easier to tie than old, stale feathers that either have come from a bird almost ready to moult again, or that have been kept by you for many years. The sign of a good feather is that it should be springy and soft, not harsh to the touch, and with a clean, even edge, not frayed by months of hard service for its former owner.

A throat of Gallina (that is, guinea-fowl—*perlehöne*, 'pearl hen,' they call her in Norway) is a good deal easier to tie on than a hackle is because the feathers are not so delicate. Gallina makes a very good hackle, too, and whether tied as a throat or hackle it makes the fly look, at least to my eyes, extremely taking, and it is the best of all imitations of the legs of an insect. In fact, the rough, mottled legs of some water-spiders are remarkably like the single strands of Gallina.

My whole aim in tying a fly is to get a lively motion in the water and, also, neatness. Nature in all her forms is always incomparably neat, and if you wish your fly to counterfeit a living thing, whatever it may be, your work should at least be neat. And amongst all the suggestions that are made as to what it is that the salmon supposes the fly to be, all are agreed upon one point—that he takes it for some living thing, making its way across his pool.

For myself, I am inclined to think that this is the beginning, the middle, and the end of the matter. The salmon was bred in the river, and for the first two years of his life ate greedily of every living thing that he came across, if it was small enough to fall a victim to his powers—flies, creepers, slugs, worms, spiders, minnows, all came alike to him. Then he is impelled to the sea, where he finds fresh myriads of creatures of the most strange forms, yet as he comes across each one he tries it and he finds that it is very good. Just consider how strange these things must look to a lusty little smolt, fast growing into a grilse, when he first comes to see a shrimp, a sprat, a sand-eel, a crab, a prawn, a star-fish or a jelly-fish, not to speak of little flounders and all sorts of flat fish scudding along on the sandy bottoms. Don't you think a prawn is quite as odd-looking a beast as any salmon fly can be? And when the grown salmon after, perhaps, two or three years' absence comes back to the river that he left as a little smolt, does he remember very clearly his tiny flies? I suspect that he looks for something much bigger than he really finds. If I might guess at the thoughts of the salmon I could fancy him thinking thus: 'Hallo! That's a rummy-looking object that has just fallen on the water over there. I believe it's alive—yes, it must be alive, for I see it swims against the current, and it is crossing the pool, too. I wonder what it can be! I remember when I was up here as a little fish there used to be some whacking big flies that tasted jolly good— great big fellows, and a decent mouthful, not like these miserable little gnats of March browns that I have seen so far, so small that you can't taste them. I wonder if this one is of the old sort that used to be so good. There he comes again, or else another one. He looks pretty fat, I'll have a go at him. Ugh, Holy Poker! what a brute! What a sting he has got! And how he held on. I'll leave that sort of fly alone for the future.'

When people talk of salmon taking the salmon

fly for a shrimp or a prawn, as many people insist they do, well, it may be so, but it is worth while to remember that big, wary trout often fall victims to the salmon fly, and they have never seen either shrimp or prawn, and they know very well what a trout fly is, and are very hard to catch on an artificial one.

XIX

KNOTS

MY DEAR BOYS,—All knotting of gut involves some risk of cutting or breaking it, and for that reason you are obliged to learn some special knots for use with the thick gut needed in salmon fishing. Even if you do not aspire to make your own casts, or even to mend them for yourself, you would have to know the best knots that are in use for tying the gut cast to your reel line, and for tying the gut itself to the loop of your fly.

The beginner may do well enough by having a large loop at the end of his gut cast and attaching his fly to it by passing this loop through the eye of the fly and then over the fly itself, and he may have a similar loop at the end of his reel line for fastening that to his gut cast. But loops are clumsy and unreliable. They use up a lot of gut, and they do not get thrown away and renewed nearly as often as they should be renewed or as the gut used for a single knot would be replaced, for on untying one fly and tying on another you naturally tie the new one upon the undamaged gut and throw away the crushed end that was employed for the last knot. And there is sound sense in that practice: the greatest strains that arise in casting always occur at any place where thick and thin stuff joins, and the nearer you get to the end of the whip lash the greater the strain on the material becomes. It is the last inch of the gut cast that runs all the risk of breakage by being cracked like a whip, through unduly hurrying your throw, and the two places where all the strain falls are the junction of the flexible loop at the head of the fly with the rigid shank of the hook and the junction of the single gut cast with this loop of the fly.

The use of a long loop also on the gut cast strengthens this latter point of weakness by doubling the gut there, but itself also tends to grow weak where the single gut joins the double gut forming the loop. The great risk is that having got a neat and satisfactory loop, either on the line or the cast, you are apt to look upon it as a permanent means of attachment, forgetting that, as I have explained, both the end of the casting line and the end of the gut cast are places where thick stuff joins thin, and places in which the best materials quickly become unreliable and gut especially so. For it is a well-known fact that gut that has become slightly 'necked' and then has got dry will stand a quite heavy pull when you begin to use it again, but after it has been wetted and used for a very short time it will snap upon any trifling jerk. The danger is, as I have said, that having got a loop ready made you are apt to go on using it until it breaks when you strike a fish,

FIGURE OF EIGHT KNOTS

and you lose at once your fly and the whole fruit of your labour. In theory you can watch each loop and can detect its weakness; in actual practice you will be sure to lose precious fish because the loop has grown weak without your noticing it.

For attaching to the cast very large and heavy salmon flies, especially those with metal eyes, such a loop on the gut is not unsatisfactory, if you watch it most carefully to see that no part of it has become necked or weakened. But for flies of moderate size or for small flies this loop is a very poor fastening. It is clumsy and conspicuous, and by its stiffness it deadens the play of a small fly, and it also involves the risk of breakage that I have just tried to impress upon you.

Both for tying the line to the cast and for tying the single gut to any fly which has a flexible loop (that is, a loop made either of twisted or single silkworm-gut or made of fiddle-string—as described on page 167), a sound and reliable knot is that called the figure of eight knot.

This knot has two forms. The first and simplest, and the best, is no more than a reef knot made with the gut and the loop on the fly, and then having the spare end of the gut where it comes out of the knot turned once round the gut of the cast and then bent back and thrust into the reef knot again before it is drawn tight, so as to be held fast in the tightened knot. The other form, which looks neater, is in reality a single hitch of the gut made on the fly-loop with the loose end of the hitch brought round and turned back through the knot in very similar fashion.

I. The simpler form—the reef knot figure of eight—is made thus : Enter the point of your gut downwards through the loop of the fly (held with the wings uppermost) and make an ordinary reef knot with gut and loop. The free end is now lying parallel with the last strand of the cast.

Lift the free end *over* the gut link, bring it round below the link, and then fold it back on the top of the loop so as to lie as in the illustration below, and pull tight.

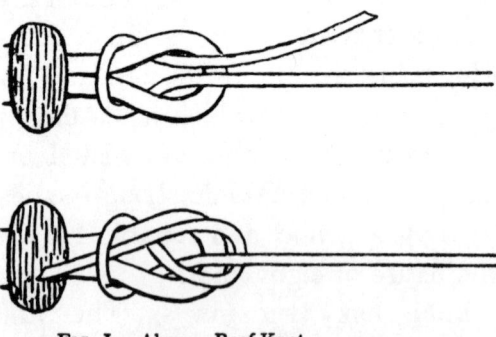

FIG. I.—Above—Reef Knot.
Below—Knot completed, but loose.

II. The knot in its other form is made thus : Hold the fly between the left finger and thumb and upside down (*i.e.* with the hook point above, not below the horizontal body of the fly). Then put the end of your single gut upward through the loop of the fly, bend the gut over away from

FIGURE OF EIGHT KNOTS 181

you, bring it round underneath the head and make an ordinary half-hitch, and leave a loose end nearly an inch long. Then turn the fly over (so as to have the hook point below the body), when it will (from above) appear as in figure II.

Next take the loose end, bring it round *below* the gut line, then bring it up, bend it back and poke it right down through the fly loop and through your half-hitch, so as to make the completed figure of eight, as shown in figure II.

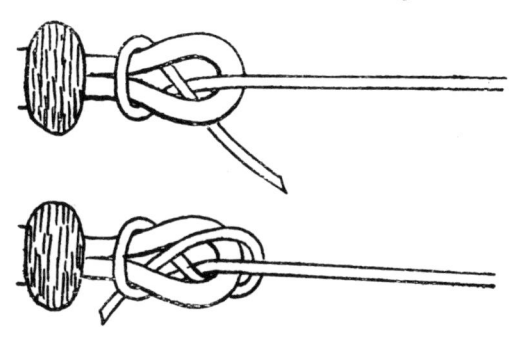

Fig. II.—Above—Half-Hitch.
Below—Knot completed.

The knot is now done, and you gently pull all tight, bringing the whole knot forward away from the head of the fly so as to lie as close as possible to the forward end of the loop. Note that the sides of the loop of the fly should be squeezed together as the knot is pulled tight, and with a quite new and unused loop it is an advantage, after drawing the knot tight, to give the sides a slight squeeze with the teeth and then give a second pull. If that be done, the figure of eight knot is almost perfection. Whatever knot you may employ, if the fly has never before been used, you must give extra care to the knot. A new, unused loop, unless perfectly soaked or carefully squeezed with the teeth after the knot is drawn together as I have described, will have grown softer after a certain amount of fishing, and on a sudden jerk from a salmon the gut is apt to cut itself in the knot—as you may see from the broken end after you have realised the loss of your fly and the salmon. Why it cuts the gut in this way is not very plain. Even if the loop is of fiddle-string, which softens at once and can be tied directly it is thoroughly wetted, yet a new, unused loop seems to resist the squeeze of the knot, and is liable to break off upon the sudden snatch of a salmon, unless extra care has been used to see that the knot has settled itself firmly in the new loop.

The figure of eight in reef knot form is a good and reliable knot for all stout gut, and it has the merit of being easy to untie. To loosen it you hold the fly close up to the knot and with the thumb nail push aside the final loop of gut (the one that you made when you turned back the loose end round the gut link after the reef knot or half-hitch). As soon as this is moved it is easy to get hold of it and pull out the end of the gut, leaving only the half-hitch or the reef knot, which is undone at once.

Whilst we are untying knots there is one useful little tip that is absurdly simple, but still may not

SLIP KNOT FOR METAL EYES

occur to your mind. One often cuts off the fly, knot and all, and then afterwards one wants to untie the knot and have the fly ready to put on again. It is by no means easy to untie such a knot, and it is, of course, most risky to try to cut the gut in the knot unless you take some means to make sure that you shall not cut the loop of the fly. Well, if you force the point of a pin under any bit of gut that you wish to cut, and then shave along the pin with the blade of your knife, you cut the gut without the least risk to your fly. The knife blade is, of course, held at right angles to the pin and almost flat upon it. This little tip can be used just as easily for removing the fly from the cast in the first instance.

For tying gut to eyed hooks or to the ring of a swivel the best knot is one of the very simplest things in the world. You have merely to thread the eye or ring upon the end of the gut, then turn that end back and give it a single knot round the gut, and then run up the sort of primitive slip knot that you have made.

It looks a quite inadequate knot, but you will find that it answers perfectly.

Detail:

1. Pass the loose end once (if the fly be a large one, *twice*) through the metal loop, then, with the end, tie a single knot round the gut above the fly (thus you form a sort of slip knot).

2. Before running up the slip knot pull that single knot firm and tight (but do not strive to

jam it hard or you will spoil the roundness of your cast at that point).

3. Work the knot quietly down upon the metal loop, pulling the gut line tight, and thus forming a sort of tightened slip knot. Figure III. shows this knot before it is pulled tight.

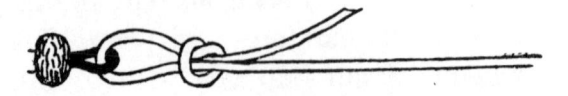

FIG. III.—Knot for Small Eyed Hooks, or for Swivel Loops.

This knot, if properly made and tightened, is very strong indeed, and very little liable to 'neck' or 'knuckle' in casting. If you do give a sudden jerk to the fly the slip knot upon the smooth metal eye has sufficient play to avoid the cracking off of the fly.

In a really high and gusty wind I do not think that any fly but one with its loop made of fiddle-string is entirely free from the risk of being cracked off when you are using a big salmon rod. If the fiddle-string loop had no other merit than this one, it would be well worth while to have a few flies tied upon such loops for use on very windy days. On such days you have quite enough to do to cast the fly clean and to get it to the place you wish, and it is a great blessing to feel that you need not bother about any risk of snapping off the fly, or of striking a fish with a fly dangerously weakened by the strains and jerks inevitable in a high wind. You have only to look at the fraying of your gut cast that occurs during a day's fishing in a gale of wind to realise what severe treatment the gut has had.

The Double Blood-Knot for Salmon Gut

MY DEAR BOYS,—I promised you a few wrinkles; here is the greatest tip that I have ever learnt about salmon fishing, by far the most valuable piece of knowledge, and one that has saved me many salmon and many, many pounds in salmon gut.

Not only is this the neatest knot that can be used to connect strands of gut, but it is far and away stronger and more durable than any other, and the knot, instead of being much weaker than the average strand of your cast, is quite as strong as any other part of it.

For eighteen years I have shown this knot to brother anglers and have never met a salmon fisher who knew it, and at the present time I believe that not one of the London tackle-makers knows how to make it. Out of hundreds of casts bought from all kinds of tackle-makers that I have seen in the hands of other fishers, there has not been one on which this knot was used, although I understand that the knot is known to one or possibly two country tackle-makers who jealously preserve their secret. I owe the knowledge of it to the accident of finding, in the post of chief engineer of a White Star liner, upon which, in the year 1892, I was travelling round the world, a keen salmon fisher, born and bred upon Tweedside. I hope that he will forgive an exceedingly grateful angler and pupil if I name him without adornment as Jock Purvis. A keener fisherman never lived, and when the thumping of his engines was substituted for the sweeter music of the Tweed, he consoled himself by making up flies and tackle, and amongst other things in studying this knot. Having obtained some casts upon which the coveted knots were to be seen, he set them in wax and cut sections of them in order that he might examine them with his microscope. At length he perceived how the knot was constructed, and finding accidentally that I also was among the salmon fishers, he showed the knot to me. But to know how this knot stands when drawn tight, and to be able to tie it easily, are two very different matters. With a good deal of trouble we could reproduce the correct knot from time to time, but the discovery of the method by which this knot can be tied with the very greatest ease by any one, and (as I have often proved) can be tied in almost complete darkness when you have to hold your hands against the sky in order to see anything at all of what you are doing—this was not made until later.

D.O.D.—the 'dear Granpa' of your baby days, to whom you and I owe so much besides fishing —found that out, and now to tie the knot is simplicity itself. The only requisite is that the gut must be well soaked before you begin it.

THE BLOOD-KNOT 187

The knot is tied thus :—

(1) Lay the ends of the two strands of gut side by side as you wish to tie them and about

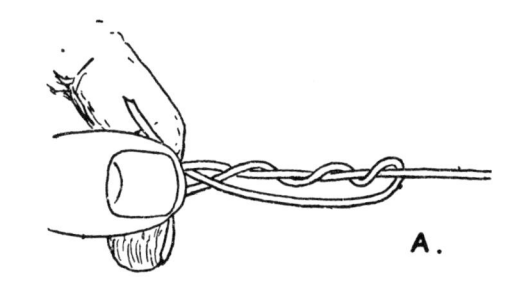

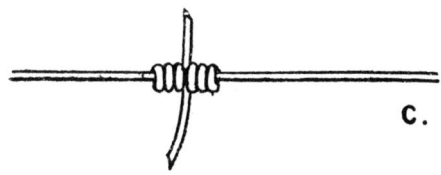

A.

B.

C.

FIG. IV.—*a.* The first half of the Knot.
b. The whole Knot, loose.
c. The Knot, pulled tight.

one-eighth of an inch apart, holding them with your left hand, the end of the left-hand strand being nearer to your body.

(2) With your right hand take the nearer end and wind it three times round the other strand (winding over and away from you).

(3) Then bend the end back and poke it down between the two strands where your left thumb was. Figure IV.*a*.

That is half the knot done: the other half consists in doing exactly the same thing with the opposite half of the knot, but reversing the twist.

(4) Reverse this half knot so that your left hand holds it, end to the right.
(5) Take this end and wind it three times *left-handed* round the link, thus giving a reverse twist. (See Appendix, Note 3*a*.)
(6) Then bend it back and poke it through between the two links so as to lie beside the other loose end, but pointing the opposite way. Figure IV.*b*.

Then, to pull the knot tight, slightly moisten the left finger and thumb, and with them hold the knot lightly whilst you pull the ends firmly and sharply. The knot will run up into a complete and translucent roll with the two ends sticking out at right angles, and they can then be cut off short. Figure IV.*c*.

The beginner will find it an advantage when he wishes to pull this knot tight to get a friend to hold the knot for him, with a finger and thumb moistened in water, so that the tier has both hands free to pull the knot tight. But with a very little practice no help is needed; you hitch the gut round the root of your little finger (or of that and the next finger), just as a woman holds

THE BLOOD-KNOT

her wool in knitting, and that leaves your thumb and finger of that hand free to hold the knot, and so both to damp it and to prevent it slipping.

> Please mark! (1) Figure *B*, p. 187 still shows the twist on each half of the knot continuous. The knot is neater and as strong with the twists reversed, as just described. But though I now usually make the twists reversed, yet if I have to tie a thin end to a thick one I still make the twist continuous (as in *B*), because thereby I can give the thin end a half turn more than the thick end. (For this see Appendix, Note 3*a*.)
>
> (2) The gut must be well soaked, and it is better to damp it before the knot is pulled tight, or, if stiff, to resoak it.

Before cutting off the projecting ends it is well to give them a good pull, and until you become well practised in tying the knot the ends should not be shaved off too closely. Soon you will tie it so securely that the ends may be cut off as close as a knife can shave them.

A great advantage of this knot is its economy of the gut. It can be tied so as to leave ends of no more than half an inch or even less, and in a strand of gut that is running thinner and weaker towards the end you can bring the knot exactly to any point that you may wish. With expensive gut or thick gut in short lengths this is a great benefit, both saving your gut and giving you fewer knots in your cast. With this knot, when fishing, you can and should retie your cast on the spot, if it shows any sign of weakness. You can, if necessary, make up a complete new cast of single gut—the gut having been soaked, of course—in from five to ten minutes. You can also—and I find this of great use for a rapid change of flies in cold weather, or when the light is bad or at any time when one intends to try a change and then resume fishing with your former fly—you can keep your change fly on a strand of gut and soak that in a tobacco tin or in a bit of wet flannel (or in your mouth or inside the stocking over your waders), and then cutting off the last link of your single gut (with the fly), tie on your new link ready tied to its fly. For any one who does not often change his flies, two or three flies, each on a good long strand of gut, will provide all his changes for the day. And the two links should be tied together whilst you may count ten, in less time than it will take even to tie on a fly, far less, of course, than the time needed to untie one fly and to tie on another.

This most ingenious knot is nothing but a double blood-knot. Each strand of the gut runs straight through the knot, both lying within it side by side and jammed together by the rolls outside it, so that the harder the gut is pulled the more firmly do these rolls jam. The great suitability of the knot for tying gut is due to the fact that each strand of gut does enter the knot in this way and go right through it without any bend whatever,

THE BLOOD-KNOT

and to the strain being taken by the jamming of these two straight pieces together.

Who was the ingenious person who invented this knot, or who first thought of applying the method of the blood-knot to tying salmon gut no one knows; but he most certainly deserves the perennial gratitude of all salmon fishers.[1]

[1] For a further simple knot see Appendix, Note 3.

XX

OF WADING, WADERS, AND CLOTHING

My dear Boys,—There are things that you can do in your youth that you have to regret and to pay pretty dearly for in after years, and among them is the habit of much wading without waders. It is all very well in summer when the water is warm, and feels only cool and refreshing as it swishes round your knees, but in spring and in late autumn, when the water is nearly freezing and the air often is actually at freezing-point, you *can* wade unprotected, and no doubt you will do it, but it is an act of boyish folly which, if you fish much, will ensure for you, as it has done for me, agonising cramps and much rheumatism in later years.

Even in warm weather it is a pretty foolish thing to do regularly, or except as an occasional venture, but in really cold waters you should be warned most earnestly, not only to wear good waders, but also to have thick clothes and warm underclothing. Standing in cold water for hours together takes all the heat from your limbs, and the moisture and perspiration condenses on the inner side of the waders, which become quite damp, and the knickerbockers that are rubbing against the damp waders are kept damp also, and this, if you fish much, brings on to a certainty cramps, rheumatism, or sciatica in later years. But if you always, when wading, will wear a pair of thick woollen drawers, you will find that your legs keep dry and warm, however damp the outer clothing may get and however thin it may be. The underclothing next your skin keeps dry notwithstanding that moisture goes on condensing on the inner side of the cold wader. Years of neglect on my part have taught me a severe lesson, for they have made cramp in the feet and thighs a dread enemy in spring and late autumn fishing, and I urgently beg you not to neglect this warning. If you do find yourself a victim of cramp, however, half a teaspoonful of bicarbonate of soda—which you can get in almost every house because the cook uses it to make her cakes light and her plum-puddings dark—in a wineglass of water, taken before you go out, will generally keep cramp away for that day.

In cold weather an extra pair of socks pulled over the feet of your stockings is a good thing to keep you warm, and so is pulling the stocking tops over one's knee instead of turning them down, as is commonly done. Quite apart from fear of cramps to come, it is worth while to keep warm because it makes fishing so much more pleasant, and because, if you keep your legs warm, your hands will not so easily get to that pitch of numbed stiffness that every salmon fisher knows when they are utterly unable to untie a knot, and when, after your day's fishing is ended, the return of warmth to your fingers can almost make you dance with pain.

Stout brogues with good nails are another essential to comfortable wading in heavy water, and to keep the nails renewed will save you many a ducking in places where the wading is bad. You should buy a few pennyworths of stout hobnails, and then you can always with a stone drive a few nails into the soles of your brogues if you find your foothold bad. If you get much fishing it is well worth while to spend a shilling or two on an iron foot, such as cobblers use to put inside a boot when they wish to hammer nails in the sole, but if you have not got such a foot, a good wedge-shaped stone slipped inside the brogue will serve the purpose. But do not hammer nails into a sole when it is very dry, or you will find that whilst you are hammering in one nail half a dozen others near it will start up and become quite loose. Soak the leather and then drive your nails into it.

Great controversy rages in the smoking-rooms of fishing inns as to whether you should or should not wear a strap round your waist when wading in dangerous waters. Many anglers assert that if you do use a belt, and do not allow the water to get freely into your waders, if you should have to swim for your life the buoyancy of your legs will drown you by causing your head to go under water and your feet to bob about on the surface like corks. I have even met men who vowed that they had seen this happen. Well, that is all utter nonsense. A salmon fisher who has been swept away by the stream may be stunned or numbed by having his head or his limbs struck hard against a boulder, or he may be dazed by the knocking about that he gets when he is trying to struggle to his feet in a swift current that is tumbling him along down the stream, but he has no need to fear the result of having air in his waders. His feet will not bob about on the surface or sink his head. I have tried it more than once by deliberately upsetting out of a boat when crossing the river in my waders, and the result is nothing of the sort. The buoyancy is enough to keep your legs well up, but it does not bother you at all, and you swim quite easily, although the clumsiness of the waders makes you very slow, and the weight of water in the waders makes it difficult to get out if the bank is high. Indeed, when the legs of the waders do fill with water it becomes much harder to swim, although you can do it well enough if you swim carefully and keep calm and go with the stream. The real danger is that when you slip in heavy water you struggle to recover yourself and get greatly knocked about and flustered in the attempt to regain your footing or to reach the bank at the point where you fell in.

You cannot be too careful when you have to cross swift, glassy currents. They are generally much stronger than they look, and when the river is rising you must be specially careful in such places—one inch more water may make them ten times more dangerous than they were before. Always, if possible, find a stout staff with which to steady yourself and to feel your way in heavy water, but if two of you have to cross dangerous water or a rising river, go in together walking abreast (facing across the stream), and let each with one hand grip fast the shoulder of the other at arm's length. Wading so, you support each other, and you can cross water where one man alone would be swept away; the upper wader breaks the force of the current and is himself supported by the lower one.

Not only when you have to cross the stream, but always when you are wading in big waters, unless the weather has been absolutely settled, you should be on the look-out for any rising of the river. In most rivers that have their source amongst the mountains a sudden rise of the water may occur at the most unexpected time. Heavy rain overnight and many miles away from you, or a thunderstorm amongst the hills, may fill the mountain streams, and many hours later, when you are fishing, with no idea of what is coming, the river will suddenly rise and give you precious little time to make yourself safe. The first signs that you will see are little straws, chips, and dry leaves floating by, and if you look at the edges of a gravel bed the water begins to swell up round the dry stones, as in a cup that is brimming over, in a way that is unmistakable. But when you see those straws

AN ENGLISH RIVER

A ROCKY STREAM IN SCOTLAND

REPAIRING WADERS

and bits of grass floating by, look about you, and make sure that your retreat is safe; a rising salmon river may be a very dangerous thing, and many of them rise very fast. I have reached the bank more than once to find that the water was already four or five feet deep where I had been wading comfortably two minutes earlier, and there are few salmon fishers who have not had pretty narrow escapes from a dangerous swim and the loss of their rod, if nothing worse.

There are one or two more points about waders. Always patch your waders before they are quite worn through rather than after waiting until they have once let in the water. As you know, the material consists of two sheets of strong twill or canvas-like material with a layer of rubber between them. Take a patch, cut out of an old wader, heat it at the fire, and you can easily split it into thinner sheets, each having the outer twill and either a thick or a thin slice of the rubber core that lies between them. Then with a tin or a tube of india-rubber solution you can mend the worn place quite easily, and the thinner patch will stick fast where a thicker one would unduly stiffen the material, and consequently would very soon have got rubbed off in fishing. The tendency to rub off always exists in some degree, but it can be cured by the use of a most excellent stuff lately invented,[1] which seems to vulcanise or harden the rubber and makes a new patch stick absolutely

[1] Called Goodrich's cold vulcanising solution and acid.

fast. I believe in putting on one very small patch barely covering the worn spot on the waders, and then putting over that a much larger piece of thin material just to protect the first patch. If you have no patching material some celluloid varnish soaked into a place that is wearing will keep it water-tight for a long time.

The fishing life of waders depends, first, on their being a good fit, for badly fitting waders wrinkle and rub together and very soon cut through at the places where they rub; and, secondly, it depends on the care used in turning them inside out to be dried and in turning them back again. Nothing destroys waders more than carelessly tugging and tearing at them to get them inside out, and you should be very sure of the persons who have to do this. It is an owner's job.[1]

As laces for your brogues you will find nothing better than a bit of common plaited blind cord, and four or five feet of the same cord makes a most useful sling with which to carry a salmon. You double the cord and make a slip knot at his tail, then pass the loose ends through the fish's gills and out of his mouth, double him up into a half-circle and knot the ends, with a half hitch or two, round the tail again. You can easily carry a couple of small fish of 8 or 10 lbs. apiece on the same string by looping your string round the tail of one, then passing it through the gills of both, and fastening it to the tail of the second one.

[1] See Appendix, Note 4.

The socks that are worn over the waders, to protect them from being cut or rubbed through by the sand and small stones that get into your brogues, should be good thick ones. It is a good plan to have the soles of these socks double knitted, or else roughly darned with coarse wool to about twice the ordinary thickness, and they will then last very much longer, and your waders will do the same.

Now, as to the general colour of one's clothes. Don't have any bright colours about you, any visible handkerchief or cuffs, and if you wear a white collar when fishing—you shouldn't—take care that it is hidden by turning up the collar of your coat. Salmon have very sharp eyes, and though you may catch salmon if you are dressed in white clothes or in all the colours of the rainbow, yet your chances of catching them will be much better if they have not already seen you when the fly comes to their notice. As your mother says, you seem to catch more if you look like a tramp. Sober colours that suit reasonably with the colour of banks and trees are much the best thing to wear.

A big-brimmed, soft felt hat is a great joy in heavy rain. It keeps out the wet and does not get sodden and heavy, and it acts like an umbrella in keeping the rain from running down your neck inside your clothing. Such rain as soaks through one can be endured, but I have yet to meet the fisherman who is really happy when the rain is running down his neck. And salmon take well—or often take well—in heavy rain, so don't be persuaded to take shelter or to stay at home just because it is raining hard. That is the very chance on which I have many a time taken the best fish, but when I do fish in rain I like to have a good hat to turn the rain. On very wet days, too, the short cape taken off an old ulster and put round the shoulders, and buttoned or tied only at the neck, makes a very good waterproof to fish in. It throws off nearly all the water, and does not make you hot and impede your fishing as the usual fishing mackintosh does. But the cape should be a very short one and fairly heavy.

XXI

TACKLE AND ACCESSORIES

MY DEAR BOYS,—There is no need to repeat the A B C. These things you may find in many books. I have said something about rods in an earlier letter (No. 1). If you choose a rod, be sure that it is not a very whippy one. A rod that feels as if it had no backbone is a bad rod for salmon fishing, but if for trout it is a perfect curse. And though a whippy rod undoubtedly has merits in the eyes of some anglers, there can be little doubt that it is the worst possible form of rod for a beginner. He wants not a heavy rod, nor necessarily a stiff rod, but one with a quick, springy action, bending more at the top than in the butt. I think that split cane without a steel centre gives very nearly the perfection of action. A perfect greenheart can fully equal it in action, but is not so durable nor so free from risk of purely accidental breakages, and such greenhearts are not so common as are perfect rods of cane. For salmon fishing, as you know, I use rods with steel centres, because I happen to have three beautiful rods of that kind, but I think the steel centre is a mistake, and the rod, if it be really well made, is not only cheaper but better without a steel centre, and the action is 'sweeter' and more lively.[1]

For the joints of the rod no vaseline should ever be used, unless it is quite pure and free from all trace of acid. A bit of hard mutton fat—the cold fat of any cooked joint of mutton—is much the best thing to use. It will keep sweet for weeks, and the least rub of it will prevent the joint from sticking and help to keep the wet out of it.

To free a sticking joint there is a contrivance called the Spanish windlass. Double a bit of string and twist it round the upper ferrule so as to bring the loop close to the joint. Then put a similar loop of string twisted round the opposite way on the lower ferrule. Put a bit of stick through each loop, and then a very great leverage can be got to twist the ferrules in opposite directions.

I learnt a useful lesson in 1899 from a Norwegian boatman. Whilst he was trying to get a $4\frac{1}{2}$ lbs. yellow trout into the landing-net the trout suddenly dashed under our boat and broke the top of my rod short off at the joint. After the fish was secured we went ashore to refit. There was a spare top in the net handle, but the difficulty was to get out the brass part of the broken top, which was stuck fast in the joint with only a quarter of an inch projecting. We were miles away from home, and I thought the game was up, when Olaf began to run about and picked up an enormous piece of stone weighing about 40 lbs., but having one very

[1] See Appendix. Note 5.

sharp edge. He got me to hold the broken joint on a round boulder, then he carefully placed the sharp edge of his rock on the projecting quarter of an inch of brass and bore heavily upon it. Of course this held it like a vice, and I was able with ease to twist off the sound part of the rod and put in the spare top.

Reels.—Always see that your reel is firmly fastened on the rod before you fish for salmon. In the excitement of the fight you are very apt to loosen it, and quite a number of times I have known a fisher's reel fall off and generally the fish has been lost by it. It has happened to me—I think more than once—and only a fortnight ago, on my last day's salmon fishing, I saw it happen to a friend landing the third salmon of his life, a fish of 26 lbs., foul hooked in the back fin. However, help was at hand, and he was able to get the reel on again and ultimately to land the fish, although it had been actually ashore on the opposite bank and was leaping and splashing eighty yards away from him when he got the reel in its place again.

You ought to get a good reel, and they are not cheap. But a cheap reel is seldom a really reliable one, and any injury by a slight blow or by accidents which are often quite unavoidable at the river-side may cost you a day's fishing or more. You ought to have two reels, one with a light and one with a heavy line, ready and in working order, and you are then reasonably independent of accident. Never lay a reel down upon sand. A few grains of sand may choke or spoil it altogether.

Lines.—Your lines must be dried every night, and before being put away for the season should be fully put out and left to dry for two or three days. A good plan is to wind your lines round the legs of a table, and there is nothing equal to the lumpy legs of a billiard-table for winding lines on. Twelve yards go to each round, and you can easily put three or four lines out on one table.[1]

Hooks.—See that your hooks are as stout, stiff, and rigid as possible. A great many hooks are unreliable, they bend open or even break behind the barb. The best that I have found are Adlington's Dublin hooks. And the points should be extremely sharp, and the line of the point should be parallel to the shank, not turned out. The latter is a fad based on the fallacy that the line of the shank is the line of the pull, and that to turn the point out a little will ensure its burying itself deeply. Just think : a *flexible* line is attached to the head of the fly and is pulling the point of the hook against something. Take a fly with a foot of gut or string and try the effect of putting the point against anything and pulling on the string. You will see instantly that the line of pull is directly from point to head.

I have found bronzed hooks generally to be badly tempered, and often in the present patterns the point is made so finely tapering that the extreme point is apt to break off in the fish, leaving

[1] See Appendix, Note 6.

HOOKS

you with a blunted hook, which you may not notice until you have lost a good fish or two which have risen and have not been held.

Sharpness is vital, the fish's skin is tough and shiny, and you must always have a tiny slip of whetstone and see that every hook you use is as sharp as a needle.[1] The point often gets blunted whilst you are landing a fish by his rubbing it against the gravel, and often gets blunted by a careless cast slashing the sand or the bank behind you. If in casting you touch a stone behind you with the fly you may hear a click and your fly has now neither point nor barb. If you do hear your fly touch the gravel, stop at once and examine the point. How many dozens of good fish I have known lost from this cause.

Double hooks I do not like; my own experience of them is altogether unfavourable. But in very dark or heavy water they help to sink the fly. In repeated trials that I have given to double hooks I have lost an enormous number of fish upon them, both by failing to drive the hooks home at the rise, and by their coming out later on. And in October 1900 I landed a fish of 16 lbs. upon a large double hook, and I noticed that it was then held by the left hook only. But there were five other holes quite near the existing hold, and the place where the other hook had held was cut to ribbons. Each hook had penetrated to the bone and had been levering the other out as the fish ran about and the pull came from different direc-

[1] See Appendix, Note 7.

tions. But the loss of a fish of over 40 lbs., as I believe, on the 15th September 1903, ended my last trial of double hooks. After eleven minutes' play from the time when I was able to look at my watch the hook came away, and I found that the fish had grubbed and scratched the exposed hook against the stones until he had opened out the hook that held him. With a single hook he had been mine.

For very small flies I like eyed hooks. They last longer and are easily changed; they are cut off the gut and a new fly is tied on in an instant with the sliding knot. The time when you are driven to your small flies is the very time when you wish to change the fly fairly often.

I think the best thing in the way of a box to carry one's salmon flies is an aluminium pocket cigar-case, with a slip of flannel or of old blanket gummed into each half, in order to hook the flies in it. This will hold about forty flies, and a couple of spare casts will go comfortably round under the rims. The common tackle-makers' cases, with metal clips to hold the flies, rust the hooks unless you never put a wetted fly back into them. Whatever form of fly-box you use it should be left open to dry after wet flies and gut have been put in it, or else some fine day you will find a lot of your best flies and gut totally rotten.

As a bag to carry salmon (or waders) there is nothing to equal the ordinary carpenter's basket, called a 'frail.' You want a slip of sacking to keep the frail clean. With a good frail and a stout stick for the shoulder you can easily manage to carry three big fish or four smaller ones. Besides, you can carry the frail and a rod over the same shoulder, leaving one hand free.

Freeing tackle. At first you will often catch the bottom towards the middle or end of your cast. The beginner, to free his fly, keeps on pulling, but that is not the way to do it. Whether you are fishing fly or anything else, directly you find that you have caught the bottom you should cease to pull and let the line go slack so that the water may wash the line and gut down-stream of the point where the fly is hooked up. Then after a few seconds, if you raise your point firmly, you will generally find your hook comes free, the actual pull on it having come as a down-stream pull from the gut which has been carried past it by the current. Now as to gut. I do not think staining the gut any strong colour, black, blue, or yellow, is an advantage. I think clear gut with no glitter is the best, and you will think so if you hold it against the sky beside a stained strand. And the glitter can be wholly removed by a few rubbings of the new gut cast with the crushed leaf of an alder. The alder grows by every river-side; its leaf stains the outside of gut green. The gut looks like a thread of grass until the green colour washes off, and in a very short time all glitter disappears also—a most invaluable tip for sunny weather.

XXII

ON SPAWNING SALMON

MY DEAR BOYS,—John Kirkbride in 1837 published his *Northern Angler*, and in it gives the best description that I know of all the old north-country flies, whether hackled or winged, and whether for trout or salmon. But he also gives the view of salmon spawning that was current in his time, and he tells us the kind of stuff that had been solemnly sworn to by the greatest pundits of that day. He says: 'According to Mr. Halliday and Mr. Little, two witnesses examined before a Committee of the House of Commons, spawning is accomplished in the following manner. The male and female fish select a suitable place in the running water where the bottom is gravelly, and play round it for some time. They then begin to make a furrow by working up the gravel with their noses. When the furrow is made they throw themselves on their sides and rubbing against each other shed their spawn into it; and they cover the furrow with loose gravel as they proceed upwards. . . . Although the roe of the female contains from 17,000 to 20,000 eggs, only one can be excluded at a time. The fish, therefore, continue daily increasing the number of furrows for several days and form a bed about twelve feet by eight or ten. The spawning bed is easily known by the thrown-up gravel ; by some it is said to resemble an onion bed. Mr. Halliday states that he has seen on one spawning bed three pairs of fish at one time. Should the male fish be destroyed in the act of spawning, the female leaves the bed and retires to some deep pool to find another mate. . . . The ova remain in these beds completely covered with loose gravel for several weeks or till the genial warmth of spring occasions their evolution. From the gravel the young fish, their tails appearing first, are said to spring up like a braird of corn.'

What a pretty picture, isn't it ? These subaqueous onion beds with the little fishes sprouting up out of each parallel furrow in the gravel in thick rows like sown corn, and ' their tails appearing first.' Such a masterly touch of detail intended, as W. S. Gilbert says, to give verisimilitude to an otherwise bald and unconvincing narrative. I should think even our Members of Parliament must have opened their eyes as they gulped down these fables.

Well, to this day statements which to me are very surprising are copied into some of the very best books on angling.

Even Mr. Gathorne-Hardy, in his charming little book on salmon (which you should most certainly read as soon as you can), says of the spawning salmon that ' the eggs are hidden most cunningly and covered with gravel *to some feet in depth.*' I have been quite unable to find any eggs after the surface gravel has once been scraped away, although I have found plenty scattered about among the loose stones at the top, or very lightly covered with the sand and small pebbles disturbed by the splashings of the spawning female. And in our hatcheries covering up the spawn to any depth has always, I believe, resulted in failure. Certainly the constant practice is the exact reverse, the eggs, both of salmon and trout, being kept in shallow troughs with a constant stream of water flowing over them.

A very recent book by one of the 'champion fly-casters,' who write books to instruct salmon fishers, makes the *male* salmon *with his nose* dig a hole in the gravel *two feet deep*, after which the fish place their spawn at the bottom of this pit and then fill it in. None of your furrows and onion beds here. I wonder if the author has ever tried, even with a stout shovel, to dig a hole two feet deep in the gravel in a rapid stream. If he had, I think his views of the feat performed by the salmon would be somewhat modified. The fish wouldn't, I think, have much nose left by the time his hole was dug.

I once met a gallant sportsman in Norway who informed me, as of a fact which brooked no discussion, that the gib of the male salmon was just a digging tool to delve this grave in the gravel, and that this was so was proved beyond all doubt by the fact that the gib was gone in the spring, and it could only be worn away on the gravel. I hope that I do his argument no injustice, but this belief is by no means uncommon. However, I think that most people now believe that the use of the gib is for fighting. It is rigid only when pressed from the inside of the mouth, and when so pressed a distinct though blunt and smooth point can be felt, and its apparent handiwork in the shape of handsome whitish scrapes or scars can be seen on many of the males in spawning time. Besides, it is the males alone that have the gib, and so far as I could see in many watchings the male never did anything that could disturb the gravel. It is the violent kickings of the female, which has no gib, that seem to be the cause of the gravel washing away down the stream. Besides, the common trout spawns on redds or spawning beds formed exactly like those of the salmon, and the trout develops no gib at all.

For about fifteen winters I have very seldom missed going to see the salmon spawning, and I have watched closely some hundreds of salmon actually spawning, and the fish that I have seen do not appear to be doing what has been so often described. But it is not very easy to see *accurately* what is happening on a gravelly bottom, perhaps in stained water and nearly always in a swift, rippling stream, which is the position commonly chosen by salmon for the purposes of spawning. But twice I have seen fish—big salmon—spawning in water which, though clear and fairly swift, was running over a smooth gravel bed and was not rippling water, so that the fish could be seen perfectly, and even the eggs coming from the female could be seen from time to time, and in each of those cases nothing of the kind was taking place; no trench was being dug, no perceptible amount of gravel was being disturbed; when the fish had left the place one could see that they had done nothing to cover over their eggs with gravel, nothing had been disturbed except possibly a little sand amongst the stones. Of course it is unusual to find fish spawning in such a place; they generally choose rough streams with loose gravel, and then the gravel does wash down and the hen fish almost always has a certain amount of disturbed gravel below her, sometimes only a small patch a couple of feet wide and three feet long, sometimes, especially in strong streams and where many fish have come to spawn, a patch five or six feet wide and eight or nine feet long, and occasionally one even larger than this. But even in strong streams fish often have to spawn where the bottom consists largely of stones not yet rounded by the water, and there I have many times seen them hard at work, but with no visible disturbance of the stones anywhere near them. I do not feel at all positive about this matter, but from what I have seen I think that the disturbance of the gravel is not a mechanical digging or stirring of it up, but is an incidental though probably beneficial result of the violent struggles of the fish in spawning in a gravelly stream. And I certainly think that the spawn does not drop into the gravel straight below the fish in the slight hollow in which she is usually lying, but, being only just heavier than water, is carried down the stream by the current and rolls into crevices in the gravel, and the disturbance of the gravel by the fish causes a certain amount of fine gravel and sand to wash down and helps to conceal the spawn from ducks and eels and its other enemies. If, many yards below where a fish has been spawning, you stir up with a shovel the surface of the gravel, you can easily see the peas of salmon roe that you have disturbed being swept away. They do not keep on the bottom, but swirl up with the water, almost, but not quite, able to float. They are obviously only a very little heavier than water. Roe in the fish itself, or roe that has been stripped artificially from the fish, is in colour a fine bright salmon pink; but roe quite ripe and spawned naturally by the fish seems to be generally of a translucent, purplish pink colour, by no means easy to see amongst the gravel, though visible enough the moment that you stir it up into the current. But some of the peas, even in the river, are of an almost chalky salmon pink colour, and are very easily seen. These I rather suspect to be dead or infertile eggs.

But, you may say, why the kicking that one

can see, unless it be that the fish is trying to rout up the gravel? My answer would be twofold. First, that I have seen the female kicking with the greatest vigour in the usual way when she was spawning over hard gravel which she was not touching, and was not disturbing, and also on rocky, or rather rough stony bottom, when she was unable to disturb the stones, however much she wished it. Secondly, that her violent wriggling or kicking is, I believe, done to promote the extrusion of the spawn. At Christmas of 1887 or 1888 I was with your great-grandfather upon the Tees near Dinsdale netting salmon in order to obtain spawn for the fish hatchery. The method which he discovered and adopted in order to 'strip' the female fish of her spawn was to get one of his men to seat himself on the bank, and to hold the fish between his knees, belly upwards, putting one hand under her back and with the other gently forcing her tail downwards, when the ripe peas of roe were squirted out in a continuous stream.

I am going to reprint for you his experience of seeing salmon spawning, but as I was intending to write a letter to you on this subject I determined to take the first really good opportunity of again seeing the fish spawning and to write down on the spot what I saw without reference to any preconceived theory of what I expected to see or thought I ought to see. Well, yesterday and to-day the chance came to perfection, and I did write down on the spot, as I saw it, what was happening, and here it is :—

On Sunday, January 3, 1909, a glorious mild winter's day, I went up to the Devil's Water, a tributary of the river Tyne, with one of you boys to see the salmon spawn. The stream is about twenty to thirty feet wide, and on the shallows was then about eighteen to twenty-four inches deep. We reached the water at 2.30 P.M., and here are the notes of what we saw.

Three single fish were lying above the railway bridge. One was a splendid cock fish of 28 to 30 lbs. One fish about 7 or 8 lbs. lay within two feet of the bank below our feet, and we could see that not a fin was moving, though he lay in quite fast-running, shallow water, but resting quite still upon the stones. You, D., may remember touching him with my walking-stick, to make sure that he was alive, and nearly falling on the top of him when he dashed off, splashing the water all over you.

One pair, each fish about 18 lbs., was spawning, but too far out to be seen very accurately. They lay in about two feet of water, and the disturbed gravel below them rose to within sixteen or eighteen inches of the surface. Dozens upon dozens of patches of disturbed gravel showed the spawning grounds used by earlier fish, and the farmer's ducks were greedily going over all the shallower places and evidently doing themselves very well indeed. Higher up the stream a fish could be seen splashing from time to time, doubtless another female spawning, but the water was so broken where she lay that nothing could be made out precisely.

Then we went below the bridge and presently saw a splash. Coming opposite to the place we saw that it was a female fish about 10 lbs., showing a very bright side when she turned on her side to spawn, and we could see her companion, a red cock of 12 or 14 lbs., keeping a foot or two below her, but occasionally ranging alongside. We crept to the bank, sat down and kept quite still. Presently a big wave appeared, coming up out of a deeper pool forty yards below, and then a big cock fish of 19 or 20 lbs., with a white mark on his nose and several more along his back, sailed up to the spawning pair, followed by a female fish of 24 or 25 lbs. of a light pinky red colour. The original male sheered off across the stream, but his female only edged into the shallower water, a couple of feet nearer to us, and continued to spawn, whilst the big new female was throwing herself from time to time, her big male keeping beside her, sometimes a little above, sometimes a little below her, and overlapping her by about half his length.

Owing to her brightness, the throw or struggle of the smaller female is very clearly seen. She comes to the surface turning half on her side (and three out of four times on her right side), arching her back, and then she gives five or six vigorous, shuddering wriggles or kicks, curving her body and violently straightening it again, and during this series of wriggles she moves upstream about eighteen inches or two feet. Then she sinks to the bottom and remains quiet for about three minutes. She throws every three or four minutes, but the male less often. The big female throws at long intervals, and when she does so she turns almost flat on her side.

Presently, after fifteen minutes, the big female turned and went down the stream, followed by the male. The smaller red male then came across the stream and lay beside his mate for six minutes. Then leaving her he forced his way splashing up the fast but very shallow stream above where they lay for forty or fifty yards, and after a few minutes he came back down the stream with a new sweetheart, passed his former mate, and the two then turned and ranged up in the stream some seven or eight yards below her. She continued to spawn alone, and threw four or five times at intervals, without any mate near her.

She was lying in only eighteen inches of swift water beside a rather deeper rush. No gravel was disturbed under her head, but disturbed gravel began to be visible (by the lighter side of the stones showing) about the level of her tail, and some continued for perhaps seven or eight feet below her. She lay in hardly any perceptible hollow; certainly the water there was not six inches deeper than that over the gravel below her. Presently her mate left his new friend and came up to her. Two or three times he came alongside and a little below her and gave a slight kicking, but there was no vigorous shuddering such as the female gave.

Then after a time we went down the stream to look for more fish. Presently we saw a small, bright fish's head lying in the water. About twenty yards below was the tail half of the fish, a fairly bright little grilse of about 4 lbs., eaten away, backbone and all, as far back as the ventral fins, no doubt at all by an otter. I went down and cut open this tail part, but there was no sign of milt or of roe inside it.

At twelve minutes to four we returned to our former spawners. The female was still at work; we could see plainly that she always rose to the top to throw the spawn, that her nose during this struggle was not on the bottom, and that she moved up-stream a little more than a foot in the process, but sank back to rest at the same spot each time.

Presently a male appeared outside her, came close behind her and threw, and remained lying with his head overlapping her tail. He threw with ten or twelve wriggling kicks much less vigorous than hers, with his back fin and back showing out of water, not visibly on his side, and each time he spawned he moved up two feet until nearly level with the female. He did this four times, between 3.50 and 4 P.M., and after four o'clock he continued to do so every minute

A RESTING SALMON

for some time. Probably he was there when we arrived and had moved off into deeper water on seeing us come, for he returned to the female directly we sat still.

Then we had to go home, but at 4.15, above the bridge, we saw a fish of 12-14 lbs. again within three feet of the bank in eighteen inches of water, which was running at the rate of about two to three miles an hour, yet the salmon was lying absolutely motionless on the bottom, his right pectoral fin pressed by the current against the upper side of a stone, and the tail and all the other fins slack, except the left pectoral fin, which was held tight at a slight angle against the current.

XXIII

ON SPAWNING SALMON—*continued*

MY DEAR BOYS,—To-day, the 4th January 1909, you two boys and your mother and I went again to the Devil's Water, and I took up my short waders and a stout shovel. Here are the notes of what we saw :—

On a redd above the bridge lay a cock fish of about 20 lbs. weight, with many white marks or scars along the back and on the gill covers. He was alone and was lying in about a foot of water, and the redd, five feet below him, rose to within five to six inches of the surface, the water having fallen several inches since yesterday. A small hen fish about 6 lbs. was lying close to the bank about twelve feet away, and almost opposite the former fish.

Below the bridge there are no fish at the place where we had seen them so well yesterday, but two hundred yards lower down the stream we can see the frequent splash of a fish lying just above the next pool on a swift shallow where we saw freshly moved gravel, but saw no salmon yesterday. When we get there we find that the splashing fish is a big female of 18 lbs. or more, and lying beside her is a male of 12 or 13 lbs.,

ON THE REDDS

with many whitish marks along his back and a strongly marked white patch on his nose about the size of a shilling. He lies slightly to the right side of the female with his nose just level with her tail, and he makes no visible movement at all, although she throws herself repeatedly to spawn, with violent splashings and strugglings, and after each effort sinks in the water and drops back to her lying-place near him.

Presently a second male swims quickly up and ranges alongside the first male, and then goes over to the other side of the female and lies nearly level with her. Number one takes apparently no notice for a minute or two, then he turns and glides down the stream into the deep water below, followed after another minute by number two, who had apparently done nothing at all but come up, lie for a minute quiet beside the female, and then go down. The female continued to spawn alone. Every few minutes her splashings began, and each time some male fish came up towards her out of the deeps—though not always coming quite up to her—and then dropped back again.

After half an hour a big male appeared and made a rush at the spotty twelve-pounder, who had returned to his mate, and who now bolted down-stream and hovered about, some seven or eight yards below her. After another half-hour a second pair of big salmon appeared and lay at first quite close under my bank and three or four feet from the other pair, and there the female threw herself once to spawn. Then she edged out across the stream until she came alongside the other pair, her mate following her, and then the four salmon lay side by side and almost, if not quite, touching each other. Upon this I slowly worked myself down the bank until my face was close to the water and within four or five feet of the nearest fish. Then one of the males came over towards me, saw me, and bolted back full tilt into the others, and all but one female ran down-stream. Then after a few seconds she also seemed to see me and dashed off. Then the spotted fish of 12 lbs. came up in the edge of the stream within arm's length of me, then moved out to the lie or hollow, but immediately saw me and bolted away again. I moved back a foot or so and pulled up three or four dry seed stalks of dock which had been bent down, and made them stand up beside my head so as to break the outline of it, and within a few minutes of doing so the four salmon came back with two other much larger fish, male and female. All six fish lay side by side, five of them apparently touching each other, and the sixth lying about eighteen inches away from the group. The actions of the male fish were very odd; one male, a very strong dark red in colour, but without a mark of any sort and of about 16 lbs. weight, showed no hostility to the smaller spotted male which lay beside him, but kept sliding up against the female on her right side, pushing her head slightly across the stream with his shoulder, and getting his own body across the current which washed him down under the female, lifting her back quite out of water until he had been washed right down under her body. This he repeated five or six times with only a very short interval between them, and it is the only time I have ever seen that done by a fish. Later on two fish left the redd and went down-stream, and when the four were left together one big male kept crossing over the backs of the other three fish, apparently sliding himself over their backs, but always keeping his head very much up-stream so that he slipped across their backs in a slanting direction. Possibly he was shedding his milt over them so that it might be washed over the eggs lying in the gravel; I cannot tell. The current was very fast—quite a swift rapid—and the water was about fourteen to eighteen inches deep in the hollow where the fish lay. The gravel below them rose to nine or twelve inches below the surface, and a bed of disturbed gravel extended about eight or nine feet below the tails of the fish where they lay. I put on my wading boots and went in to measure the depth of water, and to see if any spawn could be seen and where it was; whether it was buried or whether it was on or near the surface. I found that the gravel below the lie of the fish was (as one supposed) all loose, and at the tail of the stream, where the water deepened, the gravel stood up quite steeply, obviously washed down over the old unbroken gravel of the pool.

When I stirred the gravel with my shovel I could see at almost every stir of the shovel a few peas of salmon roe being washed away, but found it very hard to bring up any of the peas of roe on the shovel. By digging out solid spadefuls deeper down in the gravel I found only one or two peas of roe out of many spadefuls, and could not be sure that even those few were really buried deep in the gravel. But by scraping together some of the surface gravel and then getting up a big shovelful of that, I was able to gather a good many peas of spawn, though many, indeed most, were washed away as the shovel full of gravel was being lifted in the current. I could get no roe at all in the hollow just where the fish were lying, and I am quite certain that they were not depositing any large quantity of ova there to be covered over later on, for I should have seen the peas of spawn there on disturbing the surface of the gravel as easily as I saw them lower down, but I could see none in the hollow, none whatever.

Again, I could make out pretty clearly that the spawning female fish was not disturbing the gravel with her nose as she threw the spawn, but that she rose each time to the surface with back and side often well out of water, giving vigorous, shuddering kicks, or violent, sudden wriggles.

STIRRING GRAVEL

One female, the biggest of all, got almost flat on her side each time that she spawned, the other two not so much so.

Several times, out of very many, with extremely violent struggling the water was splashed about, and sand and mud and gravel were stirred up, but I was unable to make out that any part of the fish had touched the bottom. It appeared—but I could not be positive of this—that it was only the violent surging of the water with her tail that caused the sand and gravel to be stirred up and washed down the rapid. Only very rarely was sand or gravel visibly stirred up. Each time that I saw gravel and sand stirred up the fish shifted her position across the stream a yard or more with much splashing and swirling of water, and at each stirring the fish was *not* on her side but was swimming upright, though making a swirl in the water like that made by the blade of an oar. From the almost invariable formation of a redd, and always below the spawning fish it is, I think, pretty clear that the disturbance of gravel is intentional, and is done to provide cover for the spawn or clean gravel for it to lie on, or possibly for both purposes, but how far the fish attempts any gravel-moving operation except her natural kicking in a strong current running over gravel, I cannot determine. But I do not think that there is any touching of the gravel, and I am almost certain that there is no grubbing with her nose whilst she is throwing the spawn. Possibly she may do something with tail or fins to loosen the gravel whilst she seems to be quiescent on the bottom, for a spawning fish does not keep absolutely still like a resting fish, but (and more especially the male) moves up and down the stream, swimming, not merely resting on the bottom.

I have said that generally there is a redd, or stream of disturbed gravel, below the spawning fish. Several times I have seen fish spawning where they had made no such redd and no disturbed stones were visible. Once in December 1902, in a big, clear water, I saw a good female salmon spawning on a hard, gravelly bottom in two feet six inches of water and without a single disturbed stone being visible. Every time she threw herself, a grilse and a couple of sea-trout, lying six or seven yards below her, moved hurriedly up and had a dash at the roe a few feet below her, and once or twice her mate swung round and scattered the plunderers, chasing them right away, but no sooner did he return to his place beside his companion than they also drew up to their posts below her.

To return to the 4th January 1909. What struck us most—for the whole family was there—was the way in which the males came and went, and apparently without jealousy. Only once did we see a fish attack a smaller, and repeatedly rival males of different sizes were ranged side by side in perfect amity.

EGGS NOT COVERED UP

Having seen all that we could on the redd, which we had watched for well over two hours, we moved up to the place where continuous spawning had been going on the day before. The water was a good deal lower and the fish had left this place, so that, according to accepted theories, the hole in which they had been lying should have been filled with spawn and then carefully covered in with gravel by the fish. I went out with my shovel to examine it.

The hollow was exactly as it had been the day before. Only one pea of roe could be found in it, and none by digging up the bottom, though many were found scattered amongst the surface gravel over some twenty or thirty feet below—not merely amongst the disturbed gravel which extended for only about eight or nine feet below the little hollow.

Well, that was the end of our day. It began to grow too dark to stay any longer, and the dog-cart was waiting for us, so we went home, after putting a few peas of roe with some gravel into a bottle in order to try the effect of a little amateur fish-hatching on the part of two very small boys. The eggs all went bad one by one, each turning first to the chalky salmon colour that I have mentioned before, and then to a dull, lifeless white.

It was almost impossible to desire a better view of the fish than we had during these two days. Some results of these observations did not agree with my former beliefs nor with what I thought I had seen in earlier years. We saw practically no fighting among the males, and very little fear or jealousy. The milting of the cock fish was done very quietly, and, as far as any movement showed, very seldom. For longish periods the females were alone, yet went on spawning busily. It seems to me that there is room for a lot of accurate observation before we shall be very sure of what really does happen in these wintry waters of ours.

XXIV

TALES OF A GREAT-GRANDFATHER

MY DEAR BOYS,—I have mentioned already your great-grandfather, John Clervaux Chaytor, who gave me my first lessons in fishing. He lived almost all his life at Croft on the Tees, and he caught his first salmon in 1820, when he was fifteen years old, and his last in the year 1889. He was a member of the Tees Fishery Board, and was a very close observer of the habits of all fish, and about twenty years ago he printed for private circulation an account of his observations in a small pamphlet of some twenty-seven closely printed pages. But now very few copies exist, and I count it a pious act to reprint here those parts of his notes which deal with his observations upon the spawning of the fish, and also a few of his general observations. One most valuable wrinkle he gave me which has often enabled me to detect even at a distance the poacher of salmon smolts. From the old bridge at Croft he saw a man at least a hundred yards lower down the river catch a sturdy little fish. He said, 'It is a smelt, though it is a big one. You will see him throw it back.' I could not imagine how he could possibly tell this. It was done by knowing the fact that a young salmon, or a parr or smolt of any other kind, when lifted out of the water, kicks and wriggles vigorously until actually secured by the hand, whereas a small trout lifted out on the line almost always hangs quietly or at most gives but a few kicks. It is an absolutely certain way of knowing a young trout from a parr or from a smolt.

Notes by my Grandfather

When the frosty nights of autumn set in, and the leaves begin to fall, the fish are impelled to the exercise of their reproductive functions. They keep to the streams, and the roe which has been slowly maturing in them increases rapidly in bulk, and at the end of October or the beginning of November a little fresh water will set them to work on the streams. Many of the early-running fish ascend the tributaries; and an old kipper fisher, who was a native of Lunedale, told me that they began to look for them in the Lune about the 5th November; and I have found on the first of the month a spawning bed in the main river that must have been made at least a day or two before. Before the operation of spawning, as it is seen in the Tees, is described, mention may be made of two persons who might be expected to adhere to facts. Dr. William Chambers, in an article in *Chambers's Journal*, says that the fish deposit their spawn 'agglutinated together'; and Sir Humphry Davy, in *Salmonia*, says that they make a trough in which they deposit their spawn, and then cover it up with gravel, the male fish in particular being so energetic that he gets the end of his nose turned up. Both these writers are very wide of the mark: the ova are not agglutinated, the fish do not make a trough, and the male fish does not get the end of his nose turned up, and neither the female nor the male makes the slightest effort to cover them up. The roe consists at first of a mass of membrane intermixed with blood-vessels and small granular bodies like sand. As these blood-vessels increase in size a separation into two lobes becomes distinct, and the ova acquire the well-known salmon colour, at the approach of the spawning season occupying nearly all the cavity of the abdomen, which is then greatly distended. The milt, or soft roe of the male fish, consists of two vessels which extend the whole length of the abdominal cavity, filled with a white leathery substance which remains firm and solid till the time when it has to sustain its part in the reproductive process. Then it is gradually converted into a thick milky fluid, beginning to liquefy near the vent from which it exudes as it is required. Omitting for the present the question of colour, the female undergoes little change except in bulk. The male, however, puts out a remarkable excrescence, not from the nose, but from the under jaw. This gib, as it is called, wears a cavity in the nose, and sometimes grows so long that the nose is actually divided by it; sometimes it grows on one side, and misses the nose entirely. In very young males it is merely rudimentary: that of the scurf (sea-trout) is smaller in proportion to its size than that of the salmon, and so also is that of the bull-trout. The gib disappears soon after spawning, being rapidly absorbed. The condition of the fish being sufficiently advanced, they proceed to select their ground, which is by choice where the stones are not too large nor too fast for them to move, nor too loose so as to close in upon them. The strength of the stream and the action of the fish cause the uprooted gravel to form beds frequently several yards long when the fish are numerous, among which some of the ova find a resting-place, being covered to a depth of several inches, while the greater number are carried away by the stream. When they find the conditions unfavourable they seek a fresh place, though where there is a considerable stretch of bad ground they will persevere notwithstanding. They usually begin near the head of the stream, the smaller fish in the shallower and weaker, and the larger in the deeper and stronger parts of the stream. The operation is considered to last about two days more or less, but it is not always continuous, as a flood or other disturbance may retard it. Occasionally a combat takes place among the males, and they fight furiously, sometimes inflicting on each other serious injuries. I have seen a hen fish which had apparently been pinched all along the back from head to tail. The wounds, however, were not deep, and did not hinder her from spawning, as she was taken on the redd along with several others. It is not easy to get a clear view of what happens beneath the waters of the Tees at the time of the year when it would be most interesting to see what goes on there. Wind, rain, snow, cold, hush, floods, light and shade, in various combinations, contribute to cut short or to destroy altogether the chance of seeing clearly, and it is not surprising that some inaccuracy should occur ; but some fail to see, and others to comprehend, what is before their eyes, and substitute fancy for fact. Avoiding that error as far as possible, I will describe what I saw on the most favourable opportunity that I ever had. On the 6th November I went to the low stream at Dalton Batts, and found everything favourable. At a height of twelve or fourteen feet some large branches of a plane-tree projected horizontally over the stream, and on one of these I stood. Where the streams met at the bottom of the island there was a ridge of gravel terminating in a point, which formed two channels in the river bed. In the middle of the nearest channel there was a depression occupied by a pair of fish which were at rest. The male had some skin rubbed off his nose, which showed a white mark. A few yards farther away, near the top of the ridge, another pair occupied a similar hole, the first pair being 5 or 6 and the other 7 or 8 lbs. At intervals the females, applying their noses to the gravel, threw themselves on their sides with their nose pressed against the ground, and with rapid jerks of the tail expelled a portion of the ova, the males remaining perfectly still. Suddenly a small fish, which had been close to the edge of the water and directly under my feet, rushed in behind white nose's mate, and instantly fell back again. This manœuvre, evidently for the purpose of getting the ova, was repeated every time the spawning fish 'threw,' and only then, but was put an end to by a large fish which came bustling up from the deep stream below. He made straight for white nose and his mate, and settling himself in their hole, which he completely filled, sent them both adrift; then he went to the other pair, and did the same to them. Finally he swept away the pirate, which was a female, with his tail, and disappeared after the others in the stream below. Next day the water was more discoloured, and only one fish was to be seen. This was the larger female, and she was working by herself with her tail above water, having apparently found the gravel more easily worked downward. Then came white nose towards his own hole, but quickly departed again, doubtless knowing that the big bully was not far off. The latter, indeed, soon appeared, darting in various directions, chasing away the small fish, but not pursuing them far. I made out that he had found a mate as big as himself, who had just begun to work at the lower end of the ridge in the deeper water, and I could trace the mud which she had stirred up for several yards down-stream. Then a large male fish, which appeared like a yellowish shadow, came up on the other side of her, but disappeared again pursued by the first male, reappearing from time to time when the other returned to his station beside the female. In many years I never had so good an opportunity! and I have endeavoured, at the risk of being tedious, to be accurate, which is the main requirement. Intending to get a good haul of spawn for hatching, I returned at dusk with a lantern, a bait-tin, two milk cans, a shackle net, two old kipper fishers, and a policeman. The occupant of the ridge was still there, but as soon as the pole touched her tail she made off. Lower down, where the pair had been seen, I netted the male, unfortunately without his mate. He was a grand fish about a yard long, but, being of no use by himself, was turned out of the net into the water, where he lay like a log, making no attempt to escape, as frequently happens when the fish are handled at that season. The old kipper fishers were emphatic in the expression of their opinion that it was a shame that such a fish should be allowed to escape; but I was inexorable, so we returned as we went, *re infecta*. On another occasion the luck was equally bad, for a man who had released a trout from the bag of the net which was then in use forgot to tie it, so that the fish went through, and the rising of the water put an end to the operations. The salmon often backs out of the net; the scurf pushes forward and tries to force its way through. In a dark night they can be distinguished from each other by putting the finger into their mouths, when the strong, sharp teeth of the scurf are easily felt to differ from the smaller and less prominent teeth of the salmon. Reverting to the spawning: the female is much exhausted by the violence of her efforts to expel the ova, and quits the stream for the still water, while the male continues to hang about the place, probably because the milt is not ready all at once as the roe of the female is; and it may be that its gradual exudation may reach such ova as may be deposited by the female in his absence, besides insuring his presence in case other females should turn up. The number of males taken with nets by the Tees water-bailiffs for hatching purposes is much greater than that of females, the numbers for this season (1886-87) being eighty-four males and twenty-eight females, and they had as many as nine males without a female in one draw of the shackle net. With the rod the numbers are reversed, that of the females greatly exceeding that of the males. The female does not always eject the whole of her spawn; some few ova frequently remain in her. In one case a fish taken with the rod in March had more than four hundred left in her; the exact number was not ascertained, as the counters tired when they got to four hundred. It would seem that in the rough and ready process of spawning above described, some of the ova might not get covered at all, while some would get too deep. Doubtless both these things happen. While the egg is covered up among the gravel, it is impossible to trace the changes which take place before it emerges as a fish, and it is necessary to have it in a position where such changes can be observed. My own contrivances for that purpose have been of a very primitive order. The first was an ordinary bait can, into which I put ten eggs taken when I was assisting Mr. Samuel Wilkinson and Major Flamstead, active members of the Esk Angling Association, who were desirous of restoring the true salmon to the Esk at Whitby, and whose efforts to that end, I am happy to say, have been successful. Recovering from an accident which confined me to bed for several weeks before the hatching was due, I found one fish alive, and forthwith transferred it to a pie dish. When the time came that it had to be fed, lean meat and fish of all kinds were minced very small and given to it, and it ate them indiscriminately. When it was wanted to feed the water was stirred with a penknife, and the current immediately set it on the alert. It took only such particles of food as were in motion, taking no notice of those which settled to the bottom. It became so tame that, after the water was set in motion, it would rise to the surface of the water where the food was being introduced with the point of the knife. After some time it took those particles only which were sinking below itself, indicating that it was losing its sight. This proved to be the case, for a white speck was forming on the upper part of the eye, which, growing larger, at length obscured the whole sight, and the fish died. The water was only changed occasionally, just enough to prevent fouling by the unconsumed particles of food. In all succeeding experiments there never was another so apparently tame, because when the numbers were greater they alarmed each other. Of those which came to life in a pie dish, two survivors throve fairly well for a time, the water being changed two or three times a week. This water was brought from the river, and the last canful contained two young minnows, which consisted chiefly of eyes and shadows, so transparent were they. No sooner did the little salmon perceive them than they followed them about, and examined them attentively. They did not attack them that day, but next morning both the minnows were gone; one of the salmon was dead, and the other so shaky that I turned it out into the river. This fish had only one eye. To return to the egg, which at first is perfectly round, though it gradually becomes pear-shaped, and which is so transparent that what takes place in the interior can easily be seen, at least in the first stages. Little drops that look like oil separate and rise to the top, where they form a sort of nucleus, about the centre of which vital action originates. The drops vary in size, in number, and in intensity of colour, and the darker they are the stronger the fish that comes out. When the egg comes to rest this action begins almost immediately, and any material disturbance is fatal after they have remained motionless for about twenty-four hours, the vital forces which tend in an upward direction being apparently unable to sustain the shock of a sudden reversal, neither can they endure a sudden violent change of temperature. They cannot, indeed, be moved with safety until the fluid contents of the outer membrane become sufficiently consolidated, and that is not till the eyes are visible. This is in about fifty-eight days; but no precise date can be given, as there is sometimes a difference of a week in the hatching of eggs taken from the same parent at the same time, and undergoing precisely the same treatment. The outer membrane, at first transparent, becomes opaque and apparently thicker, but not so as to hinder the growth of the young fish from being seen, somewhat indistinctly it is true, but still it can be discerned curled up in its narrow cell. In about eighty days the membrane bursts and the young fish emerges, the back generally being the first part to appear. Sometimes it requires a little assistance to free itself from its covering, which then resembles a piece of white skin. Immense eyes, a transparent body with a large yellow bag beneath it, and a gaping mouth give it a helpless look. After a short rest it begins to try its locomotive powers, and darts about at intervals like a small balloon, sometimes head first, sometimes tail first, and apparently without any definite object; but when more accustomed to the exercise of its new powers it uses them instinctively for the purpose of hiding itself, and the greatest numbers are to be found crowded together in the darkest corners of the breeding-place. While they are transparent they are particularly well adapted to be viewed under the microscope; the intermittent current of the arterial blood running from head to tail, and the continuous flow of the venous blood in the opposite direction being very interesting. In one that was resting on the bottom of a dish (the coloured figures on which were visible through its body), close to the opening of the imperfect gill cover there was a seeming ciliary motion of the gills, which a magnifying glass showed to be the pectoral fins in extremely rapid motion; and the question suggested itself, was this an effort of Nature to cause a flow of water through the gills which did not exist in the dish, but which would always be present in the running stream? There was no response from the pie dish, and the question remains unanswered. The whole process is extremely interesting from the time when the little oil drops begin to form the nucleus wherein starts the first throb that indicates the site of the future heart, and whence the first streak of red blood begins to permeate the yolk, to the time—one hundred and thirteen days—when the yolk is entirely absorbed into the body and the perfect fish is there. Three days after the latter stage young fish fed with almost all kinds of fish, flesh, and fowl, free from fat, seemed to take them all equally well, and when wanted to feed they invariably responded to a current made by stirring the water. When moved into a tub with stones in it they chose their stations after the manner of their elders, and the big ones took precedence in helping themselves to the food. Here they seemed to keep their condition pretty well, but could not be kept after they had been discovered by the cats, when they had to be turned out into the river. When they cease to be transparent dark marks like saddles may be seen on their backs, which indicate the position of the so-called brands or finger marks. It is not easy to keep them in confinement after they get to be about two inches long, as even then they show a quarrelsome disposition, attacking each other from behind and trying to have a nip at the tail fin. Though they may have been reared in a dish they seem to be by no means at a loss how to act in the river, for they immediately betake themselves to cover under the stones as if they were quite familiar with their new habitation, and comport themselves exactly as their congeners who have begun life in the usual manner. These latter may be seen in the early summer darting about from stone to stone when disturbed, quite near the edge of the shallow water, as if aware that there they were safe from their enemies; but their growth is wonderfully rapid, and by the middle of June they may be found five or six inches long basking in the sun in the shallowest streams, and feeding voraciously during the long summer day. In the autumn they may weigh as much as four and a quarter ounces, but such a weight is not common. During the winter progress does not seem to be so rapid, but here we are met by the constantly recurring difficulty, viz. the impossibility of keeping the same individual under continuous inspection in the natural state of life. An unsuccessful spawn-catching expedition on the 16th December 1876 resulted in the capture of three brandlings, the largest of which was about seven inches long, and the smallest three and a half inches and the other five and a half. They were put into a pump trough half full of water, with some stones and bricks for shelter, and a worm or two given to them occasionally. They lived through the greater part of the winter, and the little one saved itself under the stones; but the middle-sized one suffered from the attacks of the big one, which contrived to nibble away half of its tail fin before meeting his own end, which came to pass through the trough becoming too full of water. He was found on the pavement, and no doubt he went overboard in making one of his rushes at the other. The death of that other, probably from want of proper food, left the small survivor at peace. He did not grow but was healthy and lively, and came out from his hold nearly every day to take his worm; but at length a day came when he did not respond, the next day it was the same, and on the stones being lifted he was found crushed to death, the victim of idle curiosity on the part of some stupid person whose clumsy manipulation caused the fatal result. The disappointment was grievous, and the more so because the spots and brand marks were nearly faded away, and in a few more days there would have been a perfect miniature salmon; now there are only the dried remains. In April those smelts which are prepared to migrate to the sea begin to drop down-stream into the tideway, and this movement continues till 'the first flood in May takes all the smelts away,' leaving those which still answer to the description of 'brandling,' and which belong to the succeeding generation, though a chance 'blue back' may sometimes be found late into June. There are also a few brandlings left whose size would seem to indicate that they ought to have passed into the smelt stage, being quite as large as those which have gone away to sea. These are almost without exception male fish. One remarkable exception, however, has occurred in the shape of a female brandling about eight inches long, which did not differ in outward appearance from a male, but which was full of roe of a dull yellow colour, the roe itself being composed of small ova, like grains of sand, interspersed with nearly full-sized ova, while the cavity nearest to the vent was crammed full of the burst skins of the larger ova, any outlet from the ovary not being perceptible. This was the only occasion when I found ova in the female brandling; the reproductive organs of the male fish were, at the same time, quite rudimentary, though at spawning time in autumn they would be in full activity. 17th April 1843, caught a fresh-run fish, weight 12 lbs. 12 oz., only contents of the stomach three March brown creepers. In the same year a fish taken 6th November, weighing 5 lbs. 10 oz., contained 1 lb. of roe; 412 eggs to the ounce, 6592. 13th November, fish 10 lbs. 4 oz., roe 2 lbs. 2 oz.; 417 to the ounce, 14,178. 14th November, fish 14 lbs. 5 oz., roe 3 lbs.; 313 eggs to the ounce, 15,024. Then finding that only hen fish took I gave up for the season.

The young of the common trout go through their earliest stages, which are just like those which the young salmon go through; but their distinctive marks soon begin to show, and differences in shape and colour become more and more apparent as they advance in age. The young salmon has some red spots along the lateral line, and from one to three dark spots on the gill covers; the brands are mostly in pairs, equal above and below the lateral line, equal in number on each side, and usually in pairs of eleven, nine, and seven. The least numbers that I have seen were seven on one side and six on the other; the greatest thirteen and fifteen on two of the Lune fish hatched at Stockton for the Board. The brands of the bull-trout are disposed with less regularity; the gill cover and the back fin are spotted with many dark spots. The pectoral fins of the bull-trout are of a bright orange colour, the other fins white, with a narrow black fringe to the tail fin, while the young trout of the same size have all the fins more or less yellow. The dark spots on the back of the young salmon are much fewer than those on the backs of the trout and bull-trout, and are seldom found below the lateral line, while those of the two last are found both above and below that line. On the common trout brown and red spots are intermixed, the brand marks not extending much above and below the lateral line, and soon disappearing entirely. The scales of the salmon smelts are easily rubbed off, the brand marks fade away gradually, and the spots decrease; the back of the young salmon taking a steel blue shade, and its fins a green colour, sometimes running whitish in the lower fins.

In order to test their rate of growth, I had about three hundred smelts marked in 1867 by cutting off the button fin, which does not grow again. I caught fish so marked repeatedly before they went to sea, from whence the greater number never returned, at least not to my knowledge;

but on the 1st October in that year a marked fish [1] was taken weighing 4¼ lbs. Taking the smelt to be only 1 oz. when it leaves the river in May, that shows an increase in weight of four hundred times in sixteen months after hatching.

With the male salmon at the time of spawning, his combined black, brown, olive, yellow, red, and gold sometimes form a gorgeous pattern which reminds one of an India shawl. These colours soon fade when spawning is over. I have seen salmon literally black all over, but I never saw either the scurf or the bull-trout black, or arrayed in the gorgeous colours above mentioned; [2] only a light yellow tinge on the scurf, and more and larger spots on the bull-trout. The dark tinge caused by peat water is evanescent and soon disappears, either on the clearing of the water or the death of the fish; but while it lasts it is sometimes impossible to distinguish the bull-trout from the common trout by the colour. The best indication is the difference between the heads, and especially the teeth. A 2 lb. bull-trout being young, his teeth are small in proportion to his size; but the 2 lb. trout will have such a gang of teeth as may be expected to belong to a veteran tyrant of the water—sharp, crooked, and larger; and after being out of the

---

[1] It is doubtful whether this was not a fish which had accidentally lost the button fin.

[2] I have often seen in other rivers female bull-trout with belly and sides as black as ink; at the same time the males looked like glorious golden yellow trout.—A. H. C.

water for twenty-four hours the bull-trout will have become much the brighter of the two. In most fish, indeed, the colour induced by contact with coloured substances gives place soon after death to what may be called the natural hue. I have taken a salmon of a dull lead colour, and two others of a delicate rose colour, which faded soon after they became dry, and which I thought might possibly have been caused by contact with the red sandstone. The sea-trout only take on a yellowish tinge at spawning time, but they remain longer in the river, and look like a flash of silver when they spring out of the water in the light of an April sun. I have sometimes caught trout in the Tees which had their sides covered with a pink tinge like that on the tip of the button fin, and occasionally brandlings whose sides were as yellow as a buttercup. In fact, shades of colour, changing with changing conditions, are almost endless.

Leaving out of account man—the universal enemy—the adult salmon have few enemies to contend with in the Tees. The seal has disappeared from Seaton Snook. The otter can only supply a hunt once or twice in a season. Far different was it when the old otters and their young might be heard and seen on a fine summer's night, whistling and playing about in the Brig pool, and when the sound of the cow's horn on Croft Bridge would bring together a jovial crew to join the hunt with their dogs and otter spears, seldom without a find. All the same, the salmon were not much better for the destruction of their four-footed enemies by the otter hunters, for the same men were expert with the leister and the trows, and rarely allowed a fish to escape in the summer, besides spearing them on the streams at spawning time. The otter is said to be very destructive to salmon by reason of a habit which it has of biting a piece out of the shoulder, and leaving the rest of the fish. If that be so, what becomes of it? I have for many years carefully looked out for signs of otter: I have frequently seen their seal where the sand would take a print; I have seen the backbone of a salmon stripped of flesh; I have seen the lower half of a large trout left on a rock in midstream; I have seen many skeletons of small fish left where the fish had been eaten; I have seen ova among the otter's spraint, which had passed through its body undigested; and I do not believe that the otter confines itself to taking a small piece out of the shoulder of a salmon. Such unqualified statements only mislead.

The young fish have more numerous enemies. In addition to the danger of being devoured by larger fish of their own or of other kinds, which is common to all fishes, they are liable to suffer from the depredations of the heron, the kingfisher, the water ouzel, and, more rarely, the seagull. The destructive power of the heron is well known; fortunately none of the birds named are numerous in the Tees. There were a good many kingfishers in the Tees, but a great many perished in a hard winter between twenty and thirty years ago, and they have been scarce since then. The water ouzel chiefly frequents the upper waters; the gull seldom comes far inland—and probably the damage which they all do is not very material. The brandling (parr) forms the most attractive bait that I know of for pike, perch, and chub. Two of the latter have been seen to chase one as a brace of greyhounds course a hare. After many turns it was driven ashore on a steep gravel bed, from whence it fell back and was devoured by its nearest pursuer. I don't know whether I ought to class spiders among the enemies; but one morning I found in my hatching dish a large spider, and a very handsome one he was, striped with longitudinal bars of light and dark grey disposed alternately. He was covered with long hairs; and, on being disturbed, sank in the water, taking with him bubbles of air adhering to his body just as I have seen the water ouzel do. The dish was standing on a table in the middle of the room. Where he came from, and how he got there, I know not; but appearances were against him, and I did not like to trust my newborn infants in his company, so I made him scarce.

There are not many very large fish taken in the Tees, and probably there never will be. In a river so small and so hard fished, it cannot be expected that more than a chance fish now and then should be allowed to live long enough to grow very large. James Teasdale's sea-trout, which weighed 38 lbs. when it was caught, is by far the largest fish of which I have heard. I saw it before it was stuffed. It was a male, and the milt was whole though it was taken in April. Several years ago, on the motion of Canon Tristram, the Tees Fishery Board resolved to try the introduction of fish from the West Coast, where fish much larger than the Tees fish were said to be far from uncommon. It was left to Canon Tristram and myself to carry out the resolution. Canon Tristram was unable to go, but I went to Kirkby Lonsdale twice, and procured another consignment of ova to be sent. I did not see any fish larger than I had seen in the Tees, and I have not hitherto seen any increase in size which can be traced to these Lune fish, or to the thousand Rhine salmon which Mr. Buckland gave to the Tees Board. It is too soon to look for the effect of the Tay fish which were turned into the river last year; but, reasoning from analogy, it may be expected that the introduction of fresh blood will lead to improvement.

It has been supposed that my long experience would enable me to say something worth hearing about fishing matters; but, unless the above-written notes may be so considered, I hardly think that such is the case. In these days of floss silk lines, drawn gut, and dry fly, I can't pretend to teach. The scientific modern angler would rate me little higher than an old fossil ; being, as I am, one of the primæval sort whose 'fettlements' were principally composed of a tangle of coloured silks, bits of cobbler's wax, hooks, gut, feathers, etc., very much mixed : who sat down on the bank and imitated, as well as his skill, or want of skill, would allow, the fly that was 'on,' or perhaps mended his rod top with his knife and a bit of waxed thread. In fact, a great part of the amusement consisted in the making and mending of his own 'graithing.' Except March brown, green drake, and Mayfly, his flies were mostly known to him by the names of the materials of which they were made, as woodcock and orange, snipe and yellow, swift and purple, etc., or as light and dark blue, the colours indicating what silk was to be used. When I began to fish the use of the running reel was far from being universal.[1] To the top of a two-jointed rod a hair loop was fixed, to which a corresponding loop on the line was attached. The horsehair line, about the same length as the rod, tapered to three hairs, and ended in a loop to which the 'stintin' or cast of flies, numbering from one to four, was appended, the drop flies being called 'jacks' and the line itself a 'taime.' When not in use the line was wound round the

---

[1] He caught his first salmon in 1820, and in his later years used to use light spliced rods up to twenty-two feet in length. I remember his telling me that when fishing with his friend, John Errington, on the North Tyne, he had seen the village schoolmaster at Warden take a number of fine salmon with such a rod as he has described with a hair line and no reel at all, and without losing a fish.—A.H.C

hand, and fastened to the rod at a convenient height above the butt-end by means of a piece of stick put through the wound-up line, then behind the rod and through the line again.

In the long-run the man who believes in his fly and sticks to it is more likely to do well than one who is perpetually changing. It appears, too, that the capture of fish is not absolutely necessary for the enjoyment of angling as a pastime. I have seen men fishing away very contentedly in water so clear that they might have seen that there was not a fish within yards of them. To beginners, I say fish with your heads, don't be in a hurry, keep up your rod top, and never have any slack line in the water.

J. C. C.

XXV

NATURAL HISTORY AND OTHER POINTS

MY DEAR BOYS,—Almost every point in the life-history of the salmon has been the subject of bitter controversy. The water keeps its secrets well. From the earliest times down to a year or two ago no man knew even where the common eel spawned or whence the swarms of elvers appeared in our rivers. The wildest theories were believed. Eels were supposed to be generated spontaneously out of mud or slime and even to grow out of horse hairs that fell into ponds and ditches. Now at last it has been found that every eel in the remotest inland pond, and not only in our own country but in France, Holland, and even Russia, has made his way there from breeding-places in the depths of the Atlantic Ocean beyond the five hundred fathom line, and imagination proves almost less strange than fact.

So of salmon. Not until the experiments of John Shaw of Drumlanrig, in artificially hatching and rearing the ova of salmon, were made known about 1840 was it established with certainty that parr and smolts were both the young of the salmon. Many believed parr to be a different fish, though by rubbing off the silvery scales of the smolt the 'brandling' or parr marks, and the red spots too, can plainly be seen beneath them.

Systematic markings of fish, both by private persons and lately by the Board of Agriculture and Fisheries, have at last begun to accumulate evidence of a fairly definite nature as to the main facts of the salmon's life-history. We know, for instance, that he does often find his way to strange rivers, at times even to rivers far away from that in which he was born; that the smolt, after spending one to one and a half or possibly two years in the sea, may return to the river for the first time either as the grilse of one year or as the small spring fish of the next. We have even got on his scales some rough chart of the salmon's life, thanks to the discovery—by Mr. H. W. Johnston —that the scale under the microscope reveals concentric lines of growth varying in closeness for summer and for winter feeding, and showing plainly the fraying caused after spawning by the great shrinking in bulk undergone by the fish as a kelt. But for the details of all these things you must read some of the latest books dealing with the life-history of the fish. At the present moment Mr. Calderwood's book [1] is the best that I know. But even he assures us

---

[1] *Life of the Salmon* (Arnold, 1907). It seems plain that the salmon often stays at sea till his fifth or sixth year, and returns first as a great fish of 20, 30, or 40 lbs. weight.

that the eggs of the salmon are laid in a trough and then covered up by the fish, a statement that, I think, is demonstrably erroneous, yet one that still is copied from one book into another without any proper examination into its accuracy.

Again, 'Do salmon feed in fresh water?' What angry quarrels and what oceans of controversial ink that simple question has been responsible for! I am not going to argue it over again. Blue-books have proved—as we all thought—by scientific evidence that the stomachs of salmon during their stay in fresh water undergo some change whereby they are not in a condition to digest food. After a decent interval other 'scientific gents.' have then proved equally clearly that the first scientific gents. were all wrong, and have proved that the condition seen in the earlier examinations was due to the very fact that the stomach of the salmon *had* the power of digestion and had digested itself after its owner's death. In a copy of the *Field* that is before me now, a gentleman writes from Aboyne on the Dee to say that he has just taken out of the mouth of a clean spring fish of 8 lbs., killed on a flight of bait hooks, a half-digested salmon parr, three and a half inches in length. I myself have found the mushy head of a small trout stuck on a triangle after landing an autumn salmon on the minnow, and have caught a salmon on a bunch of worms and found the hook embedded in the actual stomach of the fish.[1] Your great-grandfather, on the 17th April 1843, found three March brown creepers in the stomach of a spring salmon. And many other anglers have at times found food in salmon in fresh water. But still, in almost ninety-nine cases out of a hundred, no food is found inside salmon that have been examined. Why? Well, they *can* eject it if they want to do so. My fish caught on the worm *had* ejected the worms and left the bare hook in his belly. But I do not think that is the whole explanation by any means. The fish are rolling fat, and food is not essential to them. I think that is proved, and it is also proved that they eat very little. But I think it clear that they do eat.

In 1894 and 1895 two gentlemen, Messrs. Gray and Tosh, examined 1694 salmon from the lower reaches of the Tweed, of which 1442 were caught in the Berwick nets. The examination of the stomachs of so large a number of salmon, as might have been expected, was most instructive, and the results were as follows:—

Of the fish caught in the months of March, April, May, and June, 43%, 37%, 16%, and 13% respectively were found to have food in their stomachs. In the months of July, August, and September the proportion of fish, in the stomachs of which any food was found, fell to 1·7%, 3·8%, and 2% respectively. These records show pretty

---

[1] See *ante*, page 107.

SEA-LICE

clearly that in the early months of the year and in cold water salmon do commonly contain some food, and that they eat less and less as the summer comes on, until they reach the minimum in July, after which month there is again a trifling increase. These fish, too, were caught at or near the mouth of the river, and in the sea admittedly salmon do eat—must eat—yet the proportion having any food contained in the stomach diminishes almost to vanishing point by midsummer. The food found in the bellies of these fish was chiefly herrings, with occasional sand-eels, whiting, and haddock, and there was also found in them

- 1 caterpillar,
- 4 feathers,
- 1 beech leaf,
- and moss, blades of grass, and sedge.

Another point of controversy is the period during which sea-lice can remain on a salmon in fresh water. In some experiments made by the Fishery Board at Aberdeen with living salmon placed in a sea-tank which was then gradually filled with fresh water, it was found that the lice no longer adhered to the salmon after four or five days in the fresh water. But I am convinced that most people are unaware that there is a common fresh-water parasite much like the sea-louse, which adheres to salmon in summer and autumn in the same way as the sea-louse does, and of course gives no indication as to the length of time that the salmon has been out of the sea. Some years ago, noticing that these parasites—commonly regarded by anglers as sea-lice—were to be found in August upon trout as well as upon salmon, I collected a number of them, and by the courtesy of Mr. W. E. Archer, of the Board of Agriculture and Fisheries, lice taken from yellow trout, from bull-trout, and from salmon were submitted for examination to the official expert, who reported that they were all examples of the same species of parasite, namely, *Argulus foliaceus*, which is a fresh-water parasite, and only rarely or accidentally found on fish in the sea. Now this fraudulent little beast is almost the same size as a sea-louse, but looks rather like a translucent greenish wood-louse flattening itself against the body of the salmon, to which it sticks not only by its shape, but by means of a set of concealed feet armed with relatively large, flat suckers. The sea-louse has a waist and a sort of tail—is shaped roughly like the figure 8 with a tail.

When, therefore, you are tempted to assert that some salmon caught forty or fifty miles above the tideway is proved, by the presence of sea-lice, to have been only a day or two ago in the sea, it would be as well to make sure that you are not founding that belief—as I am perfectly certain that many people do—upon the presence of *Argulus foliaceus*, which you mistake for *Monoculus piscinus*. Pretty names, aren't they!

CLEAN OR KELT

I have already told you the way to tell, by its incessant kicking when lifted out of the water, a parr or a smolt from a small trout. It is also a help to the beginner, anxious to do right, to remember that parr or smolts, moreover, are very seldom more than seven inches long. I will try now to give you some idea of how to tell a clean spring fish from a really well-mended kelt. It is a question that has caused agonies of doubt to the inexperienced fisher, or to the fisher who has had but little spring fishing, because if he brings home the wrong fish, besides breaking the law— which probably won't trouble him so much— he will incur the merciless chaff of his friends. In the first place let me warn you that a silvery brightness is no proof of the fish being a clean fish. On the contrary, a clean fish, though often very brilliant, is not such a dead white as a good kelt. In the water the clean fish flashes rather a golden colour, the kelt a dead or silvery white. But if, when a fish is landed, a rosy pink flush—a peach-coloured opalescence—can be plainly seen along the belly and sides, that fish is a clean fish. But then that fish will be such a good fish that no doubt is possible on the matter. He will be short and thick and 'as hard as a board.' The real difficulty arises with spring fish that have been a long time up from the sea and have lost something of their condition; even then they are shapely fish, and that, after all, is the very best test of the question clean or kelt. Thickness is the one thing that the kelt never has. If a fish looks long and lean, put him back; he is a kelt, however bright he may be and however clean his gills. But if the gills of a lean fish are infested with that maggot-like parasite (*Lernæa salmonis*), then that makes his keltship undeniable; the great majority of kelts have this horrible parasite devouring the fringes of their gills, or else show the whitish lumps and scars where they have been at work. But the presence of this parasite is not absolute proof that the fish on which they are found is a kelt. I have seen one or two, though rarely, on the gills of undoubted and unquestionable fresh fish.

A slack vent also indicates that the owner is a kelt; the vent of a clean-run fish is hard and firm and will not protrude, as does the kelt's, if the stomach near by is pressed in.

A really good new-run spring fish will generally have all the fins clean and hard, and will show no sore or redness on the lower ray of the tail. A kelt, on the other hand, will generally (but not always) show a frayed and raw tail, and some signs of scraping and redness along the whole under side of the fish. This redness and fraying is a bad sign, but not necessarily fatal. A spring fish that has lain in the river for some time will often show some redness of the lower ray of the tail fin, and may show other abrasions and redness along the belly.

Of the points I have mentioned no one item is

decisive, but the accumulation of several almost always makes it fairly clear what your verdict ought to be upon the question kelt or clean.

The signs of the kelt are :—

1. Gill maggots.
2. Leanness, or rather a want of plumpness, and an apparently large head.
3. A slack and easily protruded vent.
4. Frayed tail and fins.
5. A fishy smell, and scales coming off easily.

The characteristics of a spring fish are :—

1. Shapely form, in particular depth from back to belly.
2. No fishy smell.
3. Clean gills.
4. A hard, firmly closed vent.
5. Generally dark fins, not abraded, or very little abraded, by lying on the river bottom.

The flesh also is harder and firmer than that of the kelt, but this point is more easily noticed after death, and you must make up your mind promptly whilst the question of life or death hangs in the balance. And when you decide that the fish is a kelt you must not merely take him by the tail and fling him in, neck and crop, unless you have landed him very quickly and have got the hook out instantly and without holding him down. If you have played him for long, and have had to hold him down firmly to get out the hook from his jaws, the fish will be much exhausted, and if you fling him in carelessly will very probably turn over on his back and die. You must slip him gently into the water, and if he does not quickly swim off you must prop him upright in the shallows between two stones in a current and with his head upstream, and there he will slowly recover his strength. But if a kelt has been much exhausted you will often find him still lying there like a log a quarter or even half an hour after you have left him. Then it is as well not to leave him so, or he may be attacked by foxes, otters, or herons. If you walk up to him he will bolt off into deep water and will be safe, but if he does not bolt, you must leave him.

A salmon, as you know, has frequently got a great many black spots (or X spots, as they are called, from the shape which they generally take) along its sides, and sometimes it is not very easy for a beginner to tell whether a fish is a salmon or not. But the spots afford one a useful guide, and it is this: on the true salmon, and, of course, on the grilse, there are no spots below the medial line except two or three on the gill cover, and occasionally one or two close to the gill cover and just below the line.

XXVI

THE OLD SALMON ACTS

MY DEAR BOYS,—My old master, F. W. Maitland, the Downing Professor at Cambridge, first showed his brother scholars what masses of general historical knowledge are to be found in the old legal records of our country. The salmon has been held in high honour for centuries. Lawgivers and lawyers have watched and fought over him, and in Scotland, more especially, Acts of Parliament have been many for his protection; and most of these stood unrepealed until our own days. There are, at least, seventeen acts of the Scottish Parliament before the year 1504 dealing with the safety of salmon and smolts. Let us look at some of these old acts, and whilst we do it, we shall not be less worthy salmon fishers if we spend a little time in picturing the state of the country when those laws were made.

The first Scottish act that I know of is one of 1318, in the reign of Robert I., the victor of Bannockburn—King Robert the Bruce. It provides that all who have cruives or fisheries, dams or mills in tidal waters, shall allow the little salmon or smolts, or fry of other kinds of sea or fresh-water fish (*salmunculi vel smolti seu fria alterius generis piscium maris vel aquæ dulcis*) to ascend and descend by having clear spaces not less than 'two thumbs in length and three thumbs in breadth,' and, for penalty, provides that the offender shall have forty days' prison, and shall nevertheless be heavily fined. And it adds: '*Et defendit Dominus Rex ne presumat piscari ad salmones, vel salmunculos, temporis prohibitis, super antiquam pœnam,*' thus showing that there were still older acts or ordinances forbidding fishing at certain times.

Doubtless other acts followed, but the next that I have found are two passed by a Parliament at Perth under James I. of Scotland in the year 1424. The first of these is entitled '*Of slauchter of salmonde in tyme forbodyne be the law,*' and the other '*Of crufis and yaris*' (cruives and yairs, *i.e.* salmon traps and salmon yards or dams).[1] Three other acts of this year are interesting. Chapter 11 (of the Record edition) is '*Of playing at the fut ball*'; chapter 20, '*Of rukis biggande in treis*' (rooks building in trees); chapter 21, '*Of murbyrne*' (moor-burning). Others are against her-

[1] This act of 1424 is as follows:—

'Item, It is ordanyt that all crufis and yaris set in fresche watteris, quhar the see fillis and ebbis, the quhilke destroyis the fry of all fisches, be destroyit and put away for thre yeris to cum, not gaynstandand ony privileges or fredom geifyn in the contrare, under the payne of IC£. And thai that has crufis in fresche watteris that thai ger keip the lawis anentis the Satterday slop (the Saturday slap) and suffer thaime not to stande in forbodyne tyme under the said payne. And that ilk hek (heck = the space between the bars) of the foresaidis crufis be iii inch wyde, as it is requirit in the auld statutes maid of befor.'

etics and Lollards (*anentis heretikis and lollardis*), of stealers of green wood and breakers of orchards, one '*Of stollyn wode fundyn in uthir lordis landis*,' one '*Anent stalkeris that slais deir.*' Others are against harbourers of thieves, reivers, and rebels, and '*Of wapynschawingis*'—weaponshowings, four times each year, says an act of 1491, a constantly recurring title telling of the care taken to ensure that all men were properly armed for the defence of their country, a salutary lesson to our less manly days.

The first act of the year 1426 is one '*Anent the custom of salmondis and uthir fische.*' There is one regulating the price of work made by craftsmen, and one '*Of the fee of workmen*,' another '*Anent the sawing of quhete* (wheat), *peis and benis*,' and another about the building and repairing of castles and manor places.

In 1427 comes an act '*Of crufis in watteris*' (cruives), and another '*Anent wylde foulis*,' and a few delightful others. Cap. 5, '*That baronis ger seik the quhelpis* (go seek the whelps) *of the wolfis and sla thame*'; cap. 10, '*That na man cum to courtis with gaddering*' (gathering, *i.e.* with a multitude of retainers). Occasionally the records go into Latin, but they soon return to the native tongue.

In 1429 cap. 22 is '*Anent the act of the fishing of salmonde.*' Caps. 8, 9, and 10 are sumptuary laws: '*Of the array of knychtis, lordis, and utheris*,' '*Of the array of burgessis and their wyffis*,' and '*Of the array of yemen and commonis.'* Caps. 11, 12, and 14 are '*Anent the maner of grathing* (furnishing) *of gentilmen and utheris for weir* (war),' of yeomen for war, and of burgesses for war.

In 1431 is an act '*Anent the selling or barteryng of salmonde out of the realme,*' then come acts '*Of the persute of thaim that committis slauchter*' (murder), and '*Of the slaar fugitive from the law and proclamation to be maid not to resett* (harbour) *him.*'

In 1436 is an act '*Tuiching the selling of salmond to Inglis men.*' Foreign trade was in the air. Another act is '*Anent Inglis clath and uthir gudis,*' another '*Of bying of wyne fra Flemyngis of the Dam.*' Other acts deal with night-revellers, with holding courts '*for juging of thevis,*' and another is about the selling of thieves (as slaves) by lords of regality, sheriffs, or barons.

In 1438 is an act for arresting and taking surety of rebels or '*unrewlful men,*' harboured or holden within castles or fortalices. 'Unruleful men' is very pretty. In 1449 is an act '*for the keping of trewis* (truce) *on the bordouris,*' and another '*for the away putting of sornaris* (a sorner is one who takes food and lodging by force or threats), *fenyet fulis, bardis and sic like rynnaris aboute.*' The poets of to-day would not like to be classed with these vagrants. The year 1452 seems to have been a year of scarcity. Parliament met in August and passed three acts : '*Anent the thresching out of corne,*' '*Of halding wittail in gyrnall*' (garner), '*Of bying and halding wittail to a derthe.*'

In 1455 an act provides for '*Ane ambaxat to the pape,*' and again in 1485 for '*an ambassat to our haly fader the paip.*' Trouble was brewing with England. Acts passed in October provide for the punishment of any giving warning of the riding of '*ane host*' into England, and that none pass into England without leave, and that no Englishman come into Scotland '*withoutyn conduct or assoverance*' (safe-conduct or sureties), then '*That na Scottisman bring in the realme ony Inglismen*'; and after several warlike statutes comes one, '*Thir saide statutis to be proclamyt at raidis maide in Inglande.*' Apparently 'Inglande' retaliated, for the last act of 1455 is for laying of garrisons upon the '*bordours,*' and in 1456 we get '*Of the supple of the bordouris,*' '*Of the defence of the realme,*' and then three '*Of cartis of weir,*' '*Of the sending to France,*' and '*Of the pestilence and governance thereof.*'

In 1457 Parliament is very active. There are acts '*Anent the slauchter of rede fische*'—foul salmon, of course, for the very next act is '*Anent ingynis that lat* (let or hinder) *the smoltis to pas to the se.*' Other acts are '*Anent plantacione of woddis and heggis and sawing of broum*'; '*Anent the sawing of quheit* (wheat), *peys and benys*'; '*Anent the destroying of rukis, crawys, and uthir foulis of reif*' (of reiving—theft); '*For the destruccione of wolfis*'; '*Anentis the slaaris of haris and destruccione of cunnyngis'* (coneys); and *'That all personis sall cum to courtis in sobyr and quiet maner.'*

But it was one thing to pass laws, quite another to have them obeyed. The last effort of this Parliament is an *'Exhortatione be the thre Estatys to our Soverane Lord tuiching the diligent execusione of thir actis and statutis.'*

In 1446: *'That na Inglis man have benefice within Scotland'*; *'That na schip be frachtit* (freighted) *without a charter party'*; *'Licence to merchandis to sale to the Rochel Burdeus, France and Noroway.'*

Here is a title that is common: *'Of the mone.'* In 1467 we get *'Of the cours of the blak mone.'* Try to guess it! You will do it easily when I give you other acts of 1467: *'Of the cours of the quhite Scottis pennyis,' 'Of the cours of the Inglis penny,' 'Of the cours of the mone of uthir realmes, and of the blak pennyis.'* Blak, or blac, mone is, of course, copper money, as against the white or silver penny, and the coin called *'the crounite grote.'* The coinage is a source of constant trouble, *e.g.* in 1485, *'Anent the plakkis and half plakkis*; 1486, *'The crying doune of the new plakkis'*; 1491, *'Anent them that refuse to tak gold that is crakkit.'*

In 1469 salmon again appear: Cap. 13, *'For the multiplication of fisch, salmon grilses and trowtis.'* In 1478, *'For observing of the act anent the cruvis sett in watteris,'* and another, *'Of the*

THE BARREL OF SALMON

bind of salmonde' (the bind seems to have been a measure, (?) a barrel, like the English statutory barrel of salmon = 42 gallons). Again in 1487, 1488, 1493, 1573, 1584, 1661, and 1696 are acts ' *anent the barell of salmonde, the pakking and mesure of the samyn.*'

In 1481 there is more trouble with England. In March and April the Scots Parliament sits, and their acts reflect their mood. ' *Of the breaking of the trewis be the revare* (reiver), *Edward calland him King of Ingland*' ; ' *The maner of redynes* (readiness) *for resisting and aganestanding of the said revare Edward*' ; cap. 7, a grant of 600 men of war to be laid in garrison on the borders ; cap. 8, of the places that the said men of war shall be laid in ; cap. 9, ' *Of the captanis of the saidis placis*' ; cap. 10, ' *Of the waigis of the capitanys foresaide*' ; ' *Of an ambaxat to the King of France for help and supplie.*' Then from April 1481 until December 1482 is blank. *Inter arma silent leges:* Dec. 2, 1482, chapter 1, ' *Of pece and aliance with Ingland.*'

But to return to our salmon and smolts, cruives and yairs. Further acts follow, *e.g.* 1488 (*of cruffis and fisch dammys*), 1489 (*cruvis and fisch yardis*), 1503 (*slaughter of red fische*), 1535 (*off red fische, smoltis and slaying of salmond in forbodyn tyme,* and a second act ' *off cruvis and yaris* '), 1563 (*cruivis and fische dammys*), 1567 ('*anent blak fische, cutting of grene wod and slauchter of smoltis* '), 1597 (*cruvis and yairis, slauchter of reid fische and smoltis be wandis or utherwyse*). Almost identical acts in 1581, in 1594, and in 1597 culminate in an act passed in November 1600, declaring '*Slaying of salmond in forbiddin tyme to be* ANE CRYME OF THEIFT *in tyme cumming.*'

There we will leave them, but I cannot part with these old Scottish acts without giving you one or two more of their jewels.

'*Anent the dampnable opunyeouns of heresy*' (1525) ; '*Anent them that schutis with gunnys at deir and wylde foulis*' (1551) ; '*Anent the chesing of sic ane personage as Robert Hude, Lytill Johne, Abbottis of Unressonn or Quenis of Maij*' (1555). Poor Robin Hood and Little John were out of favour in these stern days. A letter received from Queen Mary in France is said to be from '*Fontane Bellew*' (Fontainebleau). Forestry is encouraged. '*Anentis the planting of woddis, forrestis, orchardis and parkis*' (1555). In order to detect stealing, it is enacted in 1563 '*That beif, muttoun, veill and like bestiall be brocht to mercatis* (markets) *with hyde, skin and birne.*' 1661, '*Against sueareing*'; 1695, '*Against prophaneness.*'

Here are two acts with a curiously modern sound : '*Anent the makaris and upsettaris of plackardes and billis*' (1567) ; '*For instructioun of the youth in musik*' (1579).

In an act of 1592 anent the common good of boroughs, this glorious phrase occurs : '*nocht-*

withstanding of quhatsumevir.' Even Scottish caution could no further go.

The Old English Acts

In England we cannot show such wealth of statutes, but in 1225, in the ninth year of King Henry III., it was provided that '*all weirs [1] from henceforth shall be utterly put down by Thames and Medway and through all England, but only by the sea coasts.*' Then in the famous Statute of Westminster II., in the thirteenth year of King Edward I., that is 1285, is this enactment :—

'It is provided that the waters of Humber, Owse,[2] Trent, Done,[3] Arre,[4] Derwent, Werfe,[5] Nid, Yore, Swale, Tese, Tine, Eden, and all other waters wherein salmons be taken, shall be in defence for taking salmons from the Nativity of our Lady unto St. Martin's Day, and that likewise young salmons shall not be taken nor destroyed by nets, nor by other engines at mill-pools from the midst of April unto the Nativity of St. John Baptist. And in places where such water banks are there shall be assigned overseers of this statute, which, being sworn, shall

---

[1] Weirs are Kidelli, in the Latin version, and the word 'kiddle' is still used, meaning stake fences set in the stream for taking salmon, the Scottish yairs or yards. In this English version of the statute, 'but' only by the seashore means 'save' only, etc. It is a mere confirmation of section 33 of the Great Charter of our liberties (A.D. 1215), which said this : *Omnes kydelli de cetero deponantur penitus de Thamisia et de Medewaye et per totam Angliam nisi per costeram maris.*

[2] Ouse.   [3] Don.   [4] Aire.   [5] Wharfe.

oftentimes see and inquire of the offenders; and for the first trespass they shall be punished by burning of their nets and engines, and for the second time they shall have imprisonment for a quarter of a year; and for the third trespass they shall be imprisoned a whole year; and as their trespass increaseth so shall the punishment.'

Packing and barrelling of salmon, as in Scotland, was dealt with by statute. The 22nd Edward IV., c. 2, provides for the true packing and gauging of salmons and eels in butts, barrels, and half-barrels, the butt to contain 84 gallons and the barrel 42 gallons 'well and truly packed' under pain of vi. s. and viii. d. '*The salmon is to be well and truly packed, that is to say, the great salmon by itself, without meddling of any grills or broken-bellied salmon with the same, and that all small fish, called grills, should be packed by themselves.*'

A statute of 11 Hen. VII. recites this earlier act, and regulates the payment of the overseers appointed to search the barrels, to enforce the law at the sum of '*one farthing per barrel and no more.*'

XXVII

ON TAKING A FISHING

MY DEAR BOYS,—If you wish to rent a piece of salmon fishing, it behoves you to be very wary indeed, or you may find that you have wasted not only your money but your holiday as well. I am sorry to say that many attractive offers of salmon fishing are nothing less than swindles, and that rivers are let year after year on records made in some altogether exceptional season. There are records which are carefully built up by incessant prawning and worming throughout the whole season, and there are known prawn fishers who get rivers offered to them at nominal rents, in order that the owners may obtain a record of this sort. Even honest records of catches made by fly fishing may mislead you, unless you ascertain that the fish were taken during the very months in which you intend to fish, and that it was not in some altogether abnormal season. On many British rivers the bulk of the fish are taken at the very end of the season; on most Norwegian rivers at the very beginning, and there is a large class of Scottish rivers in which fish are caught freely in early spring, and again in late autumn, but in which through the summer and early autumn the fish will not take the smallest notice of a fly—or of any bait or lure—although fine salmon are splashing about in every pool. Let me remind you of a few points that it is well to consider :—

(1) Go and see the water for yourself, or at the very least go and see some trustable man who has fished it. A river in which salmon are actually to be caught may yet be a mere sluggish ditch, fishable only in a wind, and hardly worth fishing even then, or maybe not wide enough to fish with any pleasure. If you cannot see the river, get photographs : they may give you some information ; but it is better in all cases to insist on being put into communication with some one who has fished the river as a tenant.

(2) Find out how many pools there are that are good salmon pools, what length of each of them is usually fished ; and as to each pool, whether it is fished from the bank, or by wading, or from a boat, and if from a boat, whether by casting or by harling.

(3) See the actual fishing books, over at least three or four *consecutive* seasons preceding the proposed tenancy. See how many salmon are caught with the fly each year over the very period that you are proposing to fish, and whether they are distributed fairly regularly over that time, or are got

chiefly in a few lucky periods. If the former is the case, you may feel pretty safe, but if the latter, then it probably means that fish can only be taken after floods, and you will be absolutely lost unless you are lucky enough to get floods also.

Do not easily accept explanations that there are no regular records. For waters that are let there *are* records, unless it is known that they could not bear inspection if they existed. Unless you know the man who makes them, be very shy of excuses for poor records, such as that the river was very little fished, or that the anglers who fished the water were unskilful. You will almost always find that your results will be much more like the worst than like the best that they show you. If everything is not fully and frankly answered to your satisfaction you should resolutely refuse to go further with the proposal. A bad salmon fishing is a most expensive luxury, and is a daily and hourly disappointment. You had much better go off to Norway or to Ireland and get some decent trouting. Salmon-fishing is almost always let on a rental based on the best takes of the best years, and very good salmon years are few and far between.

(4) Find out whether previous bags were made by keepers or with their assistance. They

are on the spot early and late, and more than you can ever hope to be. A catch made by strangers to the water is much more promising for you than an equal result achieved by resident anglers who know every mood of the river, and almost every stone of each pool in it.

(5) Ascertain most carefully whether you are to have the *exclusive* right of fishing, and over *both* sides of *all* the water. If you are not to get this, then find out who usually fishes any part of it, which side he has, and whether he fishes fly only or what baits he uses, and to what extent he and his guests usually fish. Many a good stretch of water is rendered almost useless to you by having a persistent prawner constantly fishing up and down the opposite bank. Even minnow fishing can be very annoying to a neighbour, though I have been guilty of that myself. You can never have the pleasure of leaving a pool quiet if some one else has the right to fish it when he chooses. And find out whether your *vis-à-vis* uses a boat or no upon your pools.

(6) It is just as well to have it made quite clear beforehand who is to pay the rates and taxes on the fishing rent—the rates often come as an unpleasant surprise to the fishing tenant.

(7) Of course such things as accommodation, boatmen, if needed, means of getting to and from the water, and distance of available shops for supplies must be considered; and they will occur to any one.

If you are going to have a long lease consult your lawyers, and see that you have in it the right to cut, or to require to be cut, willows, alders, and other bushes, which may interfere with the fishing. An alder or a willow which is a trifle whilst you can pass your rod over it, may become an obstacle of the most annoying kind in a year or two.

Other minor annoyances there are that local inquiry may reveal. You can inquire as to bad or slippery wading, muddy bottoms, and frequency of droughts (always find out whether the river in dry weather shrinks so much as to be hardly worth fishing; and when you go to see a river inquire carefully what is its *normal* height). A bull or even a lot of cattle depastured beside your best pools may be a source of intense annoyance. Bulls are queer-tempered beasts, especially with persons who fear them, and with strangers strangely dressed. However, if you engage a rustic with a stout cudgel, he will look after the bull and take care of your tackle on the bank at the same time.

XXVIII

A POSTSCRIPT

My dear Boys,—There are a few miscellaneous hints that I should like to give you, though most of them are not connected with salmon fishing.

The first one, however, is, or was so, for on cold days on getting home from the river we used always to find ready for us in the fender a jug of the most excellent brew that I have ever tasted—a hot mulled claret, and this is Falshaw's receipt for it :—

Take a shred of lemon rind, three cloves and two egg-cupfuls of water, and simmer these together for a few minutes. Then add a pint of claret and warm until it is nearly boiling. Add four to five lumps of sugar and, if you wish, two to three teaspoonfuls of cherry brandy, and serve in a small jug with claret glasses.

It may be worth while on a fishing excursion to know how to make and bake decent bread. Mr. E. B. Kennedy, in his delightful book, *Thirty Seasons in Scandinavia*, tells you how to do it.[1]

---

[1] His receipt is this :—Take 1 lb. wholemeal flour, rub into it a pat of butter, three or more teaspoons of Yeatman's baking powder (or yeast, if you can get it), add thin skimmed milk to make all consistent, mix quickly, and bake forty minutes in a quick oven. In Norway, as he tells you, wholemeal flour is sold as '*Graham's hvid mel.*'

FERRETING

With a loaf of fresh bread, a lump of butter (which can be pressed into a hole cut in the side of the loaf), and either a tin of sardines or a lump of cheese, any keen fisher may in the most out-of-the-way place have a luncheon fit for a king—too good, I think, for most of them.[1]

All boys love ferreting. Now, I *have* known the ferrets to lie up in the holes, and cause a trifling wait of an hour or two before they could be got out again; indeed, most people think that ferreting consists chiefly in waiting with frozen feet for the ferrets to come out. Generally the delay is caused by one or more failures to pick up the active little wretches when they come out to sniff the fresh air and to see, I suppose, whether you have gone home, before returning to worry their rabbit. Every ineffectual grab made at the neck of a ferret makes it more wild and more wary. If you use a bit of stout cord about eighteen inches long you may save yourselves all this trouble. Make a small loop at the end of the string; put a slip knot round the ferret's neck; draw it close and then make it fast and 'non-slip' by putting the loose end through the string collar that you have thus made and taking a half-hitch. Then the loose end, about a foot long, is towed about by the ferret as he works the holes, and when he appears at the entrance, and you come near to pick him up, he usually backs a little way down the hole, leaving the string now lying in front of him. You have only to lay hold

[1] See Appendix, Note 8.

of the string and lift him out at once. Not only does this save all trouble in picking up your ferrets, but they soon become very tame and very easy to handle when there is no longer any snatching at their necks as they dodge back into the hole.

Another tip, now, to clean your gun quickly and easily. Take the 'jag' of your cleaning rod, or take any other straight rod, and round the head of it wind and tie some string so as to make a small lump. Then keep three or four bits of oily flannel about four or five inches square—one always for the first wipe through, one or two for a further polish, and one well oiled for a last rub. You will only have to place a square of flannel on the lump at the end of your rod and you can not only push it through the barrel, but the string lump enables you to pull it back again, and to push and pull as often as you like. You can, indeed, rub the barrels quite warm in this way, and you can clean a gun in a couple of minutes, the same set of rags serving for dozens of cleanings.

Another tip to destroy rats—which are about the worst enemies of game eggs and chicks—is this. Carry an old jam-pot or a jar full of bisulphide of carbon, and, with a stick, dip a lump of rag, cotton wool, or waste of any sort into the liquid and push it as far as you can down each rat hole, and at once bung up the hole with earth. Every rat will be 'scumfished.' Bisulphide of carbon is very evil-smelling and very inflammable, so you must keep it well away from your face and

ODDS AND ENDS

from any light, but with ordinary care it is a perfectly safe thing to handle. Of course it will do only for rat holes in the open, in banks or hedges, and so on; in buildings the fumes are not in a sufficiently confined space to stifle the rats, even if you don't mind killing them there. And I need hardly add that rabbits in your young plantations can be exterminated in the same way.[1]

To taint out rabbits from their burrows for shooting days, a certain stinking oil, sold under the names of 'oil of hartshorn,' 'Dippel's oil,' 'animal oil,' or 'foxes oil,' is far the best thing to use, and there is no need to buy the same thing under a fancy name and at a fancy price to do the same work.

Also this oil painted on the stems of your young trees, or put on bits of rough string or sacking tied round the trees, will prevent rabbits from barking those trees for a whole winter.

[1] Don't put a match down the hole after the vapour has mixed with the air. You will remember a cousin doing that in Sussex and the explosion that followed, which shook a great oak tree over the hole and scared the keeper badly.

XXIX

SOME BOOKS ON FISHING

MY DEAR BOYS,—As I have said, books on angling are almost innumerable. Walton's book, published in 1653, is still the freshest and the most delightful of them all. But what he wrote about was chiefly bait fishing, and nothing that he says will help you at all in fishing for salmon or trout. But you must read him, though his book appeals less strongly to the keenness of boyhood than it does to older fishers, to those who are willing not to hurry, who can lay down their rod on a May morning the better to feel the mere pleasure of being alive, and who can enjoy to the full the temper of a writer ' whose ways are ways of pleasantness and all his paths are peace.' One, Colonel Venables, who, in 1662, wrote a book called *The Experienced Angler*, knew a great deal about fly fishing for both trout and salmon, and Charles Cotton Walton's friend, who wrote the latter part of the *Complete Angler*, was a real trout fisher in the sense we now understand fly fishing, and he was a scholar, who could write, too, about other things than fishing. What do you think of these few lines from some of his verses, as a picture of the

ANGLING BOOKS

long shadows of the setting sun on his Derbyshire hills?—

> 'A very little, little flock
> Shades thrice the ground that it would stock,
> Whilst the small stripling following them
> Appears a mighty Polypheme.'

But the number of good modern books upon fishing is great, and I can only tell you of a few of them. Of Scrope's book, *Days and Nights of Salmon Fishing*, I have already spoken. It tells you of the lawless days in the early part of the nineteenth century before the present Salmon Acts, when fishers were few and fishing cheap, and when you fished fairly in good water and poached foully with torch and spear, when the river fell and the fish would not take the fly to your satisfaction. Henderson's book, *My Life as an Angler*, published in 1879, is a most interesting account of Tweedside salmon fishing and of north-country angling generally, and to you, my boys, I would commend what is said about your great-grandfather at page 22, and also the absolutely convincing and detailed account of the extraordinary increase of heavy fish in the Tweed which followed the passing of the Acts which protected the kelts from capture. The author was one of a party of Durham anglers who fished the Tweed for about thirty years, from 1840 onwards, and two of the best-known salmon flies took their names from them, the Silver Wilkinson and the Durham Ranger. At page 164 also he tells you how to cook a trout by wrapping it in five or six folds of wet paper and thrusting it amongst the ashes of a wood fire.

Another really good book is Stoddart's *Angler's Companion to the Rivers and Lochs of Scotland* (1847). Stoddart's book expresses, and to my mind perfectly, the very best practice of north-country fishing, though he devotes more attention to trout than to salmon. It is a delightful book, though marred by his savage and insolent attacks on Shaw of Drumlanrig, the true pioneer of all accurate knowledge of the life-history of the salmon. Another book that you should most certainly read is *The Angler and the Loop Rod*, a book written in 1885 by an old Scottish cobbler named David Webster, who every summer used to fish the Clyde and the Tweed for his living, and in the pages of whose book there is more sound, practical advice for beginners than in any other book that I know. But the larger part of his book also is devoted to trout fishing.[1]

Amongst the very recent books I will pick out only two of the best. Mr. Gathorne-Hardy's little book on Salmon in the ' Fur, Feather, and Fin' series of sporting books, and Sir Edward Grey's book on *Fly Fishing*. Each of them will give you much pleasure, but of the last I cannot help saying that it is the very best book, without any exception whatever, upon fishing as practised now. But still the book is a very short one, and

[1] Really Webster supplied the material and the late Dr. Livingstone of Wishaw wrote the book for him.

the author has spared only about forty pages to salmon fishing.

These letters of yours are not intended to compete or to compare with any of those books. They are intended to teach two boys salmon fishing so far as that may be taught with a pen, for, since we have removed into the county of Sussex, I may not be able to teach you with a rod. Well, they are done, and for the present, at any rate, my salmon fishing is done, and, like Robert Roxby, the Northumbrian fishing poet, at the end of his life describing what he believed was to be his last day's trouting on his beloved North Tyne, I say:

> 'And now I'll reel my tackle up,
> The fisher's craft resign,
> And bid farewell to rod and reel,
> To hackle, hook, and line.'

APPENDIX

ON PRAWNING

My dear Boys,—When this book was first published some of my very kind and friendly critics pointed out that, though I had written on worming for salmon, there was no reference to fishing for salmon with the prawn.

Well, I have certainly caught more salmon on the prawn than the two which are all that I have got with the worm. It may be, perhaps, forty or fifty in all caught with prawn. Being all caught in hopeless fishing weather, they took a good deal of fishing for, but still I am very far from being an experienced prawn fisher. In truth I rather dislike fishing with prawn, for several reasons. First of all, the fish have never played as well when hooked on the prawn as they did when taken on the fly, or even when taken on a minnow. I do not know the reason for this. Possibly to some extent it is because my prawning has been done in dead-low water when fish are apt to be less vigorous, but anyhow I am quite sure that the same fish would have fought much better on the fly.

Another reason for which I avoid much prawning is that it is a boring and messy business to bait the hooks, even with fresh prawns, and the preserved ones are just as messy, and generally have an offensive smell. Also I cannot think it quite fair and sportsmanlike, if one has guests or neighbours, to be constantly dragging great red prawns through the pools that they will have to fish with fly the same day.

Still, a good many times on a hopeless summer or

autumn water, I have got a good fish on a prawn, and on one foggy September evening, when we had not thought it worth while to fish for some days, I got with four prawns five big salmon, the best a very short, handsome fish of 27 lbs. All were got out of the upper thirty-yards run of one pool, and in the course of an hour and a half. The last fish destroyed my last prawn, or I should perhaps have got still more fish that night, for I should certainly have fished once through the whole pool before going home. I don't think one fish that evening let the prawn pass him, and they all took it savagely, with a plunging tug followed by a prolonged thrashing about on the top of the water before they settled down to fight. Well, as far as experience of prawning goes, I am still in 1915 just where I was in 1909, for I have prawned no more. But now, finding myself unable to leave my billet for a few days, whilst on quite another kind of sporting expedition in Northern France, I think that I had better write my letter on prawn-fishing at once, lest another chance may not occur. For accidents of all kinds are a recognised feature of these 'expeditions.'

Well, what has struck me about prawning is this. First, that there is nothing like having fresh prawns, however soft or damaged they may be. When bought even fresh prawns are always boiled, and therefore red. (People say that salmon do not care for unboiled prawns. I must say that I can't believe this; I hardly think it has been fully tried.) Secondly, I found that, in dead-low water at any rate, the best chance to catch the salmon is the very first time that he sees the prawn. Then you have a really good chance of catching him, however sluggish or hopeless the water may be; but after that, often for days and days, you may put a prawn over him in vain. You may get him on it, of course, but there will be nothing like the probability of getting him that there was the first time he saw it. Another thing that strikes one is the great difference in the way in which different fish take the prawn. Often they take it so gently that you doubt whether it can be a fish at all. It is often not even a faint nibbling, but only a mere touch, that you feel, less than the drag of a floating leaf against the line. In fact, often one has only known it was a salmon by knowing that a salmon lay there, and that nothing but a fish could touch your prawn there. And at times you confirm that by getting the fish, or an unmistakable pull from him, at the next cast. At other times salmon take a prawn with a tremendous and delightful snatch, followed by a violent rush off. This is no doubt because they have seen the prawn some way off, and have dashed across to intercept it, and then turned quickly to go back to their starting-point. At times they follow the prawn, and then make a violent dash for it as it nears the bank and threatens to escape from them. This I have often seen them do; sometimes with the result of a violent tug upon the prawn, but more often they fail to seize it, even though the rush of the fish at the last moment seemed most determined. Perhaps the angler on the bank is seen in time. On one occasion I am sure that was so, as the fish sheered off, and bolted right across the river and up the shallows on the other side.

Another thing about prawn-fishing is that owing to the size and colour of the bait you can see it working in places where no other lure could be seen, and often during the whole of its course. You not only see the fish attack it, but you learn a good deal about the way the currents run in your pools, that you might not have noticed before. With the weighted tackle that I will describe it is very easy to cast and fish a prawn, and when you are tired by fishing without real hope in your fly pools, it affords a welcome rest and change to take the light spinning rod and try a prawn in the deep slack water that won't swim a fly at all. There are quite a number of different ways in which the prawn can be fished, most of them requiring the use of a spinning rod and tackle, or at any rate of a casting reel.

I have been told that the prawn is deadly when fished like a worm, and either downstream or upstream, and I have tried it so occasionally, but without any success. I have read and heard also of its killing fish when thrown in heavily weighted and pulled down to within a very short distance of the nose of a visible fish and left there till he took it. It doesn't sound very sporting, but it might be tried perhaps on a hopeless fish. But it must be a fresh prawn, I understand. I have been told too, that in Ireland—where I believe it is often called 'the shrimp'—a prawn is sometimes fished through the pools dangling from a large cork or float.

But the simplest method of all, where it can be worked, and that by which I caught the five fish I have already spoken of, is to stand at the head of the pool and let the prawn down yard by yard to the fish. I think it is better to use a thin line, at any rate when the water is low and clear, and the prawn should have the tail broken off to facilitate its being pulled backwards against the current. Backwards is, of course, the way a prawn ought to go, for, like a shrimp or a lobster, he swims in swift backward jerks caused by a sudden grab of the water with his powerful tail. As you are letting the prawn down, therefore, you let out the line a few feet at a time, and then give several sharp jerks to the rod to cause the prawn to jerk back in the stream, and as the line that is out gets longer these jerks have to be very powerful, in order to allow for the elasticity and stretching of a long line. You can hook and hold the fish at a great distance below you. I have caught them fifty and sixty yards below me, and once a fish that could not be reached in any other way, I caught by letting down a prawn to him when he was not, I think, less than eighty to ninety yards below me. Of course, when you hook a fish far off, you should give him a few violent jerks to send the hooks home, and then you must reel up as fast as ever you can. Very often he will come upstream, but if he does not, you must be prepared to get to land and go down to him, reeling up as fast as you can. And you want to hold him pretty hard, as it is remarkable how a salmon will shake off the prawn if lightly held. No doubt the bulk of the prawn, when jerked about in the water, gives the resistance necessary to tear out the hooks.

When the prawn has been let down as far as you wish, you may wind it back in similar manner. With three or four strong jerks you get the rod point upstream: then you reel in a few yards of line, letting the rod top go downstream as you do so, and repeat the process over again. Often you will get the fish as you are winding up, particularly if you can bring the prawn up somewhat to the side of the main current. As it goes down you should keep to the centre as a rule, or the bait is apt to sink and foul the bottom. Of course this method of letting down the prawn to the fish is only useful when the depth or shape of the river permits you to get your rod top well out over some main current, or at least above the lie of the fish. In many pools you cannot do this, and therefore you must fish them in some other way, or not at all.

Two other ways of prawn-fishing require a casting reel and also a spinning rod for comfort. In one method you fish with the prawn heavily weighted, using it rather like a minnow, but making it keep as close to the bottom as possible. You make a long cast across and down the stream, then let the prawn sink and cross the main stream very deep, even letting out more line to let it sink. Then, when the prawn has swung across the lie of the fish, keeping the rod low, you slowly wind the bait in up the near side of the stream until it is within six or eight feet of the rod top. I don't much care for this way of fishing, though I have seen a good many spring fish taken by it—much to my annoyance when I have been fishing with the fly. It is a bore humbugging about with your bait along the bottom and catching on it every now and then. But undoubtedly it is a way that kills fish. I almost always use the following way when I fish with a prawn. Using a light ten- or eleven-foot spinning rod, you wind the prawn in quite short and then cast it almost straight across the stream. In a very broad pool, or where you wish to reach fish lying opposite to you, you must cast your prawn well upstream on the far side of the current, or even into the middle of the stream as high up as you can throw it if the stream is very deep or swift. Then you let the prawn sink a few feet, and then begin to work it across the stream by a series of sudden jerks upstream, with a distinct pause between each. At the same time you wind in sufficient line between the jerks to enable you to ' keep in touch ' with your prawn, and to strike firmly at any fish that takes it. It needs a little practice to do this quickly and without flurry, but it can very soon be learnt, and is then very easy to do. This way of working the bait seems to be very deadly to the salmon. It is the old system of ' sink and draw ' fishing, as used with natural minnow applied to prawn-fishing. It is even better fitted for a prawn than for a minnow, as the latter does not naturally move by backward jerks, whereas a prawn does do that very thing always.

One merit of the prawn for occasional use is that it generally takes large fish, and that with it one may take a salmon that has been lost on the fly, and cannot be induced to rise again, but yet continues to occupy a really favourite taking place and excludes some less shy fish from it. Such a shy fish, if tried with a prawn just as darkness falls, is very apt to fall a victim to it, even when he has refused a minnow. But it is better not to try both the same evening.

I will now describe the best tackles used for prawn-fishing, only warning you that in my judgment the various tackles sold by the shops are much too elaborate. They seem to think that the more triangles they put on the better will be their chance of catching a salmon. It's quite wrong to think that. The fewer hooks you can do with the better, if any of them are to take a deep hold, and one hook well bitten in is worth far more than any number not buried well above the barb. And the pull given by a rod is not strong enough to ensure burying a number of points at once, although, of course, a fish in its struggles may bury them if it hasn't got rid of the hooks altogether before any one barb is buried. Nothing surprises the beginner more than the way that salmon will seize hard and yet escape from a prawn or a minnow that is so covered with hooks that you can hardly pick it up without pricking yourself. The reason probably is, that so many hooks had hold of the fish that no one of them ever got buried well above the barb before he felt the pricking and shook them off.

Let us pass on to prawn tackle now. With a prawn one uses a sinker of some sort. I use a round lead bullet about the size of a boiled pea on three or four inches of trout gut or fine thread, and tied to a ring or swivel in the main cast, as I have already described for worm-fishing, but about three feet above the bait. Under the prawn, too, are a few inches of lead wire wound round the gut and the shank of a triangle, just to keep it swimming right side up.

The trace by which the casting line is connected with the bait may be all of gut or all of wire. But I generally have the upper half only of wire, and three feet or so next the prawn of gut, as that allows the bait to move with more freedom. The wire above is good, as it enables you to break off your lead, if that sticks in the rocks, without losing your prawn and prawn tackle. The tackle is made thus :

Take three feet of wire. At the upper end you attach a

double swivel, just as for a minnow trace. To the lower end you attach either a small ring or another swivel, and to this you fasten both the lead, dangling on three or four inches of fine gut, and also the two and a half or three feet of gut which leads to the prawn.

The lead on its fine gut I always attach to the upper ring of this swivel, which is then free to allow the bait to turn round. A prawn always has a tendency in fast water to spin or wobble over and over, as you can't fasten it on with exact symmetry.

Now we come to the actual mounting of the prawn itself. It may be put on a single large hook, inserted under the tail and brought out at the head. But when I have tried this the prawn has generally broken up under the treatment. Once I did succeed in getting a big four-inch hook into a prawn (I believe it was by using a baiting needle, and pulling it through him shank first from head to tail). (See Appendix, Note 9.)

The first swim that I gave it a big fish took the prawn and began giving little tugs at it. It was my first trial of prawn, and I thought it was an eel that was at the bait, but I remembered that the fish were said to take gently, and should be given about half a minute to 'pouch' the prawn. But after several series of little tugs the fish moved off steadily, and I gave him a good pull. The hook seemed to have him all right, but he ultimately got off it somehow, just as I was making ready to gaff him.

Well, I haven't used single hooks, because of the trouble of baiting each time with a baiting needle. I use a simple flight (see Fig. A, p. 297) made thus:

1. Take a long strand of stout gut and lash a small triangle to each end of it. When in a hurry I use triangles with metal loops for these ends, and simply knot them on with the sliding knot that I have described in my previous letter on knots.

2. At one end (the thicker end, if either is thicker) tie on

firmly a larger triangle about an inch behind the end one.

3. Varnish all lappings well if you have time, and then wrap about one and a half to two inches of thin lead wire round the shank of the triangle last mentioned and the gut immediately above it.

4. Double the strand of gut so that all three triangles come together. Take a long darning needle (extra long ones can be bought and the thinner the better), and lay it alongside the doubled gut, the point of the needle being towards the hooks. Then with a bit of well-soaked salmon gut (or with stout cotton thread) passed through the eye of the needle, fasten the needle to the gut strongly yet loosely. To ensure that the needle can slide freely up and down the doubled gut lay a knitting needle (or a match) alongside and tie it in. Then you can pull your gut or thread and knot it hard and tight, yet on removing the knitting needle there is a small open loop left.

Your tackle is now complete. You can touch it up, if you like, by painting the triangles and the twisted lead wire a red colour with sealing wax dissolved in spirit. For low clear water you can omit the top triangle or substitute single hooks for both the lower triangles. This is a distinct advantage as it makes the roll of lead thinner, and also lessens the risk of catching on the bottom. If you have both single hooks, both should turn upwards when in use. The rear one is buried in the chest of the prawn, and the front one sticks upwards between his whiskers. There are two small tips here just worth noticing. To wind lead wire neatly round gut lay a pin or needle alongside the gut and wind the wire round both. It goes on beautifully evenly, and is easily tightened when you pull out the pin.

The next thing is that there is some risk when a salmon is hooked on one triangle only, that the knot will open or slip that fastens the gut trace to the big loop behind the prawn. This can be avoided either by very careful knotting, or, better still, by a little lapping together of the loop of the prawn tackle about half an inch from the end which is to be knotted to the gut cast.

To bait this tackle you take the prawn and snap off the spreading fans of his tail. If left on they cause the prawn to spin and also drag very heavily when it is being pulled back in a strong stream. But if you are merely going to have a few casts for a particular fish, I should leave the tail intact, as being more natural. Next you straighten out the prawn (gently, or his shell will come loose), and insert the darning needle at his stern, pushing it right forward to his chest. Then you plant the leaded triangle in his chest, its front triangle being under his nose. The other triangle you stick into the large shell on his back. Some fish their prawn unstraightened.

The prawn is very delicate, and unless you wrap it round in some way would soon be knocked to bits in heavy water. Some people put thin rubber rings round him, and others tie him round with worsted or thread, but I find both ways difficult and troublesome to work with wet fingers on a wet prawn and among a number of hook points. Here is a really useful little tip for binding the prawn. You take a strand of thin trout gut (or ten to twelve inches of red thread). Tie one end to the shank of the triangle that goes under the prawn's head. Tie the other end to a tiny eyed trout hook. With this thin gut you wrap the prawn round, and the little hook serves to anchor the end without the trouble of tying a knot.

I have found this the best way to support the prawn, which usually breaks by the head or the back shell coming off. You take the thread where it is tied to the head triangle and pass it up between the horny projections at his nose, then bring it down the centre to the triangle stuck in his back. Here you take a complete turn round the prawn and a half turn round the triangle (to prevent a side pull tearing the shell), and then continue winding back to the tail; then you come back for a turn or two and finish off by hooking the little hook into one of the hard back scales near the tail. The same tie often does for many prawns, and on one occasion I landed a small salmon which for the last five minutes' play had shaken off the triangles and was held only by the tiny eyed hook (on a foot of stout thread luckily) which had foul hooked the fish under the corner of the jaw. No doubt the thread had been hanging across his mouth when the triangles came away. I saw the prawn come away and played the fish very gently, but I found there had been no need for care as the hold was a very strong one.

I have made a couple of odd captures on the prawn. One day letting the prawn down a swift rush, I had a very heavy pull and then some slow tugging till the fish got out of the swift current. It proved to be a large eel, weighing three or four pounds I should judge. I got him to the shore, but did not pull him high and dry as I knew that he would at once roll up my tackle and destroy it. So I kept him at the edge, and in a short time he tore himself off and departed to our mutual satisfaction. Another time, in the same pool, a well-fed half-pound common trout took the prawn and was landed and eaten. That opens up some thoughts on the question of what a salmon takes a fly to be. What did that trout think a three and a half-inch prawn was? What living object that he had ever seen?

One knows many deep or sluggish reaches that are never fished, and yet fish take up their station there. It is worth giving them a trial with a 'sink-and-draw' prawn. I have taken several in that way and regarded them as a clear gain, as they never would have been taken on any other lure.

The common shrimp ought, one would think, to attract salmon. I rigged one up for 'grandpapa' on the Tyne, one hot afternoon in September 1895, when he was trying a new rod, and it killed a grilse the very first cast he made with it—and I gaffed the fish for him after some mischances. In fact it got off the hook a second before I gaffed it. But we never caught any more salmon on a shrimp, though we tried it several times.—Yours,

A. C.

MARLES-LES-MINES, 30*th March* 1915.

P.S.—Since I wrote this I have been to New Zealand again, and seen the enormous brown trout lying in their clear rivers, but absolutely refusing to look at fly or even minnow in the daytime. I think, however, that if a shrimp or the 'koura'—that is the local fresh-water crayfish—were mounted on prawn tackle, and fished like a prawn in all the ways I have mentioned, they would probably be found to take it. Both salmon and trout are very fond of shell-fish, and it would be a sporting way of taking these splendid fish which at present are taken chiefly by dynamite, or by what they call out there 'the ·303 minnow,' or by attracting them with an acetylene light at night and then gaffing them out. And for the shrimp, in those clear rivers, I should reduce the prawn tackle to two single hooks—a larger round hook buried in the chest with its point projecting through the back, and a smaller hook at the nose of the shrimp.

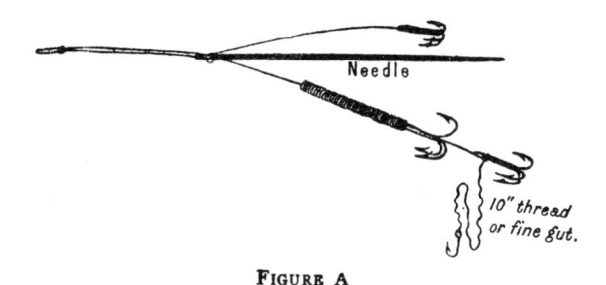

FIGURE A
A Prawn Tackle.

NOTES

NOTE 1 (to p. 50, last line)

I do not think my directions as to gaffing a salmon are quite clear. The beginner tries to gaff the fish and pull him out in one motion. It should be not one motion but two. First with a sharp twitch you pull the hook into the fish, and next with a lifting pull you draw the fish to you. If you have to get a novice to gaff a fish for you, as may very easily happen, warn him—or shall we say her?—not to try to rake out the fish in one sweep. To lessen the great risk of breaking the rod top when one gaffs or tails a fish I usually hold the line against the rod with my left hand and keep two or three feet of line loose off the reel, so that the moment I lift the fish with my right hand or my gaff I can let loose this line and free the rod top from the strain.

NOTE 2 (to p. 99, l. 12)

The metal rings of double swivels, and the ring of the swivel at the head of the phantom minnow, are round when you buy them. With a nip from your pliers they can very easily be squeezed into an oval shape. This you will find is a great improvement, as it prevents the loop of the trace from slipping round and jamming at the back of the swivel ring.

NOTE 3 (to p. 191)

There is another knot which may be used for salmon gut if your fingers or your eyesight are not equal to tying the blood-knot. It is an improved fisherman's knot. Like that knot it is two knots drawn together, but you tie each end in this way. First make an overhand knot round the other link, as for a fisherman's knot. Next wrap the loose end once round both pieces of gut and pull tight. The other half of the knot is exactly the same.

A diagram of one end will explain it. Before pulling tight the end *A* should be held close alongside the link *B*, and the loop at *X* should be tipped upwards so as to twist closely round *A* and *B* about *Z*. Then this loop, when pulled tight, will make a sort of cross with the other turn at *Y*, and these two turns should be so crossed at the finish instead of lying

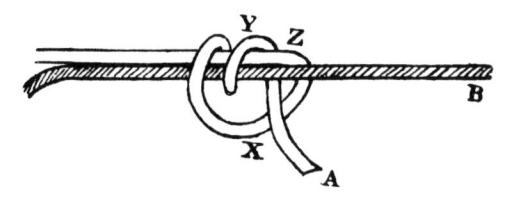

one behind the other as in the diagram. You make the other end in the same way and then draw the two knots together. The gut for a dropper fly may be put between them just as in the fisherman's knot.

This knot is less neat than the blood-knot, and the ends stick out in the wrong place, but it is a simple and strong joining, and useful for sea-trout fishing where you want to put on a dropper fly. It is better than the ordinary double fisherman's knot, where the end *A* only passes once round the line *B* and grips it less firmly.

It is less suitable than the blood-knot for very stout gut, but it may be used to make the sliding knot figured on p. 184, and if pulled thoroughly tight would seem to add strength to that knot. For tying gut-substitute to metal-eyed flies or to swivel rings this method of tying the sliding knot with half a double fisherman's knot pulled tight and slid down on to the metal has been used for years, and particularly with the 'Olympic' gut. And so has the reversed hitch, as figured in the next note. The gut-substitute should be thoroughly soaked. The plain sliding knot has been known to slip with that gut unless it has a guard knot at the end.

NOTE 3*a* (to pp. 188 and 189)

There are several explanations that I ought to give about knots that are too long to be put in the text without recasting the rest of the book.

First as to the blood-knot, I have altered my way of tying it since the second edition was printed. The late Mr. A. H. Illingworth, a great fisher and brother of an old Cambridge friend of mine, pointed out that if tied with a continuous twist the knot could not be made symmetrical, as one end must be given a half turn more than the other if the ends are to be entered side by side but in opposite directions. He thought that the knot should be tied with the twists reversed, and I fully agree with him, and have so described it in this edition. But where one has to tie a thick end to a thin one it is an advantage to give the thin end an extra half turn, and in this instance only I still use the continuous twist as illustrated at p. 187 B. On close examination of that illustration you can see that the left end has $2\frac{3}{4}$ turns and the right end has $3\frac{1}{4}$ turns. For one cannot give exactly 3 turns or exactly $2\frac{1}{2}$ turns and still put the end through between the links. The space to do that comes either just before or just after the 3 turns are completed. For stout gut I always give only $2\frac{3}{4}$ turns to each end, reversing the twists; for thin sea-trout or for trout gut $3\frac{1}{4}$ on each end, reversing the twists.

Again, in telling you how to make the left-handed twist in the second half of the knot, at p. 188 (4), I described reversing the first half into your left hand, and then I found it hard to describe the next step, except by saying that you wind the free end *left-handed* round the link. For the next step depends on which way you hold the first half after reversing it. If you have the loose end next you then you wind it first *under* and so on round the link. If you hold the end away from you you wind it first over and towards you.

Some people have been unable to see why in the loose knot at p. 187 the ends are shown going straight to the outside; but in the tight knot the twists are all outside and the rest inside the knot. The reason is that it is much easier to form the knot in this way, and the slippery gut, when pulled sharply, transfers the rolls to the outside for you and forms the correct knot. But, also, I must point out that the gut will not stay in the exact form of illustrations A or B unless it is held there. If released the end loop will at once twist round and transfer some of the twist to the part shown straight in those illustrations. When pulled suddenly tight it throws all the twists there, which is just what you want for the knot.

Just one word about the half-hitch figure of eight knot shown on p. 181. This is given in the form it was taught to me and as I used it for many years. But at times on a very violent pull it slipped or cut itself, so I took to, and always used, the reef knot figure of eight shown at p. 180. I am now told that if you end off the former knot by putting the end along on the top of the fly loop, as shown in the second cut on p. 180, instead of pushing it down, this knot is quite as reliable as the reef knot. But that knot seems perfect for its purpose.

There are many other useful knots, but one fears lest one should confuse people with too many. Mr. F. A. Wolryche Whitmore has sent several good ones that he thinks better than mine. The simplest is one for tying a line or a link of gut to a loop. It can be formed in various ways. *E.g.*: hold the loop in your left hand and put the link end upwards through it from the right. Then wind the end over away from you and round the neck of the loop once, bringing it back near the head of the loop. Then from the head of the loop push the end back along the top of the loop and under the first bit that turns away from you. Thus you get a most simple kind of reversed hitch, which jams itself by holding the end fast against the loop, very much in the same way as the end is held in the lower illustration at p. 180. Mr. Whitmore's second knot is a double knot of this same kind intended to knot gut to a metal fly loop or the silk line to the gut loop. You put the link through the metal loop in the same way, then wind not once but twice away and round the neck of the loop, bringing the second turn nearer the end of the loop than the first one. Then you push back the end round the link (as it comes up through the loop) and back along the surface of the metal loop. Thus the end lies flat on the metal loop and is jammed there by the turns already given round the loop. He tells me that he learnt these knots from Mr. Reginald Corbet, and that they have been used by many good fishers for years and are both absolutely reliable, in spite of their extreme simplicity. And he finds them **reliable also for gut-substitute and for tippets of twisted gut** in heavy waters. But I should hesitate to use this knot with any of those cheap and bad metal eyes where the curled back point only comes back far enough to touch or almost touch the shank. For such the slip knot at p. 184 is best, but made with the knot at p. 299 if the fly is large.

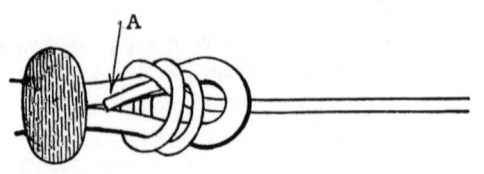

Reversed Hitch (double form).—Pull the knot tight and keep it right forward on the loop, unless the loop is of metal, when the knot may be settled on the neck of the loop.

For the single reversed hitch a guard knot may be put on the end *A*. But, unless possibly with gut-substitute, it is not needed.

NOTE 4 (to p. 198, l. 17)

There is often some little difficulty in getting the foot of each wader turned inside out without forcing them, but this can be done by the air-pressure alone if the waders, when turned inside out as far as the ankles, are rolled up from the upper end in a tight roll. This forces the compressed air into the feet, which will then turn inside out of their own accord. But even this wants doing carefully or the waders may be damaged. Any place that sticks during the turn wants humouring a little with the fingers. I do not recommend this rolling-up method for every-day use. I have used it for turning waders that had been put away and got hard and dry. But in that case you should soak the waders in warm water until they are soft, and keep wetting them with warm water till the feet turn inside out easily.

Never roll up long waders or 'boot and leg' waders to put them away. After drying them well, inside and out, hang them up for the winter. And it is a good thing to put balls of crumpled paper into the feet to make sure that they do not get out of shape. If you have to fold them up this is specially useful, or you may find the feet and ankles crumpled and hard when you need them again next year.

The combined 'boot and leg' waders are expensive, but are far the best, especially if one has to do much walking in them. With all waders, but especially with these boot-waders, which are not easy to dry, one ought to wear a second thick pair of rough socks over one's stockings inside the wader. Then this outer sock will get damp, but the inner one keeps dry and warm.

To dry boot-waders or gum-boots or felt-lined boots the best way is to have some narrow bags very loosely filled with dried beans or peas. You heat these and put them into the feet of the waders, which will soon become dry. Large beans may be used without the bags, and even heated pebbles the size of walnuts will dry the boots.

If you want to dry such waders in the sun or wind it is a useful tip to make the air circulate by putting a cardboard, or other rough division, down the middle of each leg as far as the ankle—of course you turn back the leg part as far as you can.

It is too risky to dry your waders or boots near a fire, and most unwise to let any one else dry them there. It nearly always ends in spoiling them.

NOTE 5 (to p. 202, l. 2)

As to the best length of rod to choose when you buy a rod, I think that a medium 17-foot rod is about the best for all-round salmon fishing. An 18-foot rod is better for big rivers and for strong and practised fishers, but is rather over-big for small rivers or low waters, whilst a 16-foot rod, though very nice to use, is rather small for really heavy waters and rough winds. But older men need lighter rods.

Upright rings with linings of porcelain or agate all down the rod are very highly valued by many expert fishers. They enable a great length of line to be 'shot' through the rings on making a cast, and in this way fish may be reached and taken by their aid which could not otherwise have been covered at all.

NOTE 6 (to p. 204, l. 10)

Joinings for Reel Lines.—In order to avoid large and heavy reels, which are clumsy, ugly, and tiring to use, you must have behind the 40 yards of actual casting line from 60 to 100 yards of thin plaited line of undressed silk, or of cotton or hemp, fastened to the thick casting line as 'backing.'

Whipcord or other twisted line is not suitable because of its tendency to twist and kink or tangle when wetted. With 40 yards of casting line 60 yards of backing is enough, unless one is to fish very broad or strong rivers, when 100 yards of backing might possibly be safer. A long line has one other advantage: it sometimes enables you to cross above or below a pool, and so to release your fly when caught up on the far side of the stream.

The backing should be carefully lapped to the casting line so that the join may be strong and yet may run easily through the rings. I find the quickest and easiest method is this: first scrape off any surface dressing from the end of the lines over a length of about three inches. Then lay these scraped ends alongside and get a friend to hold them taut for you, leaving you both hands free to whip them together. Take a foot or more of saddler's twist (strong thread will do) and wax it with soft cobbler's wax. Then, as your friend holds before you the ends to be whipped together, you, with the centre of your bit of thread, tie a knot round the two ends and draw this tight. This leaves equal lengths of your thread in each hand, and with these you lap the ends tightly, winding with both together but the opposite way round, like cross-gartering. And after each three or four lappings you tie a single knot (like the first half of a reef knot) just to prevent your lapping unravelling if the thread should by chance get cut or worn. End off with a reef knot or any neater finish that you may fancy.

The tighter your friend stretches the lines the easier you will find it to put on the whipping. And when you tie the knots place a finger against the last turns of whipping so that you can draw the knot tight without sawing the waxed thread against itself. You'll see what this means when you try it. I usually finish by damping the whipping with celluloid varnish, but this is not necessary.

An inch of this whipping is ample, but of late years I have always used two short lappings of about half an inch each and half an inch apart, as this gives a more flexible joining and runs more easily through the rings.

Of course a neater job can be made by teasing out half an inch of each end, then twisting the teased part into three points and locking together, or 'marrying,' these six points, as if for a true splice. Then you simply lap over the whole as described above, and varnish with celluloid. This whipped splice is the only good joining that I know if your thick casting line should get cut.

NOTE 7 (to p. 205, l. 7)

Tiny whetstones suitable for sharpening hooks can be bought under the name of 'carver's slips,' at the stores or any good ironmonger's shop. They are only an inch or two long, and very thin, and go easily into your fishing book or fly box. A file is not at all suitable for sharpening hooks. You want a hard stone to put on a polished point which will not easily rust.

NOTE 8 (to p. 279, l. 6)

In New Zealand in 1917 we learned the way to grill a fish at the waterside. You make a rough gridiron out of a few bends of fencing wire. Split your fish *down the back only*, clean it, remove the backbone, and cut off the head. Place it flat on the gridiron, skin downwards, sprinkling the flesh with pepper, salt, and, if possible, a little butter. On a clear wood fire this will, in a very short time, make the most superb grill you ever tasted. A four- or five-pound fish is a convenient size for grilling, but you can do half of a bigger fish just as well.

NOTE 9 (to p. 293)

It is not really a hard thing to put a prawn on a single hook, but there is a knack in it, and you should buy some fresh prawns or shrimps and practise doing it if you want to fish prawn in very low and clear water. You use a round bend hook and insert the point under the tail of the prawn, when you can pass it forward easily for some way. Then, when the prawn bends sharply round the hook and seems to stick, if you go slowly the prawn will break. But if you briskly force it on and, as it were, hustle it over the sticking point, all goes well and you bring the point out under the chest. Then bind the prawn with red thread or with copper wire. Mounted thus and fished rather like a worm on a very short line—often only a rod's length—the prawn is at times a killing bait. But to my mind this trickling of the prawn to the fish's nose is a niggling and rather a poaching business no better than worm fishing. People will ask why do you so greatly prefer fly fishing, and think poorly even of artificial minnow fishing, and rather despise the pleasures of prawn and worm and any natural bait. Well, it comes to a personal matter of taste and of one's own education in sport. To take extreme cases, why do we not shoot a rabbit sitting or a pheasant running? Or catch trout, as they used to do in Scottish rivers, with 12 or 14-foot rods and a string of six or eight flies? There being more sporting ways of pursuing these sports it would give us no pleasure now to do these things, which used to be done, and no doubt are still done, by what we call pot-hunters. We have all been pot-hunters at times, and with salmon the temptation is all the greater as they are here to-day and gone to-morrow, and in the meanwhile they jump out under our noses and excite our keen desire and refuse our flies for days or weeks together. But when I do catch such a salmon with a prawn I feel rather a poacher and can't take any pride in it, as I should do if I had tempted him to take a fly. Also I feel that it is rather inconsiderate to other fishers, if any have a right to fish your water, to rake the pools over with prawns or minnows or to dribble worms or prawns along the bottom past the noses of the fish they are going to fish for with fly. You practically force them to poach too in self-defence. To you, my sons, I say be first of all considerate of others. But, where you have all the fishing and that does not arise, you can form and act on your own ideas of what is sportsmanlike fishing and what gives you the greatest real pleasure, but do not for that reason sneer at or affect to despise other fishers who do not agree with you and allow themselves a greater latitude. Often it is only a question of their luck. The man who can have really good fishing can afford to stick to the fly, the one

NOTES

who has only poor water and fewer chances must make the very most of them to get any fish and cannot afford to despise any chance that may gain him a salmon.

NOTE 10

Dry Fly and Surface Fly Fishing for Salmon.—Of late years there has been a great increase in the use of very light rods and tackle for salmon fishing. So people have been using tiny flies, fished quite near the surface, and a great many fishers have been trying the dry fly for salmon, especially in clear summer waters. This is mainly due to two recent books from America, *Secrets of the Salmon*, by Mr. Hewitt, and *The Salmon and the Dry Fly*, by Mr. La Branche, who fished with Mr. Hewitt. Fishing in gin-clear waters they use short stiff rods and keep on casting to the visible or known lie of the salmon a large floating wingless fly of the palmer type, with fat body and big buzzy hackle; and sooner or later they find fish will take them in conditions that appear most unfavourable for the ordinary salmon fly. Mr. La Branche uses a double-handed 14-foot rod, and he has found many imitators in England and Scotland, some of whom have had very good sport.

Of course for many years dry fly has been used regularly for sea-trout, and many people have tried it for salmon. I had a number of large dry flies dressed on strong hooks for salmon fishing and tried them in low summer waters on the Tyne, but my only success with them was on the 23rd of May 1896, when, with a hackled may-fly about three-quarters of an inch long, I got a perfect spring salmon of 19 lb. and lost a second fish by the hold giving way. It is a pleasing memory for another reason. I arrived on Friday evening and began looking over my salmon flies. Another guest, much older, a fine fisher, but a hasty and most jealous one, said: 'What are you doing with those flies? There are no salmon in the water, and if there were I should have caught them.' So I said, 'Oh, well! I can never fish for trout until I have tried all the salmon pools.' Next morning he left, after a week's fishing, and I could not resist a postcard to say that I had got a 19-lb. fish and lost another good one. As a matter of fact I had been fishing down the pool when I saw a repeated flashing, like that of a sheet of tin, on the bottom under about seven feet of heavy rushing water. I felt sure it must be a salmon so I fished for him steadily with a winged and then with a hackled may-fly, and at last he took it. But the Tyne was not a very clear water, and I soon gave up dry fly as I found that I did better with quite small lake trout flies fished wet on a light rod and trout gut, as I have described elsewhere. But this American success with dry fly in Canada has called attention to a similar, and what I think in our rivers will prove a better, method used for some years with great success by Mr. A. E. Wood on the Dee. He has a greased and floating line, but takes care that the gut for the last few feet is not greased, so that the fly may fish just below the surface. He uses small salmon flies on hooks of an inch or less and fishes these either down, across, or even up-stream as he judges will best suit the spot to be fished; and he uses a 12-foot rod, fished with one hand. Such a rod, or even an 11-foot rod, will cast a very long line if the fly is small, but you need great skill to recover a long line from the water and then to get out a clean cast next time. You are almost forced to pull in a good deal of line by hand and then to get most of this out again by making a false cast between each of your effective fishing casts. This I understand Mr. Wood does, and he takes care to allow plenty of time before striking when he sees a rise to a cast made up-stream or across. He uses chiefly three patterns, 'March Brown,' 'Blue Charm' and 'Silver Blue,' but he is equally ready to fish with any other fly, as far as taking fish goes.

Mr. Wood has written some short notes for Messrs. Hardy's 1925 catalogue, but I hope that he will write us a much fuller account of his methods and his successes. He often uses these three flies dressed to float and kills well with them, but what he prefers and finds most deadly, when the water is right, is to cast about 25 degrees up-stream and to fish the fly wet, but only just under the surface and carried inert by the current, with the greased line floating quite slack on the water; and he very often raises and hooks his salmon at once, when his fly must be going straight down-stream. He holds that small flies are for warm water, *e.g.* Nos. 6 to 8 hooks (that is, in Hardy's scale, hooks 1⅜ to ⅝ of an inch long and of sea-trout or lake-trout sizes) are only worth going to when the Dee reaches 40° to 45° Fahrenheit. But you should get his notes and read them carefully.

NOTE 11 (to p. 17)

Casting against the wind.—In the hints to beginners as to how to cast against a violent wind, I forgot to add that some line, a foot or two at least, should be drawn in before every cast and released, or 'shot,' as late as possible and only just before the fly itself touches the water. This helps to stop the vexatious little jerk that so often, in a high wind, throws the fly back on the cast. And with a very violent gale behind you, that you can hardly stand against—the very best time to fish the slow deeps or 'dubs'—to shoot a good deal of line as late as possible in the cast helps you to fish at all even with a short line and to avoid the slashing splashes of the line on the water and the snapping jerks upon the tackle.

NOTE 12

The Curd in Salmon.—I really must tell you about sending as a present an absolutely fresh salmon without explaining the curd, the cloudy jelly which goes liquid and is not seen unless the fish is cooked within twenty-four hours or less of its being caught. As a bachelor in the nineties I was most anxious to send the best possible salmon to a house where I had often received the kindest hospitality. At five o'clock one frosty March day I caught a perfect spring fish of 15 lb., and by packing him at once caught the six-thirty train to London, and he was delivered before breakfast with a message to have him cooked at once. My friend was a hunting man, but no fisher, and he told me a few days later that the fish arrived bad and had to be thrown away. I said it could not go bad within a week at least, and more especially in frosty weather. But he said that his cook, who was a Frenchman, had cooked it at once and sent for him to look at it, and that on opening the fish it was full of a nasty cloudy mould—the curd that I had taken such pains to get for him. He does not know to this day that he threw away a fish such as money could not buy in London. I only said that I was extremely sorry, but that, if bad, some one must have stolen his fish in the train and given him a kelt.

NOTE 13

On Gulls killing Parr and Smolts.—My honoured friend, the late Colonel H. W. Feilden, of Rampyndene, Burwash, asked me to modify in the next edition my unqualified condemnation (at p. 143 of the second edition) of the black-headed gull, *Larus ridibundus*, both as to its numbers and its destructiveness to fish. He referred me to Mr. Collinge's paper on ' Sea Birds : Their relation to Fisheries and Agriculture ' (*Nature*, 8th April 1920), who puts the black-headed gull as destructive to fish only to 20 per cent. of its food, and estimates that injurious insects form 22 per cent. and marine worms 18 per cent. of its food, and considers that the bird undoubtedly does more good than harm to man. Its breeding stations in the British Isles have been set out by Mr. Robert Gurney, who says that one of the largest is at Scoulton Mere, in Norfolk, and he estimates the colony at about 2500 birds. (*Transactions, Norfolk and Norwich Society*, 1919, pp. 416 and 447.) Colonel Feilden was a high authority on natural history, and I will not add a word to what he says in defence of *Larus ridibundus*. Indeed it would be impossible for me now to contest his wishes so great is the regard that I had and have for him as the most perfect example of an English soldier, scholar, gentleman, and man of action. Trevor-Battye, who was writing his life, died suddenly at Las Palmas two years ago, and as I fear it may not now be written I will say a few words about Feilden. He served in the Indian Mutiny and in the China War of 1860, and resigned his commission in the gunners to go out to America to join the Confederate Army, where he served from 1862 to 1865 and became Assistant-Adjutant-General, and was made a prisoner after the last battle of that war. He was Naturalist to the British Polar Expedition of 1875-76, sent out under Admiral Markham to search for Sir John Franklin. He again served in the Boer War of 1881, and in the South African War of 1900, where he became a full Colonel and a C.B. In his early days he was a keen salmon fisher. After his retirement he devoted his time to natural history and to the work of various learned societies, and he became the adviser and friend of nearly every one who wanted to explore the Arctic or the Antarctic, as well he might be, for he had himself visited for scientific research Greenland, Grinnell Land, Ellesmere Land, Spitzbergen, Novaya Zemlya, and other Arctic areas. Yet in private life he was the most modest of men. You see, my dear boys, the day of knightly adventures is not long past.

INDEX

ALDER LEAF, to remove glitter of gut, 207.
Alevins, appearance of, 239-40.
  rearing, 241.
Arctic explorer, Feilden, 310.
Autumn fishing, a week-end in October, 77-87.

BACKING for lines, 9, 10, 304.
Belt round waders, wearing, 194-5.
  swimming with, 195.
Best days, 114-25.
Best fish, 150-7
Biology of salmon egg, 239.
Bisulphide of carbon, 280.
Books on fishing—
  Calderwood, 254.
  Chaytor, J. C., 229.
  Gathorne-Hardy, 209, 284.
  Grey, Sir Edward, 284.
  Henderson, 108, 283.
  Hewitt, 307.
  Hodgson, 35.
  Kennedy, 282.
  Kirkbride, 208.
  La Branche, 307.
  Scrope, 61, 283.
  Stoddart, 284.
  Venables, 282.
  Walton and Cotton, 282.
  Webster, David, 103, 284.
  Young, Andrew, 51.
Bread, how to make, 278.
Brogues, 194.
  nails for, and iron foot, 194.
Bull-trout, 245, 246.

CARRYING SALMON, in 'frail,' 206.
  in string loop, 198.
Casting, 12.
  the detail of, 13.
  secret of good casting, 15.
  casting against wind, 17, 309.
  where to cast, 17.
  casting up-stream, 18, 29, 308.
  last cast of the season, 87.
Celluloid varnish, 167-8.
Clean or kelt, 259-62.
Clothing, socks, quiet colours, hat, 199.
Cooking trout in ashes, 284.
  on grill, 297.
Corbet, R., 301.
Cramp, 193.
Curd in salmon, 309.

DEE, 255, 257, 308-9.
Disturbing fish, 21.
Dropper fly, 145, 299.
Dry fly for salmon, 307-9.

EELS SPAWNING, 253.
  taking prawn, 296.

FEATHERS, fresh, best for flies, 173.
Feeding, salmon, in river, 255-7.
  scientific theories about, 255.
Feilden, Col. H. W., 309-10.
Ferreting, 279.
Fiddle-string, loops of, on fly, 167, 179, 184.
Flies, 8, 34-39.

INDEX

Flies (*contd.*)—
  a select few, 37.
  the claret, 64.
  the white and silver, 84.
  big flies after flood, 124; and at evening, 161.
  dry for salmon, 307-9.
Floating fish home, 121.
Fly tying, 166-76.
Foam, 160.
Forty-pounder, a, 156.
Foul hooked fish, 117, 147, 203.
Frail, to carry fish, 206.

GAFFING, 50, 298.
Gib, 211, 231.
Gill maggots, 260.
Grandfather, his notes, 229.
Grilling fish, 297.
Gulls, 143, 309-10.
Gun cleaning, 280.
Gut, 8, 10, 207.
  fine gut, 32.
  testing, 10.
  old gut, 64.
  tying thin to thick, 300.
  tying stout links, 300.
Gut-substitute, knots for, 299-301.

HACKLE, how to wind and tie on, 171.
Hatching, 237.
Hewitt, 307.
Holding rod 'short,' 23.
Hold line, how to, 44.
Home, Lord, his great day in 1795, 124.
Hooking fish, fourteen consecutive rises, 25.
Hooks, keeping sharp, 44, 205, 305.
  double, 205.
  eyed, 183, 206, 299, 302.
  whetstone for hooks (called carver's slips), 205, 305.

ILLINGWORTH, A. H., 300.

JOINTS, mutton fat for, 202.
  to free sticking joints, the Spanish windlass, 202.
  a rough and ready vice for, 203.

KELT, how to tell a, 259-62.
Knots, 177-91, 298-302.
  blood-knot, 187, 300.
  double fisherman's knot, 299.
  figure of eight knot, 179-82, 301.
  guard knot, 299, 302.
  gut-substitute for, 299, 301.
  lines to gut, 179, 301.
  lines to swivels, 99, 184.
  metal eyes for, 184, 302.
  reversed hitch, 301.
  reversed hitch, double, 301-2.
  sliding or slip knot, 184, 299.

LA BRANCHE, 307.
Last day of a season, 145-9.
Lines, 9, 10, 204, 303-5.
  light, 32.
  spinning, trout lines for, 93-4.
  splicing lines, 304.
Loops on line and gut, 177, 179.
  of fiddle-string on fly, 167, 179.
Lost fish, 49.
  recovering, 67, 71.
Low water, 18, 164.
  surface, fishing on, 18, 29, 308-9.

MAORI CHIEF and BISHOP SELWYN, 129.
Marked salmon, 138.
Maxims, 22, 38.
  metal eyes, knots for, 183, 299, 301, 302.
Minnow fishing, 88-105.
  in big dark waters, 90.
  in frost, 91.
  minnow tackles, 101-4.
  casting natural minnow on fly rod, 102.
Minnows, phantom, 95-7.
  leading, 96.

INDEX

Muggy weather, bad, 160.
Mulled claret, good, 278.
Mutton fat for joints, 202.

NATURAL HISTORY, 253-63.
'Necked' gut, 10, 178.
Netting salmon, 137, 235-6.
New Zealand trout, 297.
   to grill trout, 297.
   poaching methods, 141, 297.
Night fishing, 161.
Norway and the Norwegians, 128.

OLYMPIC GUT, 297.
Otters, 126, 247-8.
   killing salmon, 131-3.
   fishing, 133-4.
   catching an otter, 135.

PAIN, sense of, in fish, 55-62.
Patience, 3, 76.
Phantom minnows, 95-7.
Piano wire, 98.
   pliers for cutting wire, 100.
Playing fish, 46-50.
Poachers, 139.
Pollution, 137.
Prawn, 286-97.
   tackle, 292, 297.
   baiting, 295.
   on single hook, 305-6.
   eel taking, 296.
   trout taking, 296.
Pricked fish, 38.

QUIET RUNS, 163.

RABBITS, 278, 281.
Rain, 159.
Redds, 212, 221.
Reels, 9, 203.
   casting reels, 92.
   overrunning, 93.
   catching salmon without a reel, 251 *n.*
Resting, salmon resting on bottom, 219.
Rifle bullet, 141, 297.

Rising water, 159-60, 196.
Rods, 6, 9, 201, 303.
   not whippy, for beginners, 201.
   spinning rods, 92.
   upright rings for, 303.
Roe, 213.

SALMON ACTS, old English, 271.
Salmon Acts, old Scottish, 262.
Scales of salmon, rings on, 254.
Seagulls, 143, 248, 309-10.
Sea-lice, 257-8.
Sea-trout, 245.
   a 38 lb. sea-trout, 250.
Seals, 137, 247.
Sharpening hooks, 205, 305.
Shaw of Drumlanrig, 253, 284.
'Shooting' line, 19, 303, 309.
Smolts, 229, 243, 254.
Snow, 69.
Spanish windlass, 202.
Spawning, 208-29, 233-5.
   little fighting or jealousy, 223, 226.
Spey, 138.
Splicing lines, 304.
Spots on salmon, few, if any, below lateral line, 262.
Spring fish dropping down river, 138.
Spring fish in October, a, 151.
Spring fishing, 63-76.
Striking the fish, 40-5.
Styles of fishing, 28, 307-8.
Sudden floods, 159, 196.
Sulking, 47, 57, 58.
Sunshine, 158-9.
Swimming in waders, 195.
Swirling pools, 18.
Swivel rings—
   squeezing to oval, 298.
   tying to gut, 184, 299.
   tying to wire, 99.
   tying to silk line, 99.

TACKLE found on fish, 49, 61.
   ancient tackle, 251.

INDEX

Taking a fishing, 273-8.
Taut line, 111.
Testing, the gut, 10; the line, 94.
Tinsel, 169.
   winding for body of fly, 170.
Trevor-Battye, 310.

UP-STREAM, casting, 18, 29, 308.

VARNISH, celluloid, 167.
   for flies, 168-9.
Vaseline, 202.
Vulcanising acid for mending waders, 197.

WADERS, care in turning and drying, 198, 302-3.
   putting away, 302.
   repairing, 197.

Waders (*contd.*)—
   socks over, 199.
   socks inside, 303.
Wading too near the fish, 21.
   without waders, 192.
   in swift or rising water, 195-6.
Wasps, salmon taking, 59.
Where to fish in various states of water, 164-5.
Whetstones, 205, 305.
Whipcord, 304.
Whipping lines together, 304.
Winging flies, 172-3.
Wire: piano wire, 98-100; lead wire, 96.
Wolryche Whitmore, F. A., 301.
Wood, A. E., 308-9.
Worming, 105.
   salmon swallowing worms, 107.
Wounded fish, 83, 137, 157.